MY ECO-WORLD,

MADE IN CHINA

MY ECO-WORLD, MADE IN CHINA

MICHAEL **LOONG**

PARTRIDGE
A Penguin Random House Company

ISBN:	Hardcover	978-1-4828-6422-9
	Softcover	978-1-4828-6421-2
	eBook	978-1-4828-6423-6

Print information available on the last page.

To order additional copies of this book, contact
Toll Free 800 101 2657 (Singapore)
Toll Free 1 800 81 7340 (Malaysia)
orders.singapore@partridgepublishing.com

www.partridgepublishing.com/singapore

Contents

Introduction

China, a huge agrarian country, has only 15 percent total land mass suitable for crop cultivation. Illiteracy is widespread. About half the population of 1.36 billion living in rural areas endure conditions reminiscent of the past millennium. The rest of the population, in urban areas, enjoys a living standard comparable to any advanced country in the world. Such income disparity is a potential time bomb of social unrest.

China used to be the biggest economy in the world. However, it closed its door to foreign trade during the Ming Dynasty (1368–1644). This isolation led to China declining in economic development and power. China suffered foreign aggression by countries from Europe, Japan, and the United States in the early twentieth century. There was widespread civil unrest. The corrupt Qing Imperial government was finally deposed in 1912 by revolutionary Sun Yet Sen thus ending two thousand years of imperial rule.

In 1937, Japan began a full-scale invasion of China and started WW2. The war ended in 1945 after two US atomic bombs were dropped on the cities of Hiroshima and Nagasaki. In 1949, Mao Zedong defeated Jiang Kai-shek of the Kuomintang Party in a civil war and established People's Republic of China.

To reconstruct China, Mao devised the massive commune farming system, but it ended in failure. In 1966, he launched the infamous Cultural Revolution that threw the country into chaos, setting China back economically and socially at least a generation. He died on September 9, 1976.

In 1978, Deng Xiaoping introduced a market economy that uplifted two hundred million people out of poverty within three decades. In 2012, China became the second-largest economy in the world, a coming-of-age epic event for the country. However, the economic progress has also generated public discontent involving corruption, air and water pollution, high cost of living, and inflation. Food contamination is widespread.

The massive US subprime mortgage debacle in 2008 caused a global economic crisis that affected China's exports, resulting in the GDP (gross domestic product) dropping to 7 percent from its peak of 12-14 percent in the past.

Grave issues confront China's future prosperity and security concerning food production, availability of fresh water, and energy supplies. China needs to find sustainable sources of energy to replace its dependency on foreign oil. China imported seven million barrels of oil *per day* in 2014. Water is in short supply. Food crops have to be imported to fill the gap of inadequate domestic production.

The Solution: Eco-World

The Chinese government decided to invest US$1 trillion in a project that creates an "eco-world" comprising four hundred eco-cities. This project will resolve the social issues of escalating inflation, unemployment, high costs of housing, education and healthcare, and will indefinitely eradicate the rural poverty that affects six hundred million people. In addition, China will be self-sufficient in food, energy, and water. Grains will be harvested on automatic eco-farms; clean energy will be taken from renewable sources; and unlimited fresh water supply obtained from diverted river water. A fully integrated fishing industry will be established to satisfy demands.

Every eco-city government will provide citizens low-cost housing; a modern, electrified transport system; medical facilities; a modern education system; and an all-weather airport. Use of fossil fuels will be banned. All private vehicles will be battery powered. Effective banking and financial systems will be established to provide funds for state owned and private industries and to preclude the sale of toxic assets. Tourism will be promoted, encouraging foreign travellers to visit China. This tourism plan is expected to earn US$4 trillion per year.

China will build four hundred eco-cities over a span of twenty years, and the first eco-city has been built with assistance from Waratah, a philanthropist organization in the United States. The mammoth Eco-World project incorporates state-of-the-art science, information technologies, social engineering, and town planning to provide a green, clean, and congenial living environment. All waste products will be recycled. Local industries are to spend more on R&D (research and development) to produce high-value, quality products. Robots will be used liberally in daily lives and in every industry and social infrastructure. The e-government will be pro-citizens, with weekly meetings between local officials and citizens to solve grievances.

The Eco-World is a game-changer for China. It will be a utopia devoid of fear of war over shortage of food, water, and energy. China will become the richest nation on Earth and will become an engine of growth for other countries. China will continue to support the United States as the "international police" to maintain order.

Two hundred years ago, Napoleon Bonaparte said: "China is a sleeping giant. Let her sleep, for when she wakes, she will move the world." The Eco-World of China will be the testament of Napoleon's prophecy.

Chapter 1

Making Waves

Sailing to Shanghai

The *Lotus* has been sailing from Los Angeles across the Pacific Ocean for the past fifteen days and is now heading toward Shanghai. It is a nuclear-powered commercial ship owned by the Waratah Organization, the world's largest and richest philanthropic organization, with its headquarters in Los Angeles. Contributions to Waratah charity funds come from all over the world. The *Lotus* has been converted and modified from a decommissioned Russian nuclear-powered aircraft carrier. A new US-made nuclear reactor is installed to replace the old one.

Docking is scheduled in two days' time. The *Lotus* will be anchored at a special berth in the port, as it is a nuclear-power ship. Captain Teng is preoccupied with numerous programs for the ship's one thousand crewmembers and two thousand passengers, including billionaire and millionaire philanthropists, dignitaries, and ex-government officials from many countries. Other passengers include eminent scientists, specialists, and experts in the fields of physics, engineering, medicine, chemistry, biology, and information technology, as well as research students from various countries.

The *Lotus* Is a Research Ship

The refurbished ship is equipped with modern equipment and facilities for various research projects conducted on board. The projects are funded by Waratah. Many of the passengers are invited as special guests of the Chinese government as they are involved in setting up an Eco-World in China, the first of its kind in the history of mankind, which has a significant impact on human social evolution.

Recognition of Waratah's Contribution to China's National Developments

On board are members of the executive council of Waratah, who have been invited by the Chinese government to attend the official inauguration of the first new eco-city of Meigui. Honorary Chinese citizenship will be bestowed upon them for their valuable contribution toward the developments of China and the betterment of the Chinese people. The brand-new city has been established by the Chinese government jointly with Waratah, which has contributed immensely their efforts in finance, materials, and time, helping the Chinese government in the concept, design, and implementation of Eco-World, which consists of four hundred eco-cities.

Two of the most important people who have contributed immensely to the Eco-World project are Huang Long, an eminent Chinese agriculture scientist, and Phil Kendall, an American entrepreneur and specialist in robotic technology and application.

Waratah Charity Projects

Waratah regularly invites member philanthropists to leisurely sail around the world and enjoy their sea journey, seeing and doing many interesting things. They appreciate the various research projects being performed and how the projects help alleviate the problems of food production and offer clean energy from renewable and recyclable sources and new fresh-water supplies. Research projects are also performed to develop humanoids to help the disabled and to perform menial, dirty, or dangerous jobs shunned by people.

Other projects involve universal Internet-enabled education, waste-material recycling systems, innovative surgical treatments, nanotechnology, carbon-free transport systems, and 3-D printing. Some project models are designed on board and tested on land to prove their feasibility and to discover potential problems.

How to Feed Three Thousand Passengers on a Ship

Several huge kitchens, mostly computer-operated, prepare every day foods for more than three thousand passengers. Most of the chefs are robots, and they prepare meals to suit the various tastes and styles of different nationalities of the passengers. It is fun to watch how the software-driven robots can be programmed to perform various ways of cooking to meet the culinary specifications set by the human chefs.

The dining hall is served by robotic waiters who can take orders for food and drinks and deliver them to the diners. Robotic cleaners are deployed to clean and mop the dining hall and kitchen, which are designed specifically for robot operation. Waste and water recycling and refuse systems have been installed on board the ship.

Managing a Community of Three Thousand People Living on a Ship

An emergency surgical theater is available to perform any operation on board via remote operating procedure. Standby power requirements for the ship are provided by two biodiesel power-generating plants. Fresh vegetables are available from the eco-farms on board the ship. The *Lotus* is self-sufficient with fresh drinking water that is produced on board. A recycling system takes care of all the waste products.

The *Lotus* is the first eco-friendly ship ever designed and operated in the world. It is like a small town, with several thousand people living in an eco-friendly environment.

Captain Teng's Duties

Captain Teng, a veteran naval commander with many years of experience, has a laundry list of activities to accomplish before the ship's arrival in Shanghai. His duties and entire program of activities have been scheduled at the head office. He has a checklist to perform before docking, like the long checklists used by airline pilots before takeoff and landing. Captain Teng communicates with his copilots and will check off their completed duties. An alarm will activate if and when a check-off item is omitted in the process.

Once the ship has completed disembarkation of all the passengers and cargo has been unloaded, Captain Teng will proceed to the Waratah regional office on land for debriefing and information-updating, including the weather forecast for the next journey. Any change to the next sailing schedule is discussed and a new list of VIP passengers received. Together with his operational staff, he will examine the cargo manifest and the detailed list of dangerous goods.

Lotus Operations

The ship will go through a thorough safety check before her next voyage. It is scheduled to depart in three days. It must leave Shanghai's port punctually to continue its voyages with a new group of invited guests to South Korea and Japan and then back to Los Angeles. Its European voyage will follow its Asian tour. It sails round the world once every six months, stopping at selected seaports. Its schedules are tightly controlled and kept secret for security and safety reasons because of the VIP passengers, renowned scientists, and precious and invaluable assets on board.

The *Lotus* is equipped with a state-of-the-art computerized system that controls the ship's operation. The system will flag any operational defect that occurs at any instant, and it will alert the maintenance crews what rectification is required. The ship is navigated by an autopilot and by GPS. The autopilot is updated constantly with the latest weather information that is transmitted via satellites. It automatically navigates the ship to avoid rough seas and strong gales that may endanger the ship's safe operations. The ship's operation and location is tracked in real time by an onshore maintenance center that downloads the information of every system of operations and control of the ship.

Chapter 2
Docking in Shanghai

The New Shanghai Port

A clear morning at the Port of Shanghai welcomes the arrival of the *Lotus*. Shanghai, the largest financial center in the world, with a population of thirty million, is a modern cosmopolitan city in a conservative China.

A fleet of shining black China-made luxurious Hongqi limousines presents an impressive sight at the VIP arrival hall to welcome the foreign VIP visitors by Shanghai's mayor and other senior officials from Beijing. The VIPs are taken to a tour of the port facility and operation. *Impressive* and *unbelievable* are two words uttered by the visitors upon seeing the various aspects of the port's design and operation. A day later, they take a flight to visit Meigui, the first eco-city ever built in the world.

The new Shanghai port exudes a feeling of freshness and serenity. Its contemporary architecture in the midst of the charm of old, historic buildings has been restored and turned into administrative offices. Shanghai City has been transformed by incorporating the latest advancements in technology, science, and social engineering. No more is this port a drab, noisy, polluted, congested, and dirty place as in bygone days. From the past monotonous design of basic functionality as the only design criterion, the port has been transformed into a modern building. Its aesthetic tastes defy any semblance of traditional seaport architecture. There is no dull, huge car park for the parking of cars, trucks, or other vehicles at the docksides. There are no more heavy transporters belching out black exhaust.

The new buildings are eco-friendly, with facilities for recycling waste products. Robotic fire-fighting systems, designed to extinguish all kinds of fire within thirty seconds, have been installed. All freight movements are performed underground, unaffected by the elements. Near the dockside are a large artificial lake and a traditional Chinese garden dotted with seasonal flowers, fauna, and flora, making a picturesque scene of a tranquil rest area for the port workers and local residents. Robotic workers are deployed to manage the garden, equipped with resting benches and public convenience facilities, including the public toilets that are designed specifically for robots to clean automatically. CCTV cameras are installed at strategic locations and managed by security workers who are mainly handicapped persons stationed at home. Most workers and residents travel by underground mass-transit system or driverless electric bus. Restaurants operating 24/7 employ robots as chefs, cleaners, and waiters.

The new Shanghai port operation resembles a fully computerized factory. Hardly a soul is seen on the dockside, an unusual sight for a seaport. Yet its atmosphere is relatively quiet, with minimal humming sounds from the electric motors of the operating machines. All the electricity comes from the power grid connected to the tidal-wave power generators, the wind turbines, solar and hydro power, and steam turbine generators using biodiesels from waste oil and renewable biomass.

Noise, water, and air pollution, common in any seaport around the world, is practically nonexistent at Shanghai Port. There is no vehicular traffic involving internal combustion engines. No waste discharges into the sea from any ship. An automatic sewage discharge system is installed at the port to collect all the waste products, including oil, which are then transported to a nearby waste processing plant for recycling. Every piece of mobile equipment or machinery is electrically operated.

Cargo Container Identification

The *Lotus* carries many containers of cargo destined for various parts of China. The containers are all tagged electronically, and their positions are tracked by a GPS system. The port operator has a computer image of the stacks of containers and their positions. All the containers and their contents, as well as the consignees are manifested and made known to the port authority and the consignees in advance via the "Automated Cargo Loading and Unloading

System" via the Internet. It is managed by the Global Shipping Society, to which all the major shipping companies around the world belong. The usual problems of missing and mishandling of cargo at a conventional seaport are nonexistent at Shanghai Port.

The massive cranes are computer controlled and have a high precision and safety record. They can simultaneously lift onto the mobile conveyors several containers. To an underground station, the containers are transferred and electronically sorted in accordance with the destinations in China. With such an automated system, the *Lotus* cargo of one hundred thousand tons can be unloaded within a relatively short period. Hence its efficiency, based on volume of cargo handled, is faster than a conventional air-freight carrier at an airport.

Technology and, hence, speed are the driving force for heightened efficiency and significant savings of time and human and natural resources. Productivity is maximized. The automated system eliminates human errors that often occur at conventional seaports, resulting in serious accidents. The latest design at the Shanghai port facility achieves significant productivity that is unprecedented in history or in other parts of the world.

The common problem of theft in many a seaport is nonexistent at Shanghai Port. The safety record is unblemished compared to previous manual systems. At this 24/7 technological advanced seaport, there are no workers' strikes, which are a common occurrence in traditional seaports around the world. Speed of operation is paramount for processing and dispatching of highly perishable and short expiry date merchandise. This is enhanced by the integrated systems of air, land, and water transport connected to the seaport.

Centralized Cargo Complex

The sorted containers are transferred by automatic electric freight trains to a centralized cargo complex operating on a hub-and-spoke principle. At the complex, sorted cargo containers are loaded onto designated loading bays for dispatch. The huge complex is fully computerized with robotic workers. The main feature of the complex design is to eliminate the traditional congestion at the seaport by road and freight transporters, as seen in many old seaports around the world. Transporters are informed via the Internet of their cargo-holding station for freight collection. Long-haul trucks are no longer hogging the roads around the seaport waiting to pick up their loads, thereby eliminating traffic congestion.

All of the port's administrative functions are fully computerized. There are no cash transactions, as all payments are done electronically. This is to eliminate any temptation of graft by port workers and administrators. An eco-port is an effective weapon to deter corruption and underworld activities that used to occur in many seaports around the world and even in the present in some countries. Smuggling is eliminated at this seaport.

The centralized cargo center is connected to the city center by a network of underground electric trains. A special dedicated train provides a direct link to the airport. The port and the cargo complex are open 24/7 unaffected by inclement weather. Robotic workers are deployed in the warehouse. Security robots are controlled by staffs comprising handicapped persons who can work from home to perform patrol duties.

Port Immigration Processing System

Immigration processing is a breeze for the passengers as they are cleared upon arrival within minutes by the automatic screening of passengers' passports and special bio-data—image of the pupil and fingerprints. The electronic immigration entry form is filled out by the passengers on board the ship using the Chinese immigration website. Passengers take a train ride to the arrival terminal to collect their luggage and personal belongings. From the terminal, passengers can take mass rapid transit trains, buses, or taxis to the city or other destinations. Private passenger pick-up points are provided. To ease the fear of overcharging by taxi operators, a passenger can buy a pre-paid ticket from a vending machine for the final destination marked by location coordinates of the residence or any building in the city. Such location coordinate is given by the Land Transport Authority (LTA) and can be found on the LTA website.

Tour of the *Lotus*

Upon completion of discharge of cargo and passengers, the *Lotus* is open to invited guests from around China to tour the ship. Many children and local citizens who perform charity works are invited to go on board to see the research projects. It takes one day to tour the huge ship. The visitors are ushered into a theatre, where they are shown, via a huge computer screen, the various aspects of living in an eco-city, a charity project, as mentioned before, that Waratah is co-sponsoring.

On board the *Lotus*, a computer simulation shows various aspects of urban living including transportation; food production; health services; social activities; parks and gardens; waste disposal, treatment, and recycling; pollution control; electrical and water supply; contamination control; water resource management; and airport and seaport designs. Computer simulation and physical models are built to allow the eco-city planners an insight into the complexity of design and integration of various organizations to ensure there is no wastage of natural resource. People live in harmony with the environment.

The visitors are taken on a tour to see the various research projects. The first site shows the neatly planted rice and wheat in enclosed troughs filled with compost. The plants grow in controlled air temperature, pressure, and humidity environments. Water with soluble nutrients feeds the roots via tiny biodegradable capillary tubes inserted in the compost and released from a central tank at regular intervals. CO_2 is pumped into the enclosure and released at a predetermined rate. The growth rates are recorded by cameras. Selected plants are dissected each week for detailed examination and biological and chemical analyses. The scientists endeavor to produce the best seedlings for a particular locale.

Other research projects being performed on land are shown via video screens to the visitors. Various engineers and scientists experiment with 3-D printing to produce exotic and complicated objects using different natural or recycled materials. Housing construction using 3-D printing methods is envisioned to be the standard for the future to construct hundreds of thousands of apartments in a massive scale across China. Other projects involve robotic applications in the fields of education, health care services, and hospitals. Robots are designed to replace human beings who detest working in dirty, noisy, strenuous, and mundane conditions without stimulation and creativity.

The visitors are amazed to see how robots can be designed to perform special tasks to aid disabled patients at home and in hospitals. One of the greatest achievements they can do in the education field is to provide uniform education of the highest standard to students from different social strata. There is no longer a distinction between elitist and mediocre schools. The Eco-World project eliminates social discrimination and provides equal-education opportunities for all citizens. China will not have problems employing well-qualified teachers to teach students in schools. They will be replaced by robotic teachers.

Chapter 3

Meeting with Government Officials

The VIPs, consisting of members of the Waratah Management Council and some senior members of the subcommittees in charge of the Eco-World project, are flown from Shanghai to Beijing to meet with the President of China and his Cabinet ministers. It is their first trip to Beijing, and they are excited about meeting with the President, who will bestow honorary citizenship on them for their efforts and valuable contributions toward the setting up of eco-cities in China. With help from Waratah, China could realize its cherished dream of eradicating in the rural areas the age-old poverty problem of six hundred million people (more than double the population of Indonesia, the world's fourth-most populous country).

The Eco-World project provides China with adequate supplies of food, water, and energy as well as unpolluted air and water for the entire population in the next millennium. The contributions from Waratah in the education field and health care services are immeasurable for the benefits of hundreds of millions of Chinese. The day it implements the project will be the day of reckoning for China to save itself from being besieged by internal strife.

The Story behind the Birth of the Eco-World Project

At the meeting with the Chinese government, the Waratah Management Council members express their curiosity as to why China abandons her longstanding urbanization projects and embarks on a new Eco-World project. The Chinese government's reply is that the Eco-World project is influenced by the prevailing domestic sociopolitical problems, international economic-political events, future national security concern, and the bitter historical experiences of foreign aggression. China needs to continue to rework and improve its policy so as to move up to the next higher level of modern socioeconomic political advancement for the welfare and livelihood of its 1.36 billion citizens.

Reasons for Socioeconomic Political Reform in China

The world is changing fast, and time is running out for the Chinese leaders to take baby steps of reworking the current socioeconomic political program. The real push that comes to shove is the fear of uprising by six hundred million poor rural residents and the urbanites who are reaching a boiling point against the rampant corruption of the Communist Party officials. The political reformists are raising their voice that unless positive actions are taken to redress the social and political problems, the days are numbered for the Communist Party to rule China. Therefore, political reform cannot be put on a back burner forever, and, hence, a political reform committee has been formed by the central government to set a timetable to implement a new sociopolitical economic policy. There is no time to wait.

The new policy requires a paradigm shift and a laser-focus innovative and proactive approach to push China to the frontier of prosperity and peace. Technology and innovation will be the driver for social and economic progress. China must catch the tailwind of the momentum of self-confidence of favorable international relationships with many countries around the world while the powerful United States faces unprecedented headwinds of setbacks in dealing with international political crises in Europe, the Middle East, and Africa, as well as the financial burden of the increasing national debt exceeding the country's GDP. The US government's monetary policy of relentless printing of non-asset backing fiat money via successive quantitative easing measures causes much concern to the Chinese government holding Treasury bonds worth US$1 trillion that might turn into a Zimbabwean dollar if hyperinflation strikes the US economy. Much of the cheap money has been used by investors buying stocks on the stock exchange, pushing the stock prices higher without due regard to the lethargic health of the economy and generating no value to the real economy.

The successful launch of AIIB (Asia Infrastructure Investment Bank) by China in 2015 with fifty-seven countries joining as founding members despite strong objection from the United States, illustrates the high international regard given to China by US allies like the United Kingdom, Germany, France, Australia, and South Korea. China has launched "One Belt and One Road" and "Twenty-First-Century Maritime Silk Road" projects to promote international trades between China and countries in the Middle East and Europe. It is an opportune time for China to climb to the center stage of leadership for global economic development, stability, and cooperation. Napoleon's prophecy of China waking up from a long sleep to move the world is becoming a reality.

Mao Zedong and Deng Xiaoping—Altruistic Patriotic Nationalists

The visitors are briefed on the recent socioeconomic political history in the eras of Mao Zedong and Deng Xiaoping. Both Mao and Deng believe Communism is only a means to an end. It is only a management tool, not a terrorist ideology or an evil religious cult. Spiritually, Mao and his colleagues were true-blue Chinese Confucianism followers who were pacifists, not hegemons. In reality, pure Communism is a strange culture totally incompatible with the five thousand-year-old Chinese culture. It might not last another decade in this cyber-world. Communism with Chinese characters is a quick tonic that can be used to cure the sickness of human corruption and inequality of basic human rights in China. Chinese social development with Confucianism, Chinese history, culture, and language will endure for a long time.

Relationship between Mao and One Billion Poor Farmers

Mao understood that most of the rural farmers were illiterate and would not care who the government leaders were or their political doctrines. They cared only about their basic survival. Mao did help the farmers rid themselves of the powerful landlords who charged the farmers exorbitant farm rental fees even during periods of drought or flood that destroyed their crops. Doing it alone without external help, and promising the farmers a better life, Mao devised the do-it-yourself commune farming system, which ended in failure with serious consequences. After many trials and tribulations, the one billion poor people remained as destitute as ever. Such a bitter lesson learned was one reason for Deng Xiaoping to seek help from the outside world for his economic reform. A one-man band cannot succeed economically in turning around a huge country devastated by ravaging wars.

Deng Xiao Ping—A Pragmatic, Caring Politician

Deng believed all political doctrines are based on theory, and all of them ignore the importance of human factors for successful doctrine implementation. Political leaders must realize there are a multitude of people with various upbringings, including social, religious, cultural, and educational backgrounds. Political doctrine is too academic a subject to be easily understood by the illiterate farmers. Moreover, many people are disinterested in politics. They are only interested in leading their own lives without fear and injustice and having a space to live, an opportunity to work, and food to eat. The government is to help them achieve their dreams. Deng Xiaoping said making money was glorious, and he encouraged people to do business. Such action was taboo in Mao's era. Deng fired a silver bullet by introducing sociopolitical reform with a market economy that uplifted two hundred million people out of poverty over three decades, a scale never attempted before. Many people took Deng's advice and made a living by doing private business, in defiance of true Communism.

Different Approach for the same Goal by Deng Xiaoping

With many sacrifices, and endurance against obstacles from foreign countries, China achieved accolades by being the second-largest economy in the world in 2012. However, with one step forward economically, China suffered many steps backward in social disorder, corruption, pollution, and widening of income disparity, with the age-old problem of rural poverty remaining unresolved. Mao Zedong, a true-blue revolutionary and a nationalist, wrote a swan song for pure democracy in China, and Deng Xiaoping, a pragmatic modern economics wizard, wrote one for pure Communism.

Both Mao and Deng happened to lead the nation and live at the right time. Deng's era of achievement cannot be replicated anywhere. It is the COCASO (an acronym standing for Communism, Capitalism, and Socialism) political doctrine, which helps China achieve economic success and improve standards of living for people living in the urban cities. The success is a combined effort of Deng's leadership and wisdom, his team members, and the masses.

There will be a modified version of COCASO to cater to the next stage of socioeconomic development when the six hundred million destitute rural residents move to a new Eco-World, where poverty will be of a bygone word. The Chinese government hopes the success of the Eco-World, a product of cooperation between the United States and China, will enable the two nations help the world achieve long-lasting peace and prosperity. The Chinese Eco-World would become the trailblazer for other countries to emulate.

Chapter 4

Recent History of China

The Isolation of China

The famous Silk Road epitomized the first large scale of international trade between China and Europe, the Middle East, and West Asia during the Han Dynasty (206 BC–220 AD). The Silk Road served as a conduit of exchange between cultures, religions, sciences, technologies, philosophies affecting China and the outside world. Until 1840, China was the largest economy in the world and contributed to the civilization of the world with four great inventions: the compass, gunpowder, paper making, and printing technology. With the demise of the Yuan Dynasty, China was closed to foreign trade as ordered by the new Ming Dynasty's (1368–1644) imperial ruler. This isolation led to China falling behind other advanced Western countries in the fields of science and technology, and declining in economic development and power for more than six hundred years.

Opium Wars with Britain: the British Empire and Opium Trade by Force

Opium smoking was introduced to China by the Europeans in the seventeenth century. Later, it was the British merchants who smuggled opium from India to sell to China to earn the silver coins that were in short supply in Europe.

Silver was used in China for commerce. An opium war broke out between China and Britain from 1839–42. The Qing imperial army capitulated due to inferior armaments. Numerous land concessions, including Hong Kong, were ceded to Britain. An avalanche of similar concession demands came from other foreign countries, including Japan and Russia, following in the footstep of Britain.

A second opium war (1856–60) was started by Britain against China when the former was unhappy with China arresting a pirate ship that flew an English flag. More skirmishes ensued between China and the combined forces of Britain and its allies of the United States, France, Japan, Russia, Germany, Austria-Hungary and Italy. They attacked and destroyed the grand opulent Summer Palace in Beijing. After defeat, China agreed to open more treaty ports to unrestricted foreign trade, especially in opium. By late-nineteenth century, China was fast sinking into a semi-colonial state, representing the beginning of "a century of humiliation by foreigners." It was a wake-up call to China of the peril of having a weak army and a corrupt government. This bitter lesson was embedded in the minds of future Chinese leaders and people.

The Boxer Rebellion (1898–1901) and the Demise of the Qing Dynasty (1644–1912)

The Boxer Rebellion (1898–1901) fought fierce battles against the eight-nation foreign armies in and around Beijing and was defeated. Priceless historic treasures inside the imperial palace were looted by the foreign soldiers, who burned the capital city and committed heinous war crimes against humanity. The relic of the burnt Imperial Palace remains standing today.

A Corrupt Government and a National Disgrace

A heavy price of war compensation was paid to the eight invading nations: Great Britain, the United States, Japan, Russia, Germany, Austria-Hungary, Italy, and France. The Imperial treasury was emptied. The frail Qing Dynasty fought many wars against foreign aggressors, ending with defeat and concessions to the victors. Taiwan was ceded (1895) to Japan, which had ruled Taiwan for five decades. Russia invaded Manchuria in 1900 and stayed put. It was the Xinhai Revolution, led by Dr. Sun Yet-San of the Kuomintang Party that put the final nail on the coffin of the fractured Qing Dynasty. The two thousand-year imperial rule ended in 1912.

"Emperor" Yuan Shi-Kai (1912–16)

The birth of the Republic of China (ROC) under first president Sun Yet-Sen had a lot of post-natal pain with General Yuan Shi-Kai who helped engineer the abdication of the last Emperor. He outmaneuvered Sun Yet-Sen to become the second president of ROC, dissolved the parliament in 1914, and changed the constitution. In 1915, he declared himself emperor. His self-proclamation was met with strong protests from the ground, and the episode finally faded with his death in 1916. Subsequent to his death, China was fragmented into regions of warlords, and the central government was a lame duck. This sad scenario lasted a few decades, until 1949 when the well-armed Kuomintang army was defeated by Mao Zedong's peasant army and "people power." The Kuomintang Party did not have the mandate from or an emotion connection with the billion-strong poor peasants.

Japanese Aggression (1895–1945)

US Commodore Perry sailed to Japan in 1854 to forcefully demand Japan open its door to trade. Thereafter, he helped start the Meiji Restoration (1868–1912) for Japan. With the acquired knowledge of science, technology, and manufacturing skills, Japan produced products for export and earned foreign exchange to procure raw materials for manufacturing armaments to wage war against its neighbors. Japan invaded Northern China in 1895, and the Qing government ceded Taiwan to Japan after being defeated. Later, it invaded Beijing in 1898, Manchuria in 1931, and waged full-scale war against China in World War II from 1937–45

Why the Chinese Hate the Japanese Warmongers

China suffered during the 1937–45 Japanese aggression period: there were between twenty and thirty-five million deaths, ninety-five million refugees, and trillions of dollars' worth of property damages. The country's industries and economy were decimated. Crimes of rape; chemical and biological weapons against civilians; burying people alive; torture of men, women, and children; sex slaves; and other sorts of heinous inhuman carnage and brutality were committed by the Japanese soldiers. Thus, hatred of Japan by the Chinese people was profoundly sown, and it would linger for a long time as Japan refused to feel repentance for crimes against humanity, even until today. Without repentance, Japan portrays an image of haughtiness toward China.

The atomic bombs dropped by the United States on Hiroshima and Nagasaki forced the Japanese army to surrender. Thus far, the samurai warriors in the Japanese political circle never admit Japan was defeated in WW2; it only cedes to the dropping of atomic bombs. They have a superiority complex because they have defeated Russia and the US navy at Pearl Harbor. The Japanese wanted to behave and act like Westerners. The Japanese government officials, during new government inauguration ceremony, wear Western-style tailcoats that signify the traditional culture of the West. In South Africa, under Apartheid, Japanese were considered white.

During WW2, twenty-seven thousand American prisoners of war were sent to Japan to work in factories as slave laborers, and all were tortured. The savage Japanese military had no respect for human dignity and war conventions. They inflicted immense suffering on the innocent people in the Asia-Pacific countries and achieved nothing worth their military adventure except sufferings by their own innocent Japanese people—in particular, the people of Hiroshima and Nagasaki. Unfortunately, there are still hardcore Japanese politicians harboring feelings of rearmament and a desire to stage another military adventure, even with declining economic output and an increasing aging population. Aggressive adventure and a culture of militaristic attitudes in Japan's politics continue to linger on. Japanese hardcore politicians recently introduced, in a frenetic pace, a bill in the *Diet* (the Japanese Parliament) to rearm and send troops to fight overseas to the aid of allies, even though Japan is not directly under threat. Unfortunately, China and other Asian countries have no choice but to accept Japan as a neighbor.

Japan Declared War on the United States

The United States was subjected to an unprovoked attack by the daring, merciless, terrorist Japanese suicide bombers. They struck the US naval base at Pearl Harbor, Hawaii, on December 7, 1940, causing 2403 casualties. That attack led the United States' entry into WW2. Commodore Perry of the United State Navy in 1854 never realized that by forcing Japan to open its door to international trade, Japan was able to learn from the West the technology and skill in manufacturing military armaments for aggression against other countries including the United States.

The Japanese war mongers, with their limited natural and economic resources, audaciously believed Japan could fight a full-scale protracted war of attrition in the vast Asia-Pacific regions, which covered a population of more than two billion people in distant countries from the Northern to the Southern hemispheres. Physical fatigue and mental exhaustion should have had a profound effect on the Japanese foot soldiers, who fought in extreme weather conditions and across rugged terrains for more than a decade away from home and family. It was illogical for the Japanese soldiers to kill the hundreds of millions of Chinese farmers who could provide them with food and water. History shows the Japanese army leaders were dogmatic, ruthless, aloof, and audacious, and it was naive for a resource-deficient country to wage a full-scale protracted war against the world. Unfortunately, the Japanese imperial ruler is powerless to control the political agenda of the hardcore samurai politicians in the government.

Chinese Civil War (1927–49)

Mao Understood "People Power"

In the civil war fought between the Communist Party and Kuomintang, Mao Zedong got the full support from the hundreds of millions of landless farmers in the rural area. The farmers helped Mao defeat Chiang and establish a new government in 1949. The farmers received free land, as promised by Mao.

One had to understand that Mao had no choice but to become a Communist because he badly needed help of all kinds from Russia, which happened to have a Communist government. The United States refused to help Mao because he was a pure Communist. Instead, the United States backed Jiang Kai-shek, a practitioner of democracy, but it was tainted with corruption and ineffective management, especially of the poverty suffered by the one billion rural residents. During the civil war, hunger was widespread throughout the devastated country. Mao lived in caves during the civil war and dined with his foot soldiers whilst Jiang enjoyed an urban living standard worthy of a *generalissimo.*

The Militarism of Japanese Culture

The US government, as the signatory to the Japanese surrender in 1945, ensured Japan would not be allowed to rearm to start another war against other nations. Showing mercy, the US government did not put the Japanese emperor on trial for crimes against humanity. With massive help from the benevolent US government, post-war Japan, within two generations, was able to rise from the ashes of the atomic bombs to conquer the world with its cheap and reliable commercial products to become the second-largest economy of the world until 2012. The Japanese people worked very hard for their country's economic recovery and to pay for the war reparations. Life in Japan was austere and simple for many years after the war.

The Unremorseful Japanese Warriors

Hitherto, the defeated Japanese hardcore warriors never performed their traditional Japanese ritual of *seppuku* or *hara-kiri,* a form of Japanese ritual suicide by disembowelment to show contrition and to honor their defeat. China is weary of the Japanese militarism spirit still being preserved by the hawkish right-wing politicians who continue to worship WW2 first-class war criminals in the Yasukuni Shrine.

The Japanese government leaders drum into the minds of the Japanese people, especially the young, that their invasion of China was justified in order to liberate the Chinese from Western colonization, a ludicrous excuse for killing innocent people. Some politicians even deny the atrocities committed by their soldiers during WW2. It is a frightening thought that these hardcore politicians could one day lead Japan into war again on its neighbor, China. They never learn from the bitter history they vehemently deny. It is doubtful its future military venture against China would have full support of the US government.

No Permanent International Friendship

History reveals that there is no permanent friendship in international relation, only permanent enemies. China believes it is impossible for the United States to continue to tie the hands of war mongers in the Japanese government, even though the United States and Japan are now military allies through a defense pact. In order to achieve their aim of rearmament, Japanese politicians stealthily create maritime tensions in the East China Sea in order to coerce the United States to rescind their prohibition on rearmament. Japan, with no remorse for their past atrocities, will not hesitate to strike against China again when its military arsenal is ready. The Japanese government is on a campaign tour of the world, spreading rumors about China threatening the peace of Asia because of the dispute over a few tiny rocks in East China Sea claimed by the two countries, urging other countries to support Japan to rearm. China names the tiny rocks as Diaoyu Island. The United States seems to have relented on its tight control of Japanese rearmament. Hence, China needs to build up its economy and military strength for self-protection. Such is the belief of the Chinese government and the people.

The US government has forgotten that China and the United States were partners fighting the common enemy of Japan during WW2. China has never invaded the United States and it has no such intention of doing so in the future because both are important trading partners for mutual benefit. China owns more than US$1 trillion worth of US Treasury bonds, which would be at risk if a war were to break out between the two nations. It is inconceivable that a war could occur between them as both possess atomic weapons.

A similar political crisis between the United States and Russia has existed since end of WW2. Both possess nuclear weapons. It is interesting to note that both the United States and Russia were allies in WW2, fighting the common enemy of Nazi Germany. Now the United States and Germany are allies and Russia is the United States' adversary. The United States could do nothing when Russia was accused of military action in Crimea. It is a strange world of international politics. The United States' wavering foreign policy also occurs in the Arab world. Saddam Hussein was captured by US soldiers during the 2003 US invasion of Iraq, and he was later executed in 2006. Saddam was a staunch US ally during the bloody Iraq-Iran war from 1980–88.

Cultural Revolution (1966–69)

Fearful of being outmaneuvered by his political opponents, Mao and his wife initiated the tumultuous Cultural Revolution. Rare historic relics, artifacts, and cultural sites were destroyed or ruined by the Red Guards. Schools were closed and intellectuals persecuted. Many innocent people lost their lives. Once again, China's economy was in utter tatters. Mao introduced the Great Leap Forward campaign (1958–60) with a nation-wide commune system for farming. The project failed catastrophically, and China experienced great famine.

Once more, after twenty years of waiting for a better future, the poor farmers went through another round of misery, this time with pure Communism. Thus, poverty has no affinity to any political doctrine. Practicing idealism of any political doctrine is impractical in a practical world that is imperfect and forever evolving. Political doctrine has no scientific proof and is based on many assumptions devoid of any human factor.

The death of Mao Zedong left a big vacuum in Chinese politics. Together with his reformists in the Politburo, Deng Xiaoping had to pick up the pieces of an economy in tatters. Boldly, he formulated the country's economic program and political reform by opening up China to the outside world. A do-it-yourself policy was not on his mind.

Deng's famous saying, "It doesn't matter whether a cat is black or white, as long as it catches mice," encouraged everyone to excel in whatever they did. "To get rich is glorious" was another of his famous sayings, which encouraged individuals to do business. This is the Chinese dream but is against Mao's doctrine and pure Communism ideology. Deng was not one to bury his head in the sand. Chinese people must not go hungry again and suffer another round of humiliation of foreign aggression. Poverty attracts no respect in international political games.

Deng understood economics was the lifeline of a country, and exports were the path to obtaining precious foreign exchange. Capitalism and Socialism ideologies were incorporated into his national developments. With his sayings and brave actions, Deng played the "Last Post Bugle Call," which bade farewell to pure Communism ideology. He believed a political ideology was only a management tool for people to manage national affairs for the benefits of the nation and its people. Old Communist tactics of encouraging unionists in the capitalist countries to strike was not Deng's political style. He wanted the world to be peaceful and friendly for his export business. He wanted customers to buy his "Made in China" merchandise.

Deng dismantled the entrenched collective farming system and sought help acquiring the best industrial and social practices from all sources, including its traditional political adversary, the United States. His market-economy policy was to concentrate the country's resources on economic development of the coastal cities, starting from the fishing village of Shenzhen next door to Hong Kong, a convenient and ready-made international seaport and global financial center. Rural residents were permitted to be migrant workers seeking jobs and living in the cities.

After creating wealth in the eastern regions, he moved his momentum to the hinterland in the western regions of China. He played courtship with US politicians on US soil. It makes sense to do business with countries that are rich. He who has money calls the shot. Money is king.

To Learn the Best from Others Is a Virtue

At age seventy-four, Deng Xiaoping did not have much time to go into the details of his epic project of building an open-market economy to feed the 1.36 billion people. Moreover, his comrades-in-arms and contemporaries in the government were all in the geriatric age brackets. Time was not in their favor. He was apprehensive to confront the politically hot-potato problem of the reunification of the British Colony of Hong Kong in 1997, and the possible consequence of massive emigration of Hong Kong residents and the collapse of the Hong Kong economy that Deng would depend on for his market economy. There was no time to do comprehensive research into the whole project and calculate a payback. An eyeballed concept and a rule of thumb were the only tools he possessed to launch his novel program. Hence, short time required immediate action.

Deng embarked on a "getting to know you" trip to several countries. He went to Singapore, a tiny country with a population of four million and a history of only thirty years, to learn what made Singapore thrive without natural resources and with a GDP per capita even higher than some Western countries. Singapore's economic success model inspired Deng to adopt a similar approach to opening up China to the outside world. Since 1992, thousands of Chinese senior government officials have been sent to Singapore Nanyang Technological University and National University of Singapore for executive-management training. Such continuous formal overseas training programs are the first in China's history for government officials.

Deng also made visits to the United States and other countries to learn the best practices of industrial and economic developments. To learn the best from others is a virtue, to reinvent the wheel is a "no-brainer." Singapore was successful in "borrowing" foreign talents to help Singapore progress economically and technically to manufacture goods for sales in the world market. China could do likewise.

Lessons Learned from Countries Practicing Democracy

The Chinese leaders witnessed Western democracy being long in theory but short in practice since WW2, as there was too much dichotomy and radicalism between the liberals and conservatives, the left and the right wings, and the polarized political parties constantly bickering on important national issues that seldom reached consensus in parliament.

Political parties indulge in money politics, buying votes during general elections with generous donations from influential people and companies with big pockets. Too much public money is used by an incumbent government to give "freebies" to voters so often that the national treasury runs out of cash. Many governments develop social policies just to pander to prevailing public sentiments without regard to their quality and sustainability or long-term national interests. Many political careerists in some democratic countries indulge in political corruption, and such is the pattern or fashion prevailing in this materialistic world of politics.

In fact, there is no selecting a good leader by the voters when both political parties in a two-party system practice pseudo-politics. The choice given to the voters is only to pick a political party to form a government and not the best person to lead the nation. There is no absolute freedom in this world, not even in the United States, to pick a person to manage a country's affairs politically, as much as no one has the freedom to choose one's parents. Presidential candidate for the United State general election is picked by the political party. Alternating political parties in a democratic government does not offer opportunity of long-term national planning. Politicians' personal greed is the common disease that kills all political doctrines. When political parties are immersed in deep-rooted money politics, the county is doomed to fail in its political and social development. Human factor is the key to success in any political doctrine.

Peasants and Politics

Peasants in underdeveloped countries do not understand political ideology, which has no relevance in their daily lives. In any case, democracy theory is written in the context for the urban voters and not for the poor Chinese illiterate farmers living in remote villages without modern amenities or basic health care services. To the poor illiterates around the world, democracy or Communist political doctrines do not strike a chord with them. Only real politics involving basic human survival is welcome by deprived human beings.

Deng Understood the Plight of Rural Residents

China needed a peaceful domestic environment and a benign parliament to conduct its business of economic development. It takes time and patience to uplift the living standard of a huge agrarian country filled with one billion poor people, and to repair the decimated economy bankrupted by foreign aggressors and WW2. The destitute in the rural areas are tired of century-old corrupt governments that show no concern for their survival. The hungry know no politics but savors the caring hand that offers relief. Deng Xiaoping offers such a hand. His actions are all about human lives filled with decency. He is not a politician shrouded with hypocrisy and grandiloquence. This is Deng Xiaoping's political reality.

Lessons from Past International Politics

Chinese leaders learned from history that hypocrisy abounds in global politics. Some self-centered and phony politicians in some countries talk passionately about human-rights violations in a huge country like China, with 1.36 billion people, but have no reservations toward supporting a war that killed hundreds of thousands of innocent people, including women and children, in foreign countries. Some "Rambo" and "cowboy" politicians subscribe to using force instead of dialogue to settle international disputes. Some radical politicians in disguise leverage religion to further their own ambition of self-importance through incitements that lead to a war. Unfortunately, all of these camouflages practiced by phony politicians, harm innocent people around the world. The Chinese people do not accept phony politicians who cannot bring prosperity to the nation. Hence, the Chinese government refrains from interfering in the domestic affairs of other countries.

A Minority Can Topple a Government Elected by Popular Vote

This is a flaw in modern politics in countries that have free elections. Even a government popularly elected by a majority can be brought down by minority public demonstrations or coup d'état. Pure democracy still has a long way to go in an imperfect world. China's Communist politics are not perfect either, with increasing social disgruntlement against the Communist Party members for being corrupt. Under Communist rule, the government can plan national development programs on a long-term basis. This is difficult for a democratic government as too many politicians spend excessive time planning on getting reelected in the next election.

Dirty Politics in the World

There are no all-weather friends in international relations, only foul-weather friends who would ditch you when there is no personal gain to be had. There are troublemakers aplenty in international politics, crying for financial and military assistance from one country against another. There are powerful politicians who could spin a false story to start a war against someone who fails to understand the message of "You are either with me or against me." Such a message to the fragile countries is intimidating. This is a real world that we live in.

The politicians with altruistic ideas serving their countries with unreserved commitment, love, selflessness, and passion seem to be light years away from this materialistic world. The only foreign country in this world that dared invade the United States was Japan, who is now a darling of the United States in their "defense" partnership, picking China as an imaginary enemy. Fact is indeed stranger than fiction as both China and the United States were once comrades-in-arms fighting Japan, the common enemy in WW2. Both China and the United States suffered immensely from the Japanese invasion. There is no animosity between the two countries, and hence, there is no valid reason for the United States to treat China as an enemy, especially when China is an excellent customer of US Treasury bonds. One makes money by trading, not by fighting, which is a waste of precious resources and human lives and causes misery to both sides.

Choice of Political System by Deng Xiaoping

Deng believed every political system, whatever its form, style, or function was a work in progress. It would have a shelf life or use-by date. Every political system has its own characters in every country depending on its people, religion, culture, history, common values, beliefs, and aspirations. With the passage of time the characters may change to suit the prevailing social, political, and economic conditions. Hence, political system in every country is never static. It evolves with time. It is a waste of time and effort for any country to try to export a political doctrine to another country. It will never work.

There is no one-size-fits-all political system. One man's medicine is another man's poison. There has never been an ironclad political system in any country. Unlike many other countries, the Chinese leaders do not interfere with the internal politics of other countries. Assassinations of heads of states are prevalent in democratic countries. Examples include President John F. Kennedy of the United States, Indira Gandhi of India, Benazir Bhutto of Pakistan, Yitzhak Rabin of Israel, and Park Chung-hee of South Korea. Bitter political rivalries in many so-called democratic countries often involve jailing the former head of state who was defeated in a general election.

Every political doctrine is based on pure theory. There are no ifs, or buts, and no assumptions are made, and there is no consideration of human factors. There can be no fair debate on the suitability of a political doctrine when not all of the citizens of a country can fully understand its theory and practicality. In Western countries, influential people in big businesses or powerful trade unionists could influence political election results. He who pays the piper calls the tune. This is not true democracy. It is money politics that favor the rich and powerful, who are the main actors. The masses are the supporting cast.

Real democracy does not give absolute freedom to any individual who can do whatever he wants to the detriment of the majority. Not every human could behave rationally and responsibly toward fellow human beings in any society. Not every electorate is rational in selecting the right political candidate in a general election. In some countries, a film star or a politician with a handsome face can win an election. Communism cannot bestow absolute power to the government to do whatever it wants to any individual, thereby incurring the wrath of the majority. People power is always the weapon of mass destruction in any country practicing whatever political doctrine. Survival is the ultimate choice of human beings, and a political system is only a means to an end to achieve survival. There is no sense to go to war because of differing political doctrines.

History Makes a Statesman of Deng Xiaoping

Deng has lived through tough times and humiliation and witnessed the miserable lives of poor farmers in rural areas. He was banished to the countryside three times. He realized the one billion illiterate and desolate people would never understand politics or care who was in political power. They were too remote from the seat of power. Various dynasties had come and gone, but their lives remained in a nadir. To them and their ancestors, time has stood still without hope of turning into a better future. Their fear was not about any upheaval in politics or change of dynasty but of calamitous weather that could destroy their crops. Famine would strike and no one would come to their help, and they hopelessly awaited an inevitable demise as their final destiny. It was a recurring historical event.

Such is the reality of Chinese history that has perpetuated for centuries and is unknown to foreigners. Where are the foreign politicians who long sang the glorious tune of democracy, demanding China practice democracy but never offering to help the destitute farmers who have been in dire need for centuries? International politics is a game often corrupted by money, rhetoric, hypocrisy, and personal greed, often under the disguise of freedom of speech, and echoed by news media controlled by a political party. Personal integrity and principles are absent in many a political firebrand and lobbyist.

A New Political Doctrine—COCASO

After the demise of Mao Zedong, Deng launched a new political system of market economy, incorporating the best of Communism, Capitalism, and Socialism doctrines. He would call it "Communism with Chinese Characters," there being no better name. Therefore, his hybrid political system cannot be cloned by others. The system could be labeled the COCASO system. The dosage of each of the three doctrines that constitute the final configuration of COCASO varies according to the prevailing socioeconomic political environment in a digital and fast changing world.

The Future of China is a Work in Progress

China will continue to improve its socioeconomic political system to keep abreast with the times and the rest of the world. There are new ailments that cannot be cured by previous medicines or courses of treatment. Relentless competition from other countries in product innovation, quality, and pricing should propel China to invest more in R&D (research and development) and human resources to satisfy its customers. Continuous improvements require continuous upgrading of social infrastructures. You need a capable political leader who has a helicopter view of world events and a ground-zero feeling and empathy for the deprived people.

Important Friendship with the United States

The United States, being the richest country in the world, has been an important trading partner of China for a long time. Hence, Chinese leaders will strive to maintain a steady and healthy relationship with the United States for long-term trading's sake. China must accept that American people despise Communism as a political doctrine, and personal freedom is their sacrosanct religion, which is not in harmony with Communist ideologies. To Americans, personal freedom and democracy are dear to their hearts. The Chinese leaders will endeavor to soft-pedal to the American people that human beings living under Communist rules also need money to survive, just like any other society—a simple logic not too difficult to comprehend by any stretch of the imagination.

Communism is a suitable medicine for China's ailment of poverty, at least for the time being in the twenty-first century. China does not pledge that Communism is the wonder antidote that can cure the disease of poverty in another country. Nor can China proclaim to the world that Communism will forever remain the perfect political ideology to govern China. China needs the United States as a business partner to trade with in order to feed its 1.36 billion people. You do not need to be a rocket scientist to realize this logic. Pure Communism is no fashionable political ideology in world politics today—not because of the United States or any country but because of lack of interest in other countries. Pure Communism is a difficult political ideology to apply to today's social environment and materialistic world. It has died a natural death.

Reunification of Hong Kong: Maintaining Hong Kong Stability is in China's Interests

That Deng Xiaoping maintained Hong Kong's status quo as a self-governing entity after reunification in 1997 was a political masterstroke. He promised no hegemonic absorption of Hong Kong into the mainstream of the mainland. He did not ask the Hong Kong people to change their lifestyle. His innovative policy of keeping democratic and capitalist Hong Kong under one-country, two-system governance for fifty years was brilliant.

He would not tolerate a massive migration of mainland people swarming Hong Kong in search of better lives. Hong Kong plays a significant and important role for China in its economic development and national reconstruction. Hong Kong provides a safe conduit in the international financial sector to facilitate payments in US dollars by foreign customers to the Chinese producers, and for Chinese importers to foreign suppliers. The Chinese foreign exchange system was not in tune with international standards, and the Chinese RMB (the renminbi, the official currency of the People's Republic of China) was not recognized as a foreign-exchange currency. The Hong Kong dollar was freely acceptable in foreign trade.

Hong Kong Is a Bridge for China to Reach the World

Shanghai, the financial hub of China, needed the assistance of financial and technical expertise and savvy from Hong Kong's local and foreign residents, as well as Hong Kong's financial institutions to help in its advancement toward a modern financial-, investment-, and foreign-exchange center and stock exchange. It is a match made in heaven for China's global trade with Hong Kong's modern air-and-sea freight terminals serving as the logistics center for China to facilitate imports and exports. Hong Kong serves as a bridge for China to reach the world market for its exports.

The Uncertainty of Hong Kong after Fifty Years

After fifty years, new generations of Hong Kong people might not have the culture and traditions to dovetail and integrate with those on the mainland, and the importance of Hong Kong might diminish as a facilitator to help mainland China in its future economic developments.

The whole of Hong Kong's political landscape has to change to meet new challenges for the reunification with the mainland. Hong Kong people are used to having a laissez-faire working and living attitude that is incompatible with the culture of the authoritarian officials in the civil and government services on the mainland. Recent scuffles in Hong Kong illustrate that the local residents are not receptive to the bad social conduct of some mainland visitors who, for example, allow children to urinate in public places, spit in public, or ignore traffic rules. There is incompatibility in culture, habit, and custom.

Nontransparency of the legal system on the mainland is another roadblock that will not be acceptable to the Hong Kong people. They have been used to transparency and independent judiciary for decades. Until the mainland judicial system and party politics are strictly demarcated and the government officials abide by the rules of law, Hong Kong people will doubt their assets are safe and personal freedoms secured come the days of final reunification. "The real taste of the pudding lies in the eating," as the saying goes. The real problem lies with the mainland—the "new mother"—and not Hong Kong, the "lost child," to assuage the fear of the people in Hong Kong. The dichotomy between the two cultures is not easy to reconcile when the laissez-faire people in Hong Kong have lived under British rule and culture since 1842.

The smooth transition of Hong Kong to mainland is uncertain. Reunification by force is not a wise proposition. Gentle persuasion and patience are good communication tools. There is a middle path for people in Hong Kong and on the mainland to tread without animosity toward each other.

The other hope is for the new Eco-World to assimilate the two different societies into a new society with common interests. Wisdom should prevail in the end. The Chinese government has some homework to do to achieve a harmonious and peaceful reunification the final lap of which has a profound effect on cross-strait relationship with Taiwan.

Half the battle could be won by the Chinese central government by providing the majority of the population of low-income people with jobs and housing. Mao Zedong won the civil war against Jiang Kai-shek because he got help from the poverty-stricken farmers who were offered free farmland. Mother China should help Hong Kong promote the film, music, and finance industries that have been the economic foundation of Hong Kong for a long time. China should capitalize on these assets further by expanding employment opportunities. By so doing, it signifies Mother China is caring and likes to connect with the Hong Kong people. Mother China must show positive action in this regard.

Hong Kong's legal standard in the business world is solid and trustworthy and, therefore, is an asset that China should endeavor to leverage for the benefit of Hong Kong and perhaps the mainland in international trade negotiation.

Under no circumstance or difficult social disturbance of public demonstration should Mother China take any punitive action against the people of Hong Kong or the local government, as the ramification of a miscarriage of justice would be too much to bear by all Chinese people and the world at large. Mother China should be mindful of foreign troublemakers who like to stir up discord in the Hong Kong community and animosity toward its central government.

Chapter 5
Deng Xiaoping and His Market Economy

Teething Problems during the Market Economy Implementation

During the initial period of implementing his market economy policy, Deng Xiaoping encountered a slew of political, industrial, social, and economic problems. Western countries imposed economic sanctions and trade embargo on China. Technical and financial aids from the trusted communist comrade the Soviet Union ceased after the bitter feud between the ideological opponents of Mao Zedong and Nikita Khrushchev in the early 1960s. Chinese industries were of WW2 vintage. Productivity and quality were of no concern to the state-owned industry-management staffs who were more political appointees than professionals. Workers were not employed by state-owned enterprise (SOE) but assigned by the government as government employees. Manufacturing skills were decades behind the West.

Deng's Only Option—Opening up China to the World

Every citizen had a job in Communist China. Hence, every SOE was bloated with staff. International trades were conducted mainly with the relatively poor communist-bloc countries with soft currencies. Hard currencies like the US dollars were treasured, as they were used to import wheat and soybeans and other essentials from Western countries. Daily essentials were rationed. Deng Xiaoping recognized that to export marketable merchandise to the Western world and meet their required standard, China would require modern machineries, and good management and production skills that had to be imported. However, this required hard currency, which was in short supply. Hence, aid from external sources was desperately needed. There was no ambiguity from Deng that opening up China was the only option.

Deng's industrialization program had to start from the lowest base, as the only thing available in China was abundance of unskilled labor. Hence, there would be a long learning curve to achieve an industrial standard comparable to that in the Western world. Deng, as the CEO of China Incorporation, and his comrades had a tough time revitalizing Chinese industries. Their task was herculean.

Consequence of Market Economy Implementation

Without reinventing the wheel, Deng sought help of all kinds from overseas Chinese diaspora, returning overseas scholars and businessmen from Taiwan and Hong Kong (prior to being returned to China by the United Kingdom) irrespective of political background. Soon, many small- and medium-sized companies began to sprout up in Shenzhen and the neighboring towns in the Delta region of the Pearl River near Hong Kong. Many Hong Kong cottage industries, mainly garments, consumer products, and toys, moved to China due to low-cost labor and overhead. Social benefits to workers were nonexistent. These were followed by less sophisticated electronic manufacturing in the consumer markets.

Gradually, many foreign companies outsourced their product manufacturing and assemblies to Chinese SOEs and other privately owned companies. The Chinese leaders will never forget all the support from the people of Hong Kong and Taiwan that initiated the miracle of modern China's economic success. Hong Kong's financial institutions and internationally recognized commercial laws facilitated the ease of foreign exchange transactions for the Chinese exporters.

In keeping abreast with the times and market demands, many sweatshops that used to employ low-paid menial workers transformed into fully integrated automatic factories, churning out mass production of high-quality garments and consumer products. Even violins, which used to be an expensive musical instrument made in Japan for the rich in the United States, had become affordable to the "man on the street" under the "made in China" label.

The United States and China—Mutually Beneficial Business Partners

US consumers reaped immense benefits from buying "made in China" products at low price with acceptable quality, hence keeping low their cost of living. The bilateral trade was a win-win situation for both countries. China became the United States' largest trading country in the world. Deng's Midas touch created in 2014 a bilateral trade of US$594 billion between the United States and China, in China's favor.

China possesses nearly US$4 trillion worth of foreign reserves in 2014. Deng lifted two hundred million people out of poverty. Shenzhen, a tiny fishing village in 1978, is now a modern vibrant metropolis with fifteen million migrants earning in 2014 a GDP of US$260 billion, which is larger than that of Greece, an advanced Western country mired in massive national debt. Modern Shenzhen was built in one generation. Such a feat is unprecedented and is a defining moment for Chinese political leaders. The student protesters at Tiananmen Square in 1989 would not have imagined in Communist China this possibility of the social advancement of the two hundred million destitute rural residents.

Deng understood basic survival is a prime objective. Mao Zedong would turn over in his grave hearing about Deng using Capitalism in government policies. In 2012, China surpassed Japan as the second-largest economy in the world. No one could believe Communist China had the ability to achieve such gargantuan economic success in such a short time. Communism has no Midas touch ability to turn China into a modern nation. China's progress comes entirely from the people's effort and commitment.

Admirable Achievements by the Central Government

With a diversified cultural and religious background and a country with more than five thousand years of checkered history, trying to unite and satisfy all the different ethnic groups under one banner is no easy task for any government of any political ideology. In China, due to its large population, the scale of social problems is often of gigantic proportion.

For example, how do you safely execute and manage a high-speed train transportation system to provide 3.6 billion passenger trips in a span of forty days during every lunar New Year period? What do you do with the surplus expensive high-speed trains after the forty-day peak operation is over?

Within a generation, China can send astronauts into space, build the world's longest twelve-thousand mile high-speed rail network (its 160 mph high-speed trains crisscrossing the whole country), and build sixty-five thousand miles of high-speed expressways. Automobile sales in China are the highest in the world. Such phenomenal socioeconomic achievement in a relatively short period is astonishing. Achievement of this scale cannot happen if the government is not caring and if there is no effective political system and dedicated political leaders.

Gradual Easing of Restriction of Political Activity

There are five to six million university new graduates annually, a number similar to the entire population of New Zealand, and it is a herculean task to find and provide employments for these young graduates. There are 480 million Internet users in China, and if 10 percent of them use the microblog to air their grievances against the government, it would be mind-boggling just to read all of the forty-eight million messages! Deng Xiaoping and his successors made an unparalleled history in China allowing netizens the freedom to complain. Such freedom was taboo under Mao's regime and ignored by touting Western foreigners and media, who constantly raised loud voices about China having no freedom of expression. It is unfair to beat down others on human rights issues when their own backyards are flooded with inhuman treatment of people of different skin colors or religions.

There are still six hundred million rural residents in China who are illiterate and can be easily influenced by foreigners with ulterior motives wanting to cause trouble. China is a multiracial country with many ethnic minorities, and it is not easy to protect them from being indoctrinated and swayed by subversive elements from foreign countries with a grudge against China. If China were to adopt the draconian policy of "You are either with me or against me," that is being practiced by some Western countries, some religious troublemakers who plot to inflame internal strife in China would have been eliminated long ago, but they are still alive today. Indeed, Chinese political leaders are tolerant toward political dissidents.

The eradication of poverty of two hundred million people by any measure is a good indicator of the dedication of the Chinese leaders who care for the people. Deng's actions signaled the success of the first industrial-cum-social-and-political revolution in China after WW2. Singapore leader Lee Kuan Yew once told Deng Xiaoping, who visited Singapore in 1978, that many Singaporean Chinese were descendants from China arriving in Singapore as indentured laborers, half-literate but hardworking. If Singapore could progress well economically with such migrant stock, there was no reason China, with many millions of educated people, could not do better. With Lee's encouragement and moral support reinforcing his conviction and courage of turning China's economy around, Deng adopted Lee's strategy of opening up China and easing political restrictions.

New Freedom of Expression and Travel

China advanced rapidly with flourishing multinational and bilateral trades, and with bloated foreign reserves. Gradually, the national sociopolitical landscape underwent significant changes, with more emphasis on capitalism and Western culture. As the government has more confidence in managing the national affairs, and the people are more cooperative in national development, there was relaxation of news reporting and the free-flowing of news and information from foreign countries. The Chinese government, allowing one hundred million people the freedom of traveling overseas for holidays and spending US$130 billion, attests to the confidence of the country's political leaders regarding personal freedom. Such a situation was unacceptable in Mao's era. Personal freedom, as distinct from democracy, is not as grim as what many foreigners imagine it to be.

Aftermath of Urbanization

With a budget of US$106 billion a year for urbanization, the huge influx of rural migrants into the cities in the past three decades has created unprecedented demand for social amenities that could not be met adequately in the areas of housing, medical services, education, and transportation. In addition, China faces grave internal problems of soil, air, and water pollution, and shortages of food production, energy, and clean water. Many children of migrant workers suffered from depression and neglect due to absentee parents. The country faced a credit squeeze on private small- and medium-size enterprises, widening of the rich and poor divide, runaway inflation, and the unemployment of university graduates.

There is an equation of economic balance. China's GDP achievement is balanced by an equal amount of wellness deficits, which are defined by costs of repairing the damages to the environment and ecosystems, additional health care costs due to air and water pollution, escalating inflation, rampant corruption, rising costs of importing oil and food grains, and the high price of housing beyond the reach of many middle-income families. With the GDP increasing each year, so too do the wellness deficits if the current urbanization program and sociopolitical system remain unchanged.

Effect of Global Financial Crises on Chinese Exports and the US Subprime Mortgage Crisis

In 2008, the financial crises around the world throttled the demand for Chinese-made goods. Chinese export earnings kept plummeting. United States' banks suffered trillions of dollars' worth of losses caused by Lehman Brothers' toxic subprime mortgage bonds that became worthless due to unpaid loans by borrowers in the housing market. These subprime mortgage bonds were the proverbial spark that ignited the wildfire across the financial world, revealing the many shortcomings of many governments around the world. The banking controllers' lackadaisical attitudes in controlling the dubious financial products that skirted around proper banking regulations opened wide the door for greedy bankers to sell financial products without substantive asset backing. The US masses were the real victims of the subprime mortgage debacle, leaving them without funds to buy Chinese merchandise.

Many European countries also faced similar financial crises, with some countries having a debt exceeding 100 percent of their GDP. Many insolvent governments were bailed out by the IMF (International Monetary Fund) and the European Central Bank. Greece is a classic example. Unemployment crisis hit the roof in these debt-ridden countries. China is now facing a world that is vastly different from when it started its market economy in 1978. China was fortunate not to face such a global financial crisis thirty years earlier.

Change of Political System in the World Post WW2

The world has evolved into a melting pot of democracy, Communism, and Socialism, with significant changes in Europe, the Middle East, South America, and Asia. Even the US government adopted Socialism by bailing out financially troubled banks like Bank of America, JP Morgan Chase, and Citigroup, as well as ailing companies like General Motors, Fannie Mae, Freddie Mac, and AIG Insurance. Taxpayer money was used for the bailout during the housing mortgage crisis in 2008. These companies were "just too big to fail," as their insolvency could have triggered untold misery on many Americans and calamity to the national economy. The US government was being responsible and pragmatic and accepted the reality by sacrificing pure democracy, maintaining the livelihood of the masses and human dignity was more important than sticking to the sacrosanctity of a political doctrine.

US Government Short of Liquidity

The decade-long American wars in Afghanistan and Iraq, estimated to cost as much as US$6 trillion, would increase the financial woes of the US government. Meanwhile, the world was flooded with cheap US dollars under a quantity-easing policy that created global inflation. The US dollar, being printed copiously in thin air and the country burdened by a bloated national debt, played havoc in the world financial system. The world is indeed in the midst of transformation, looking for an alternate stable foreign currency to supplement the US dollar. It is up to China to take the lead to make the positive transformation. Many economists predict the crash of the US dollar in the future, and such a fear is felt by China, which has unloaded US Treasury bills worth hundreds of billions of dollars. With cash redeemed, China is buying up tons of gold as its currency reserve. Many countries now see China as a positive player in the financial market and foreign trade. Liquidity is not a problem to China, with its chest of US$4 trillion in foreign reserve. It is good to do business with a wealthy country. China conserves its cash by not participating in war games in foreign countries, nor would China waste time and energy interfering with the internal affairs of other countries.

Every process has a use-by date. A political process is no exception. US politics are changing. Pure democracy expired in the United States in 2008 when Wall Street destroyed the financial and banking institution foundations, leaving behind a wake of bankruptcies of corporations being bailed out by the government. Pure Communism has expired in China since 1978. It has run out its useful life.

New Political System "Made in China"—COCASO

China has invented the label "Communism made in China with Chinese characters." This unique political doctrine is non-exportable and nonreplicable. It is a unique organic social transformation from within China influenced by bitter Chinese history and humiliation of its people. It is a functional, organic, hybrid political system for national survival. It is the acronym COCASO (Communism, Capitalism, and Socialism). The dosage of each of these political doctrines in Chinese COCASO varies and evolves in accordance with the prevailing environment. The final configuration depends on the wishes of the people. There would be a democratic process for the people to participate in the final configuration.

The crux of the COCASO system is that it favors the selection of political leaders and not a political party, resembling the old system of the Chinese emperor selecting a son capable of taking over the throne of the imperial government when the father dies. The COCASO system allows the honing of politicians through a prolonged process of working in various public administration and performance assessment by senior political leaders.

World Politics Evolving around Economics and Religion

The world never remains static. Presently, there is a seismic shift in global economy from the West to the East led by China, a prime mover of global economic development. The rapid geopolitical power shift from dictators to people-power with free elections, as seen in the Arab world, has created a new wave of a power struggle between two opposing political factions with religious dichotomy.

Cross-border politics and religious differences or rivalry between superpowers features many a proxy war in Middle East countries. Sadly, these wars take a heavy toll on civilian lives and deplete valuable resources. Refugee problems become endemic, putting a strain on world peace. It will take many years for the dust of a people-power revolution to settle down peacefully, especially when the Middle East wars are entangled with oil politics. What is the price of one million barrels of oil in terms of human lives? Only the warring politicians can fathom the true answer in an oil-related war.

The world's hot spots will continue to fiercely burn in the Middle East and will zap the energy and financial resource of the US government and human lives. It is a paradox that the formidable US military, with the latest sophisticated weapons, cannot in a flash discipline a few groups of guerilla fighters creating immense chaos in the Middle East. The United States' wavering foreign policy, switching from foe to ally and then to foe against the Middle East countries seems like a 'target shooting' exercise. There is no endgame in a proxy war involving religion, which is happening in the Middle East and parts of Africa.

In its continuous economic improvement program, and with positive momentum, China would avoid to get embroiled in the internal politics of other countries, lest the entanglement zap its energy and valuable resources without tangible benefits. Keeping the thousand-year-old Confucius teaching of morality, harmony, and peace, China prefers to let other people decide their own fate and way of life.

Chapter 6

Friendship and Birth of the Eco-World Project

The First Eco-Hotel in China

Upon arrival at the Meigui eco-city, the foreign VIP visitors are welcomed by the mayor and secretary of the local government. They are then taken to one of the new hotels, designed with features that are different from those of traditional hotels. These hotels incorporate eco-friendly features, like automatic waste-disposal systems for leftover foods, used water and solid waste. All waste materials are recycled. The room is designed to accept automated operations by robots that service the room by vacuuming, wiping the desks, cleaning and mopping the bathroom and toilet, replacing toiletries, and replenishing tea and coffee cups and pots. The bed, pillows, and mattress are designed to suit the robotic operation of changing bed sheets and covers. The final conditions of the serviced room are checked by a human quality inspector.

According to hotel management, with the rising standard of living in China, it is now getting harder to hire young and energetic chamber maids to clean guest rooms due to low salary, long hours, and high work pressure, and the job requires strength and stamina. With the one-child family policy, parents do not encourage their only child to take up such low-salary and tiring jobs. When the Eco-World project is completed, every child will have a high education that will favor a high-salary job. Hence, the Chinese hotel industries have decided that chamber maids have to be replaced by robots that can work 24/7 without complaint, and without taking sick and annual leave, thereby eliminating frequent recruitment and training of new staff. Moreover, robots provide consistent quality of service and are available 24/7, which is most often unavailable when dealing with human chamber maids, especially when hotel quests check out simultaneously. New hotel guests can now check in at any time. Robots do not need retirement and medical benefits or life insurance, thus saving the hotel a lot of expenses.

Honoring Waratah Members

The next day the VIP guests have a meeting with the president of China, who bestows honorary Chinese citizenship on the Waratah executive committee members for their services rendered to China on the eco-city project in Meigui. A similar honor is also bestowed upon Phil Kendall, who has been instrumental in getting the Eco-World project approved by Waratah, and he contributes significantly to the robotic applications in education and the automation of eco-farming operations. The Eco-World project involves the setting up of four hundred eco-cities in the new Eco-World over a span of twenty years.

Eco-World and Waratah

With the help of Waratah Organization, China can be self-sufficient in foods, energy, and water and will remain sustainable for the next millennia. With the automatic replanting of trees around the country; rehabilitation of arid lands and deserts; recycling of water; constructions of numerous canals, reservoirs, and lakes across the country, China's landscape will be completely transformed and rehabilitated to a land that is more habitable and compatible with the environment. The foreign guests are invited to live in the brand-new eco-city, Meigui, for a few weeks. They have a chance to meet with and talk to the local residents to get their feedback on their feelings and how they embrace the new style of eco-living.

Meeting of like Minds

Huang Long is a world-renowned Chinese agriculturalist who discovered many new species of rice with high yields, contributing to increasing productivity of rice production in many countries around the world, especially Asia. She met Phil Kendall, the chairman of well-known American Robotic Company that produces many different types of robots for industries and domestic applications, at an international conference held in Los Angeles. They both are members of the Waratah Organization. At the conference they were fond of exchanging ideas on how to improve human living and environmental conditions.

One day Phil asks Huang whether there is a danger of food shortage in China in the next decade. Without hesitation, Huang's reply is affirmative. From then on, they earnestly study the subject of food production and finally present a proof-of-concept proposal to the Chinese government. They propose the creation of hundreds of thousands of automatic eco-farms around China that will produce enough foods to meet the demands of China for the next millennia and simultaneously eliminate the century-old problem of poverty afflicting six hundred million people.

Although the Chinese government was impressed, some leaders had reservations about how to proceed with such a colossal project without prior experience, and some wondered how to finance it. With help from external sources, in particular Waratah, the Chinese leaders believed they could overcome internal resistance and apprehension toward the project. Waratah has tens of thousands of members with human and technical resources of any kind that is required by this project. Moreover, Waratah has experience as a project and system integrator in many industrial undertakings.

Birth of the Eco-World Project

During one of Waratah Organization's monthly management meetings, Huang and Phil make a representation to urge the management council to buy into their proposal as the premier charity project of the year. It will be a unique project in human history.

After many intense deliberations, and with considerations for eliminating starvation, mass-scale poverty, and air and water pollution, as well as the ramifications of world shortages of food and water supplies, the Waratah Management Council finally agrees to accept the project and offers financial and technical assistance to China on setting up eco-farms for food grain and biomass production and for the recycling of water. In addition, Phil was magnanimous in providing free robots in the field of education and health care services.

Benefits of the Eco-World to China and the World

Huang and Phil and other philanthropists at Waratah play a pivotal and unassailable role in transforming into reality the concept of an Eco-World consisting of four hundred eco-cities in China. They have convinced the new generation of leadership in the Chinese government that China should spearhead the construction of eco-cities to alleviate rural poverty; to be self-sufficient in food, clean water, and energy-using renewable resources; and to introduce a universal affordable education system using robotic teachers, and health care service provided by robots. The game plan is to start with the eco-city of Meigui and then proceed to building more eco-cities around the country.

The synergistic contributions of the Chinese Eco-World on the global scene are immeasurable in the terms of price and supply of food grains. Sustainable renewable energy in the Eco-World will obviate the need to import six to seven million barrels of oil per day, which has an influence on the price of oil in the market that is controlled by oil cartels and commodity speculators. Eco-World will change the landscape of international oil politics. Oil is a blessing to human living but also a curse to the environment. Past wars, related to oil politics, hopefully will no longer repeat on this planet. Many lives have been lost in these wars.

Global warming effects would take a plunge with less fossil fuel consumption. The world will see the end of the effects of high oil prices, which have a cascading effect on costs of transportation, manufacturing, and fertilizers and are a major cost driver of global inflation, thus reducing the living standards of the poor and widening the income gap between the rich and poor around the world. The world has had enough of fluctuations in oil price that have created uncertainty in business investments and economic development in many countries. The world should use renewable energy earnestly and say good-bye to fossil fuels.

Meeting with Chinese Philanthropists

A meeting is scheduled for the Waratah philanthropists to meet with potential Chinese philanthropists wishing to join the Waratah Organization. The former will narrate their stories—how they become so engrossed and passionate about charity, and the kinds of projects they would like to do in their lifetimes and live to see the results, rather than undertake projects that take decades to bear fruit. Happy they are when they see the value of their contribution toward mankind in alleviating poverty and suffering, and to see the world becoming more peaceful, harmonious, and attuned to being eco-friendly. Every potential member is invited to visit the *Lotus* ship, where they can talk to scientists doing research on board.

Many wealthy Chinese philanthropists are happy to join the Waratah Organization, as they feel their contribution would be put to greater use in value-added projects not only for China but for the world. They're happy to note that Waratah's operations, projects, and financial management are transparent and managed with an open book. Their annual reports are audited by external auditors. In addition, the Chinese philanthropists are pleased with the management and operations of the Waratah's branch office in Beijing overseeing various projects for the benefits of the needy. This office would be tasked to monitor the progress of the eco-city projects in China until the completion of the Eco-World project.

Robotic Teachers

The Waratah organization has a special passion for developing innovative ideas and curriculum in the field of education. It's also interested in promoting different languages using robotic teachers and online teaching methods. With knowledge, the future generation will be better equipped to deal with problems of the future (for example, shortages of food and water; pollution; climate change; population increases; disease prevention; greenhouse effects; and transportation woes). This e-learning will spread around the world, positively affecting poor countries where schooling is lacking. The eco-city project fits in with the Waratah Organization's goals and objectives.

Robotic Caregivers

Robots will be constant companions for human beings in the future and help improve the quality of life for the disabled and the aged. They will become companions at home and in hospitals to render 24/7 geriatric care and nursing services to the elderly, infirm, bedridden, sick, and post-surgical patients on a short- or long-term basis. The requirement for humanoid robots will increase exponentially due to the increasing life expectancy with attendant geriatric illnesses. The need is necessary for the incapacitated and aged parents when their children live far from home after marriage or work in distant lands.

Presently, few young people want to become caregivers in the field of nursing because the job requires strength, stamina, and patience to deal with difficult and demanding patients. Those who have no relatives to provide home-care services could suffer from psychological problems. Humanoids can be an emotional comforter that can be designed to speak in a tonal voice and look like a person dear to the patient. They can be designed to multitask and provide consistent quality services as programmed.

The humanoid can communicate with the patient and the patient's children, relatives, and friends through social media. Together with a robot that can cook and do household chores, the patient will have a comfortable life—albeit at a cost that might not be affordable for everyone. But with mass production for hundreds of millions of patients in an aging population around the world, the costs could progressively reduce. The robots can be hired on an as-need basis to cut costs. Charity organization could render financial assistance.

Food Production Contribution by Huang Long

Substantial grain importation affects national security. It also entails a high cost of keeping emergency food stores, especially when China encounters frequent natural disasters like droughts and floods. When China becomes a food importer in large quantity (such as many millions of tons), it will face a great problem of unstable prices in the world market. International commodity speculators would have a stranglehold over Chinese social security, as has happened in the oil market. The only alternative to solving food shortage is to be self-sufficient in grain production in the new Eco-World.

Huang—An Eminent Agriculture Scientist

Huang is a world-renowned scientist who has discovered many new strands of rice with high yields, as well as rice with enhanced nutrients. She has helped feed hundreds of millions of people around the world by increasing the crop yields. Her research into increasing the quality of grass for cattle feed has increased the value of meat. Her research teams have helped increase the unit output of biodiesel fuel extracted from plants such as Jatropha curcas, seaweed, algae and corn.

Through her efforts resulting in the discovery of Chinese herbs and advanced techniques in packaging traditional Chinese herbal medicine, Huang has received worldwide acclaim for her contributions toward making it more affordable. It has grown in popularity in the treatment of ailments not effectively treated by conventional Western medicine.

With Huang's contributions, China remains self-sufficient in food supplies, energy, and herbal medicines. The quality of life is, therefore, improved for everyone, and in particular, the six hundred million poor rural farmers whose children will not have to toil for a meager living in the future. Her contribution toward the betterment of the human race accords her the qualification of becoming a senior member of the Waratah Organization. Her legacy sets an example for others to emulate.

Contribution by Phil Kendall in Various Fields

Phil has been instrumental in implementing six major projects in China for the Eco-World project:

1. intelligent robotic teachers for education
2. robotic nurses for hospitals and home-care services
3. artificial and intelligent robotic limbs for the disabled
4. remote miniaturized robotic surgery in hospitals
5. robotic systems in eco-farming projects
6. robotic search-and-rescue missions in earthquake situations

His automatic systems of robotic technology in the eco-farm operations yield significant reduction in costs of production and increase crop qualities. Phil owns the largest robot manufacturing company in the world. Its robots are used globally in manufacturing, engineering and service industries, medical and education fields, and scientific applications. His robots and humanoids can be built with an artificial intelligence level to meet the intended application requirements.

Phil's contributions allow the physically disabled to lead a fulfilling and meaningful life. They can work like anyone else. Jobs that are dangerous, filthy, noisy, monotonous, uncomfortable, or tedious are replaced by robotic workers. Lonely elderly people will lead a happier lives living with humanoid companions. Young students will find robotic teachers, who are always knowledgeable, friendly, and even-tempered more fun to be with to learn new things. Robotic teachers lead the students to think for themselves and encourage them to search for information, eliminating the age-old problem in China of rote learning. Robotic teaching is uniform nationwide, consistent in quality, upgraded continuously, and steady in its delivery of what it has been programmed to do.

Robotic Surgeries and Advanced Medical Care

By using remote robotic surgery, many experienced doctors can perform intricate microsurgery on critical patients who might be located far from major hospitals. One experienced doctor can simultaneously train many thousands of novice doctors in many different locations using this remote robotic teaching method. With 3D printing of patients with multifarious complications and rare illnesses, robotic surgical teaching can provide near 100 percent surgical operations and experience that never existed before.

Medical costs will drop as more trained specialists become available to perform intricate and dangerous surgeries. There is no need for patients to wait months for available specialists. The pressure of work will lessen for doctors, who will feel less fatigued.

Robots in Search and Rescue Operations

Phil's company has invented a miniaturized self-propelled robot that can be used in search-and-rescue operations in earthquake disaster areas. With a miniaturized camera, electronic localizer, and sound-detection sensor, the robot can transmit to the ground an image and location of a trapped person. The passages traversed by the robot inside the rubble can be displayed on a wide screen on the ground, providing useful information to rescuers. A special robot can deliver a mini-mobile phone to the victim to keep his spirits high, and another robot can deliver a feeding tube to the victim, thus prolonging the victim's life if trapped for days. Earthquakes happen annually in China. Phil's miniaturized robots will help save lives.

Future Roles of Robots

Phil foresees the future demand for robotic workers will rise exponentially, especially in the fields of medical care for the rapidly increasing geriatric and disabled populations. The Chinese government has engaged him to be the honorary president of the Robotic Technology Academy of China to promote the use of robots in every facet of life and to encourage more R&D in robotic technology. The government is generous in providing financial subsidies to companies in robotic technology development.

Chapter 7

A New Modern China

The World is Quickly Changing

It was fortuitous that the world offered China an opportunity to have a relatively stable environment for her international export trade from 1978–2008. China's GDP of US$0.22 trillion in 1978 increased to US$10.36 trillion in 2014, catapulting China into becoming the second-largest economy in the world.

In a sustainable business, there is a willing buyer and a willing seller. China was lucky to have willing buyers for more than three decades to sustain its economic progress. It is really not easy for a third-world country like China to progress so rapidly in the production of and finding markets for its consumable products worldwide. It is a marvel that, though it possessed no technical expertise in quality production and lacked in financial resources, China's state-owned companies could establish an effective system of procuring raw materials; getting funding to set up factories; obtaining and training production staff; searching for global markets, logistics, and distribution channels; and finding efficient financial controls and sales-receipt procedures involving foreign currencies.

However, good fortune does not last forever. A global financial crisis took the wind out of the sails of China's export business when the United States was mired in a subprime mortgage crisis in 2008, causing global financial mayhem, with many banks and enterprises going belly up. Many European countries were affected by a liquidity crisis, similar to what is happening in Greece, which defaulted on its IMF debt. Greece's lackluster economy still persists today.

Quantitative easing (QE) policies seem to take center stage in many affected countries trying to revive their economy, but their recovery is still trapped. Some countries attempt to devalue their currency to stimulate exports in order to earn more foreign currencies. China encountered a double whammy, with dwindling exports and loss of labor cost parity to many low-cost countries in Southeast Asia, making Chinese exporting less competitive. Hence, China needed to restructure its economy to stay ahead of the competitive curve.

The Financial World in Flux

It is an irony that many European countries that used to be financially robust and stable could plunge into a financial catastrophe and be mired in a sovereign debt exceeding their GDP by more than 100 percent. Many such countries try to borrow money from the IMF, which is already stretched to the limit of loans given to many desperate countries.

The world indeed has changed. Distress signals were sent to China for help. It is hard to imagine Communist Chinese tourists being courted with open arms, tourist visa applications being approved within days. Not long ago a visa application took months to process and had to be accompanied by the signature of a guarantor and a cash deposit. Times have changed. Respect is measured by wealth in this materialistic world. Political doctrine is irrelevant.

Rich Chinese Tourists Spend Money in Foreign Countries

Many countries gladly open their borders to welcome rich Chinese tourists spending money. "Money talks" is the reality of life in any human society anytime and anywhere, regardless of political ideology. In the real world, pragmatism always overrides empty rhetoric and mere theatrics. Cash is king and is a sign of self-respect, power, and achievement.

Deng Xiaoping's brand of real politics made China rich. The country with the money calls the shot. When China sets up the AIIB (Asian Infrastructure Investment Bank), fifty-seven countries, including many Western countries friendly with the United States applied to join as founding members despite vociferous objections from the United States. It is wise for every country to look after its own self-interests.

It is understandable that China, holding the most foreign reserve in the world and flooding consumer goods in the global markets, faces a barrage of international criticisms on trade imbalance and foreign currency exchange issues. Many Western countries, loyal customers of China-made goods, are saddled with huge sovereign debt and national deficits. China is the obvious source of loan provider but is conscious of not being burdened by default of repayment by the debtors.

With the global economy on a downward spiral, China's export market has plummeted significantly, creating unemployment problems that require quantitative easing monetary policies to lessen the impact of social problems. China's insatiable appetite for more natural resources raises fears in many Western countries of the potential of usurping of the supply of scarce and limited non-renewable resources by China. China must play its international politics card cautiously and wisely to avoid any confrontation that could lead to disruption of foreign trade and global stability that is vital to China's economic and peaceful social progress in the next millennium.

There is always a trade-off for international mutually cordial relationships. You win some, and you may lose some. There are always jealous troublemakers who loathe seeing China becoming a leading nation. However, China, being a huge and populous country with five thousand years of history, can be magnanimous to accept some human frailty in this imperfect world. Jealousy is a sign of admiration of success.

Imminent Danger of Civil Strife

In the three momentous decades of galloping economic advancements, China experienced a slew of sociopolitical problems, such as runaway inflation; air and water pollution; exorbitant housing and food prices; water shortage; unemployment; an unfair justice system; state-owned enterprise monopolies; high cost of education and medical services; and a credit squeeze on small- and medium-size private enterprises. People complained about long lines at hospitals for medical services and difficulty in securing a school for their children. Rampant corruption deeply permeated every level of society. Unemployment of millions of university graduates remains a thorny social problem.

The income divide between the rich urbanites and the rural poor is painfully felt by the underprivileged, and the divergence is continuously widening—not a good sign for social stability. The confluence of immense poverty, high inflation, rampant corruption, environmental pollution, and shortage of clean water could create a perfect storm if combined. If left unchecked, China will turn into an inferno of social uprising by six hundred million destitute people who live from hand to mouth in the world's second-largest economy. If an uprising were to happen, China would sink into an abyss of destruction of astronomical dimensions and costs. All previous good works will be completely nullified. People-power is universally a weapon of mass destruction. The farming industry in rural areas depends on manual labor, and a small plot of land can never produce a high enough income to maintain a decent living.

Fresh Opportunities for China in the Export Market

It is interesting to note that lately the United States has moved its major military forces from Europe, where many countries are mired in financial difficulties and military budget cuts, to Asia, where many countries are prospering with spare cash. The US government's adrenaline is on overdrive, sending senior officials to engage in bilateral defense pacts with many Asian countries, seemingly picking China as its potential enemy and feverishly holding maritime exercises with many Asian countries at China's doorsteps.

Meanwhile, senior US military officers fire occasional provocative salvos of defending weak Asian nations if attacked by China. Such a chorus of beating the war drums is effective in selling weapons to a country whose neighboring country is picked by the military hardware peddlers as a potential enemy. Thus, the United States is considered by China as a troublemaker. China unfortunately has to live with the troublemaker even though it is not an immediate neighbor.

Creating fear and provocation is a precursor to starting a war, which is bad for Asian neighbors but not a distant country like the United States. Asian countries, except Japan, have been living in harmony for decades, and many have suffered humiliation from Japanese war aggression. War is not an option to settle disputes between neighbors. Those who play with fire will get burned.

China had never invaded a neighboring country, not even when China had the world's strongest economy and the largest naval vessels in the world. Successive imperial emperors spent lots of resources to build the Great Wall to protect the kingdom from being invaded by foreigners. China invented gunpowder but never used it to make bombs for aggressive military actions. China has been a pacifist country for a millennium and will remain so in the future under the influence of Confucius teaching.

In response to offensive foreign military presence at its doorstep, China has had no choice but to react in kind by building up its military forces to protect its integrity and sovereignty based on tragic experience in WW2. China does not wish to be invaded again. Such a reaction is natural and in accordance with Newton's third law of motion: "For every action there is an equal and opposite reaction." Survival is a human instinct. The greater the Chinese military reaction, the more the convincing sales pitch of the arms peddlers, aided by Western media blowing hot air about the arms buildup by China against its neighbors.

China realizes that in this real world of international politics, unfriendly foreign politicians would not shed a tear for the agony suffered by the tens of millions of innocent Chinese women and children who were maimed and killed by the heinous and inhumane Japanese soldiers during the war. China bashing is an effective election campaign tactic to win some votes in the US presidential election or a ruse to divert attention of domestic problems in neighboring countries.

The Motives of US Military Deployment in East and South China Seas

As there is no free lunch, the Asian alliance countries need to purchase military hardware—not necessarily the latest expensive models from the massive US defense industries—but perhaps from the cheaper military surplus store or retired fighter planes parked in the Mojave Desert or mothballed frigates in the naval base. Military hardware and spare parts could be worth multibillions of dollars. It is a lucrative military business, which has been the United States' strategy since WW2, bearing in mind that the United States needs to earn foreign income as its national debt exceeded US$18 trillion in 2014, meaning the United States' debt-to-GDP ratio is more than 100 percent. There is no charity in military hardware sales. The massive US defense industry needs constant customers to keep their design engineers and factory staff on the payroll and its factories humming.

The US government has reduced its defense budget with cuts on military expenditures and will remain so for some time due to its huge national debt. Hence, the East China Sea dispute over some tiny uninhabited rocks between China and Japan will be kept on the hit parade list for a long time by US military business interests. In resonance is a chorus of Western and Japanese media's incessant biased commentary of exaggerated Chinese military threat. Such daily propaganda easily influences people's mind that China is a devil and the United States is an angel protecting Japan against possible Chinese invasion. Let it be known that neither US citizens nor the US Senate would like to act like Santa Claus toward Japan for no material gain in a conflict with a third party. There is no free lunch. The US government tries hard but in vain to sell military hardware to Taiwan's government on the pretext of protection against China's invasion.

One does not need a rocket scientist to explain that the few tiny uninhibited rocks are not worth a dime for Japan to declare war on China. Never forget the relatives, friends, and descendants of the twenty-seven thousand American prisoners of war who were forced to work as slave laborers and treated with brutality and subjected to inhumane torture by the Japanese during WW2. It is inconceivable that they would support the Japanese government, an unremorseful enemy, to fight their old ally China. In any case, the United States cannot declare war on China without being sanctioned by the United Nations, in which China has a veto power.

China has a powerful friendly neighbor, Russia, who also has UN veto power and who has fought with Japan prior to and during WW2. Japan still has a bone to pick with Russia over their territorial claim on Kuril Islands, a rich fishing ground of immense commercial value that is more important than the few tiny uninhibited barren rocks in the East China Sea that Japan wants the United States to fight with China. The United States has no similar request from Japan to fight with Russia over the rich inhabited Kuril Islands. Both Japan and the United States are neighbors of Russia.

It would be a foolish thought that China would declare war on the United States while China holds US$1 trillion in US Treasury bonds. It would be unwise for China to fight a war with a foreign country on Chinese soil. The Japanese government seems to ignore the fact that China has depended on the United States for its export market for a long time. In 2014, the bilateral trade between the United States and China was worth US$594 billion in China's favor. The bilateral trade figure grows each year. China and the United States will have a mutually peaceful relationship for years to come, a fact so glaringly ignored by the Japanese hardcore politicians that it's incomprehensible. Their desire for aggression seems to be in their blood.

China will be patient to wear out the provocative rhetoric by the US-Japan military alliance as China has more than five thousand years of existence. There is no problem waiting another decade or two for the United States' seventh fleet to leave the East China Sea for good. The warships cannot stay there forever; they cost the US taxpayers a fortune.

The United States is a distant country. China will adopt Sun Tzu's principle of *The Art of War* (parts 4.2, 5, "Defend or Attack"): "To secure ourselves against defeat lies in our own hands, but the opportunity of defeating the enemy is provided by the enemy himself. Security against defeat implies defensive tactics; ability to defeat the enemy means taking the offensive." Patience allows China to wait for the right opportunity to strike with decisive victory and least costs.

Meanwhile, the cash-strapped Japanese government has to foot the bill of keeping US forces on its soil and to pay for the purchase of US military hardware. The Japanese government borrows heavily from the national pension fund to support its national budget deficit annually. One day, the Japanese government has to cease draining the pension fund when the tax contribution continues to abate due to its decreasing population and workforce. Meanwhile, the Japanese industries are aging and exports shrinking.

South China Sea Dispute

Whether the Southeast Asian countries allied with the United States are willing, at the expense of social development, to spend a huge amount of money to purchase second-grade defense equipment or retired military hardware against a populous China, which has superior military strength, including nuclear weapons and huge financial resources, is an interesting guessing game. It is wise to know that no one can demand Uncle Sam drop a bomb on Chinese soil at the behest of a third-world country.

It would also be a ludicrous thought that China would want to waste precious financial, human, and material resources to invade its small neighboring countries over the South China Sea that have been peaceful for centuries even during the period when China was the strongest country in the world (before the United States was born). Peace can be had amongst neighbors only without antagonism or interference from a third party with ulterior motives. Spending precious money on social development to improve people's lives in a less-affluent nation is a better proposition than arms buildup.

For centuries, navigation on the South China Sea has never been questioned by any country, as attested by the Japanese merchant ships that transported raw materials without impediment during WW2. It is a bizarre phenomenon but illogical that a distant country can declare unilaterally that freedom of navigation on the South China Sea is being threatened by China against its neighbors. China has no military base on foreign soil.

The South China Sea is too huge to be effectively blocked by China. China needs a peaceful world for its exports. Making war is never good for China or its neighbors. War is a game of burning money, of yielding no real economic benefits to mankind. It is a waste of material resources and human lives. All the Asian countries, including China, have had painful experiences during WW2 by the atrocious invasion of Japan. Another round of war will create hatred amongst neighbors and benefit nobody except arms dealers.

It is interesting to note that China does not want to have military alliance with other nations. There is an interesting fact about the United States possessing a gigantic offensive military arsenal that is more than capable of destroying the whole world, yet it continues to add more firepower despite having an $18 trillion federal debt. Presently, the United States has no worthy opponent in a decisive war game.

When and where does the US government intend to use such colossal military hardware, and for what purpose? It costs US taxpayers many billions of dollars daily to produce and keep the weapons in readiness to strike, yet it cannot help the world by stopping pirates who routinely hijack merchant ships in the South China Sea, where the mighty Seventh Fleet ships sail every day with all its modern equipment. It is a strange phenomenon that even the small pirates are not afraid of the mighty United States' Seventh Fleet.

Asia is a prosperous region now and, hence, it is unwise for any Asian country to start a war amongst the neighbors to spoil the peace and prosperity. Many hundreds of millions of poor people are still beset by poverty due to WW2. They need peace and not another war of grave suffering. Good neighborliness is a tonic for world peace.

China is Busy Building up Bilateral Trades on Five Continents

Casting aside senseless debate and irritating remarks on military confrontation from its neighbors and the United States, and knowing time is on the side of China with its power and wealth, top Chinese officials have been traveling all over the five continents, signing bilateral trade pacts with many countries involving investments in the local industries and commerce without any adversarial reaction from the United States. The Chinese RMB (Renminbi, or yuan) currency can be used in these bilateral trade transactions.

The Chinese massive foreign currency reserves worth US$4 trillion will be gainfully employed to divest into joint ventures in foreign countries to spur the restructured Chinese economy. The expanded Chinese trades with many foreign countries will strengthen the position of the RMB as a global trading and reserve currency in contest with the US dollar, which would decline in value when the quantitative easing program continues unabated. Diversification of international trade minimizes the undesirable effect of the recent financial debacles besetting the United States and the EU, the two top trading partners of China.

Gradually, the US dollar would reduce its importance as the world's trading and reserve currency due to the US Federal Reserve overprinting of money. China will not follow the United States' policy of using its currency as a political weapon but as a conduit of doing business. Presently, China remains the largest creditor of the United States in the world in terms of possessing US$1 trillion Treasury bills. By the next decade China will play a lesser role as a major US creditor by paring down the purchase of US Treasury bills with the concern that the US Federal Reserve continuously prints money, leading to eventual collapse of the US financial system.

With its huge domestic market accrued from the Eco-World project and expanded global markets, China will have an advantage of lower production cost per unit and a competitive selling price to many other foreign customers, not over-depending on the US market. It is interesting to note that both the United States and China play different games to promote their respective export merchandise, one for war and the other for peace, respectively. It is, indeed, business as usual. Cash is king.

The Decline of the Japanese Economy

The Japanese industries in the fields of consumer electronics and ship building, which used to dominate the world market, are on a decline due to the increasing competitiveness of the similar Chinese and Korean products of comparable quality at lower prices. The reputation of Japanese manufacturing quality was eroded when quality icon Toyota had its president, Akio Toyoda, apologize to the US Congress for the fatal defects of auto acceleration that led to the recall of ten million of its cars. Toyota paid a US$1.2 billion fine. A Japanese airbag maker company, Takata, said in 2015 that thirty-four million vehicles made in Germany, the United States, Japan, and other countries were to be recalled worldwide for defective airbag inflators, which could cause fatal accidents.

The old traditions of the dogged Japanese commitment to quality began to fade in time when the quality-conscious older generation retired. The new generations do not have similar convictions or dedication to quality of manufacturing.

Japan's national debt-to-GDP is the highest among all the advanced countries, exceeding more than 150 percent. Their future is lackluster, with declining economic activities and an aging population. The people are unhappy with the yen devaluation, making imports more expensive, and the exorbitant increase in Goods and Services taxation in 2015. To support the national deficit, the government borrows heavily from the pension funds and repays little interest. Such a fiscal situation is unsustainable and is exacerbated by the right-wing government's increasing military budget to build up offensive weapons under the guise of self-defense against China and riding the coattails of the United States' military agenda in Asia. With higher prices of imports and inflation, the Japanese will have a tough time leading a comfortable retirement life in the future.

The time is opportune for China to embark on a dedicated national program of developing industries that compete directly with Japan with the ultimate aim of crippling the Japanese industries. Japan will then relegate to a nation of aged people and decayed industries. The Samurai politicians in the Japanese government would regret refusing to offer sincere repentance for crimes against humanity during WW2 and for being hostile to its powerful neighbor. It does not pay to have a superiority complex and an attitude of hostility.

The Eco-World for the Six Hundred Million Poor

The crucial task of helping poor farmers would be to turn farming into a high-tech, guaranteed harvest and a highly productive venture, not a backbreaking, backward, nature-dependent, and uncertain harvest venture as in the past. Thus, an Eco-World project is the way to go to avoid civil strife by six hundred million destitute people.

In the Eco-World, all the farmers will be resettled in new homes in eco-cities. They will be trained with job skills that are required in the new eco-cities, and they will earn a decent pay to support their family. Rural poverty would be relegated to history. Resettlement and training would be at the expense of the government, which had already dished out many billions of dollars to aid the farmers suffering from natural disasters and hyperinflation.

The government would save annually an enormous amount of money by dissolving the huge bureaucracy that looks after the needs of the hundreds of millions of farmers and their families. Also, there will be no need for the government to spend money every year on teaching food production skills, irrigation techniques, and pest control. The farmers' miseries are compounded by lack of medical care and social welfare when diseases and ill health befall them.

Six Hundred Million Poor Will Become Middle-Class Citizens in Eco-cities

The Eco-World provides the farmers' children proper education and equips them with skill and knowledge that will place them in good stead when applying for high-value-added jobs, thereby breaking the traditional vicious circle of poverty in rural areas. When the six hundred million poor farming families transform themselves into middle-class citizens, the economic prowess of China will be the envy of many countries. These ex-farmers will no longer need handout from the government, and they will contribute by paying taxes.

Positive and prudent investment in human resources involving 1.36 billion people should yield a bumper crop of dividends. China now has the means and the opportunity to act instantly. China will gradually turn itself into a technologically advanced country, even surpassing the United States.

Enormous Eco-World Benefits for all Chinese People

In the Eco-World project involving four hundred new eco-cities, there would be hundreds of thousands of eco-farms and other industrial projects that would allow China to become self-sufficient in food, water, and energy, compatible with conserving the environment and natural resources. There will be no more greenhouse gases escaping into the atmosphere. Universal education, a fair judicial system, affordable housing and medical services, and safe food will be the hallmarks of the eco-cities in the Eco-World.

A new social system would be conducive to employment and provide a pleasant, pollution-free, safe, and clean environment for community living. The income disparity between the rich and poor would be narrowed to achieve a nation of middle-income status. The new socioeconomic political system will be constantly modified to meet new challenges in a proactive mode in order to sustain another millennium. Employment opportunities will be bountiful. Technology will be encouraged and applied in daily lives and industries. Traditional family values and cultures will be maintained to achieve a tranquil, cohesive, and harmonious society following in Confucius philosophy.

Engagement of the Waratah Organization for the Eco-World Project: External Assistance Required for This Gargantuan Project

The Chinese government invites eminent academicians and professionals in the fields of science, technology, engineering, sociology, education, animal husbandry, construction, economics, medicine, agriculture, and aquaculture from around the world to submit proposals on the Eco-World project. As the project involves massive investments and would entail financial resources of gigantic proportion, it would take at least two decades to fulfill the target of building four hundred eco-cities, each of which will accommodate four million people.

In facing future predicaments of world shortages in food production and water, and problems of environmental pollution, increasing demand for rapidly depleting natural resources, and galloping world inflation, the Chinese government is resolute in making sure the Eco-World project is sustainable into the next millennia. Widespread applications of innovations and technologies would be applied in economic policies, reduction in waste of raw materials, recycling of reusable materials, social engineering, education, commerce, industries, healthy lifestyle, infrastructures, sustainable energy, and food production.

The central government had held countless top-level meetings to discuss how best to solve the current pressing socioeconomic issues and potential future problems that could affect the security and prosperity of China. As the project of national transformation involves mammoth detailed investigation, study, and understanding of the current and future potential problems, the Chinese government decided to engage Waratah Organization to do a feasibility study and propose recommendations for the development of an Eco-World.

Another reason for selecting Waratah is that China wishes to establish a deeper cultural and social relationship with US citizens. There are many good memories of the United States, especially the contribution from the Flying Tigers and private individuals, helping China overcome pain and hardship during WW2 against the Japanese invasion.

The US-China Cooperative Project for World Peace

The United States' assistance will be a catalyst in accelerating the progress of technical and information technology improvements, creating a "Chinese dream" concept similar to the "American dream" for every Chinese citizen regardless of social, religious, or financial background. The returned scholars of hundreds of thousands strong from the United States and other countries would be helpful in the implementation of the Eco-World project. With collaboration and mutual trust, these two largest economies of the world could create a powerful force to stabilize world peace and prosperity and perhaps advancement of the human race that is compatible with the environment in the new millennia.

Chapter 8

Eco-City Design

Current Urbanization Problems

For some thirty years the Chinese government has been encouraging rural residents to migrate to the cities for better living conditions and employment. About two hundred million people have benefited from the more than seven trillion RMB urbanization program. However, some six hundred million poor rural residents are still waiting. Unfortunately, this urbanization program has created immense social and economic problems that are threatening the social fabric and national security.

Current Social Ills and Discontentment

Prevailing problems of rampant corruption and social problems; rising inflation; water, food, and energy crises; escalating air and water pollution levels; high costs of housing and health care services; and rising living costs are valid reasons for a technical stop to review the efficacy of continuing the current urbanization program.

China cannot live in isolation. The interdependent world is changing rapidly, with the United States and many EU countries still mired in financial woes that might take many more years to resolve. The Chinese global labor cost parity is losing steam to other developing countries. In the meantime, China faces a multitude of social and economic problems. It is too Herculean a task and time consuming to navigate the heaps of problems to seek an individual solution. They are too complex and intertwined and involve many self-interest groups in twenty-three provinces and in mega-cities like Shanghai, with a population of more than twenty-four million. Piecemeal fixes or touch-ups offer only temporary respite to some problems but allow others to sink deeper into quicksand. The opportunity costs are astronomical, and national security would be put in jeopardy if the can of remedial actions is kicked down the road.

Time to Rework the Urbanization Program: Revolutionary Solutions Needed to Clean up the Mess

Spending an annual budget of US$106 billion (about the size of Ghana's GDP) in order to continue the current urbanization program, thus creating more socioeconomic political problems, is, to quote some reformist government leaders, a dead-end policy. China has to modernize to survive in this fast-changing world. To clean up the current problems in one fell swoop, China will have to pull out all the stops to embark on an epic socioeconomic political revolution by establishing an Eco-World.

The eco-cities are tailor-made to suit the requirements of the residents for a healthy and congenial environment making continuous improvements in order to be compatible with the environment.

Computer Model for Designing an Eco-city

The Waratah design teams employ various processes to design the eco-city, using the fastest computers and latest software and simulations of various systems and operations that will seek optimal results for the final configuration of the Eco-World. The eco-city is built in accordance with specifications with options to expand the city boundaries.

An eco-city project costing more than US$1 trillion to build would generate many more positive trillions in return on investment, goodwill, and social advancement for the country and its inhabitants, and also for future generations to live peacefully, harmoniously, and compatibly with the environment. The crucial task is to eradicate the problem of poverty for six hundred million rural residents who still live in primitive conditions.

Design Aims of the Eco-World

The Eco-World development involves the latest multifaceted national and international ideas on economy, politics, and social and physical environments that cater to future generations. It needs to utilize the latest knowledge and wisdom to select the best practices in employing available human, economic, and natural resources in a sustainable way. The end result will benefit everyone in society in a fair and equitable manner. It would not matter what kind of political ideology is used as long as it works.

The main criteria of designing the Eco-World will encompass the necessary changes to the current society. Civil administration will be compatible with the environment so future generations will have a cleaner, greener enjoyable and peaceful living without causing harm to the environment and without wasting natural resources. It encompasses every aspect of modern living, incorporating the best of science and technology, the best practices in social engineering, agriculture, food, and energy production, transportation, education, medical and health services, finance, public administration, natural resources, and environment preservation.

There is no previously existing model of an eco-city design to use as a reference. This will be the pioneer endeavor. Living in an eco-city should be a feast not only for the stomach but for the soul. There will be plenty of mini-forests, gardens, parks, lakes, and recreational facilities for leisure and appreciation of nature. Every citizen will be taught to be civic-minded and courteous in the community, with a self-reliant and self-disciplined spirit, and less dependency on government for handouts. Traditional Chinese festivals and cultural activities will be preserved and celebrated to keep the Chinese culture forever in continuity.

Eco-city living is fun, enticing, pleasant, peaceful. and environmentally friendly. Chinese leaders believe only an Eco-World can help China sustain a healthy and peaceful lifestyle for the next millennia with its increasing population and demand for limited natural resources. With every increasing output of human ingenuity in science and technology, and with new discoveries and inventions, the world should advance faster than ever before—so much so that another new Eco-World would need to replace the current one within the next ten to fifteen generations in order to meet new challenges.

Eco-City Design Objectives

A comprehensive computer model of the new eco-city design is used to define all the design objectives of various components of the eco-city government, social amenities and infrastructures, industries, and transportation and productions of food, energy, and water supplies. Each aspect of the design objectives goes through an iteration of computer simulations to find optimal results. The final configuration involves the complete integration of various components of the design objectives and will incorporate the salient features of a smart city using technology to enhance living standards. Many simulated trial runs will be conducted before the final configuration is selected.

The blueprint for building an eco-city encompasses the following objectives:

1. The eco-city life span should last two hundred years with sustaining non-polluting industries, self-sufficiency in production of food, clean water, and energy, and with continuous improvements.
2. recycling of river waters, constructing canals, reservoirs, and lakes for flood control, and creating sufficient water resources for human, industry, agriculture, aquaculture, animal husbandry, and ecosystems
3. lifestyles compatible with conserving natural resources and protecting the environment
4. parks, gardens, public amenities, and sporting fields generously provided for healthy living
5. restoration of deserts, dried lakes, and wetlands, and planting of trees in the open fields and in the cities throughout the country
6. Every business and enterprise, privately or publicly owned, must obtain an ISO 9001 (International Organization for Standardization which specifies requirements for a quality-management system) certificate to ensure quality and safety not be compromised.
7. a social system that provides equitable medical services, friendly public administration, and a fair justice system
8. a public road transportation system that is convenient, safe, comfortable, pollution-free, and affordably priced
9. Canal water to be used for firefighting in the city and forests. Every block of building has a built-in automatic firefighting system that can be operated within thirty seconds of activation by remote control.
10. To reduce road accidents, vehicular traffic is separated from pedestrian traffic, and special lanes are allocated to cyclists. All public transport roads in the city are constructed underground to allow the free flow of traffic even in adverse weather conditions. Real-time traffic conditions are displayed on Internet and on-street electronic signboards. All vehicles must install GPS and transponders for vehicle location and identification and a yaw sensor to detect drunk and fatigued driver.
11. an education system using state-of-the-art online and robotic teaching, and promotion of learning by interacting, and personal development in building character and practical application of theory

12. encouragement by government to promote civility and social grace in society, during family time, while walking in the parks, gardens, and forests, and while enjoying music, concerts, opera, and stage plays, and promoting community spirit
13. a political system based on trust, fairness, competency, respect, integrity, and a corruption-free administration
14. government providing tax incentives to encourage industries and factories to adopt the use of robots and mechanization in production and manufacturing with the latest IT and software for maximum productivity, and the employment of physically disabled persons who can work from home
15. government will encourage R&D to develop more robots to take over vacant jobs due to decreasing population
16. an equitable and affordable housing policy that allows every family a chance to own a home
17. industrial estates are provided with mass rapid transit systems and bus stations
18. ample facilities and infrastructures are to be provisioned for retirees, the aging population, and disabled persons
19. the eco-city incorporates features of lakes, ponds, gardens, parks, nature reserves, tree-lined streets, open sports stadiums, and closed-door recreational facilities
20. factories and industries located far from residential areas. Factories dealing with chemicals will have trenches built around the building to prevent spills from spreading. Every factory will have a pollution control inspector employed to ensure compliance with ISO 9001 standards.
21. the eco-city site will be big enough to accommodate a maximum population of six million with an initial population of four million
22. the topography allows building an underground mass-transit system
23. The site selected has the natural beauty of hills and mountains in the surrounding areas
24. The city will encourage online commerce to reduce cost of living and to save time. All online merchants must possess an ISO 9001 certification and provide a 100 percent guarantee of product quality and after-sales service

Chapter 9

An Eco-Airport in Eco-City Meigui

The World's First Eco-Airport

After arriving in Shanghai, the VIP visitors take a flight to the new eco-city of Meigui in Shanxi Province. Shanxi is a province that falls behind the coastal provinces in terms of economic development over the past three decades. It is the first eco-city of the world. Within an hour, the airplane lands in Meigui's state-of-the-art airport, the first of its kind in the world to operate with a miniscule carbon footprint. At the airport arrival hall, Transport Ministry and Meigui Airport officials welcome the visitors, who are later taken to a tour of the airport and shown a video of the airport's design, operation, and maintenance.

Objectives of Eco-Airport Design

An airport model is displayed in the meeting room showing a bird's eye view of the gigantic facility. The design incorporates the latest technology and past experience of airport operation. The objectives are to reduce costs of operations and to provide convenience to passengers and maintenance staff. The airport operation is user-friendly. Safety is paramount.

This eco-airport should usher in a new era of aviation industries for higher safety, productivity, and efficiency, and a model for other airport operators to emulate. Two notable features are the reduction of its carbon footprint and its all-weather operation, especially during snowfall in winter. Near the airport is a huge eco-farm that produces adequate supplies of biofuel for the airlines. Underground pipes are used to transport all the biofuel to the airport from the eco-farm factories.

User-Friendly Passenger Handling and Service Systems

After clearing immigration, passengers will proceed to collect their belongings from the baggage carousel. For ease of identification and avoidance of mistakes by passengers taking the wrong bags, all bags will have been prominently tagged with a color-coded seat number at the original departure counter. Passengers will match their baggage tag number with their retrieval ticket number. Porter services are available by pressing a call button at the service station.

To eliminate long lines by international passengers and to reduce staff at the immigration counters, international passengers will use the immigration checkpoint portal on board the flight to log into their personal travel details. As they proceed to collect their baggage, they walk through a gate, where they are fingerprinted for identification and their passports deposited.

At the next gate they will collect their passport, visa, or visit pass approval. Traditional long lines are eliminated. A dedicated lane is provided to process infant and disabled passengers. For the benefit of tourists and visitors, the airport passenger service center provides a ten-minute video of the city's features, facilities, places of interest, and cultures.

Transport from Airport to City or other Destination

Transportation choices to the city include train, bus, or taxi. The airport offers a hotel service station that advises hotel guest which bus or train number to take to reach the hotel, as well as cost and a time schedule. Train and bus stations are located conveniently next to the arrival terminal.

The Land Transport Authority (LTA) gives every building and residence a location coordinate code, which can be obtained from a Chinese BeiDou GPS map or the LTA website. Along the way the bus or train passengers could connect their smartphones or laptops to the Internet as the whole city is wi-fi wired. The electronic display screen inside the train and bus will show the names of various stations and roads on the way. The passenger can view his or her cell phone to look at the map and final destination.

A passenger wanting to hail a taxi must purchase a ticket from a taxi vending machine using the destination coordinate code for the fare. The taxi driver will issue a receipt with his name and taxi number printed on it together with a telephone number that the passenger can call for a complaint or compliment. Such system eliminates communication problems between the taxi driver and foreign visitors who cannot speak Chinese and eliminates the possibility of overcharging by the driver.

Every hotel in China issues a room booking card online that has the hotel address coordinate code printed on it and the nearest underground and bus station. The underground train service between the eco-airport and downtown stations is unaffected by traffic jams, snowstorm, heavy fog, or thunderstorms. Passengers can check in at certain underground stations that are connected to the airport.

Eco-Airport Design Objectives

Foreign visitors are impressed by the design objectives of the eco-airport. The design theme is to minimize greenhouse emissions by incorporating advanced computerized systems of airport operations, waste recycling, and eliminating surface traffic of vehicles propelled by conventional internal combustion engines using fossil fuels. The greenhouse effects are further reduced with the airline's full participation and adopting an integrated approach to passenger and cargo operations systems and management throughout the country. The state-of-the-art airport, with automation and robots, significantly helps airlines and airport operators in the following areas:

1. avoiding long delays or cancellations due to inclement weather, thereby saving millions of dollars in compensating passengers on hotel accommodations and ancillary expenses
2. increasing productivity of airplane service with faster turnaround times and higher levels of serviceability with a reduction in maintenance costs and time
3. reducing amount of fuel for the flight sector
4. enhancing longevity of airplane systems and components
5. improving overall efficiency and safety of airline operations with more technology and less manpower and human error
6. reducing carbon footprints
7. optimizing airport operational efficiency with highest productivity

Biofuel Supply

High energy consumption is a critical issue of an airport operation, especially during the nights in winter. Power requirements involve lighting up the entire apron and tarmac for airplane operations, and the concourse for movements of passengers, freights, logistics, and administrative services. Emergency power backup is necessary for a 24/7 operation. The airport energy needs come from the power grid connected to the nearby thousands of wind turbines, solar panels, and power stations using renewable biofuels extracted from corn, Jatropha, and algae plants to operate the steam turbine generators.

Biofuels are piped from underground storage tanks to refuel airplanes on the tarmac, which can be refueled simultaneously from several pumping stations, reducing delays and airplane down time. The dispatcher, with inputs of passenger load, freight, reserve fuels, flight operations, and engineering requirements would use the latest computer software to calculate the flight plan fuel requirement and the fuel distribution for the wing, center, and tail tanks. The final fuel uplift information is transmitted to the flight operation center, where the pilots are briefed before flight.

All-Weather Runways

An aircraft can land on the all-weather, full-visibility runways with latest automatic guide slope and transponder equipment, and with crosswind speed detection and control. Lining both sides of the runways are windbreakers to prevent wind shear effects. Runway heating is automatically turned on when ice is detected. The upward slope of the runway helps shorten the airplane landing distance, saving the aircraft from having to deploy thrust reversers, which are noise and maintenance-cost generators, thereby reducing airplane maintenance and fuel costs. Similarly, on the same runway with a downward slope, airplane V_2 takeoff speed is reached at a shorter time and distance, helping achieve higher airplane payload and, as a result, profitability.

Instant Firefighting System

On the runway, cameras can detect any debris that might have fallen from departing airplanes. The debris can be washed away immediately by the powerful firefighting water jets that can be raised from underground, and a robot will suck up the debris. Fire drills will be conducted regularly to ensure crises can be effectively controlled and the rescue team deployed to test its response time, readiness, and proficiency. Foams are available via the powerful water jets to fight any fire that engulfs a disabled airplane on the runway.

The water jets are remotely controlled and operate instantly when a fire is detected or reported. Fire hydrants connected to an underground water supply system can be raised at various airport locations to fight fires. Water comes from a nearby reservoir.

Congestion-Free Tarmac Operation

The tarmac is constructed with two tiers. The first tier or ground level is meant for airplane parking and towing, and passenger and staff movements. The second tier or underground tarmac is meant for cargo, airplane servicing, and maintenance operations. This design is to minimize traffic congestion often found in conventional busy airports, resulting in frequent ground accidents between vehicles and tarmac users, and between aircraft and ground equipment. With reduction in human and vehicular crisscross activities in the new eco-airport operation, accidents should reduce.

During winter, underground pipes are raised to blow hot air over the wings and fuselage to prevent ice accumulation on the airplane surface. Therefore, airplanes will not need deicing, which can take hours to complete in severe conditions. This will save precious time for airline and airport operators in winter. Airlines also save on deicing equipment and manpower costs. A snowbound airport is a show stopper, creating chaos and inconvenience to all passengers and airline operations. The economic loss is immense. Airport closures due to inclement weather are common in the northern part of China.

Because the tarmac is debris-free, there is no worry about debris causing punctures to airplane tires or being sucked into engines. Moreover, the airport authority does not need to spend resources to clean up the tarmac frequently as happens at conventional airports.

Automated Tarmac Washing

On a scheduled basis, the tarmac is automatically washed by a ground washing system operated remotely by a computerized system. A supervisor will monitor the operation by remote cameras to make sure dirt, sand, small stones, and other debris blown from the surrounding vicinity onto the tarmac or runway is removed.

Airplane Towing, Eliminating Ground Accidents, and Improving Efficiency

After an airplane has landed, it will turn into the first taxiway toward a transit pad, where an automated plane-towing system is installed. From there the aircraft nose wheel is attached automatically to a towing platform, which will tow the aircraft to a designated arrival gate. During towing, all the main engines are shut down, eliminating carbon footprints and noise. During congested periods at busy airports like Los Angeles, London, Tokyo, airplane taxiing time could take fifteen to twenty minutes, including frequent stops and starts due to traffic jams, thereby increasing tire wear and aircraft operating time, and, hence, increasing the costs of airline operation and prices of airline tickets. High traffic density on the tarmac and taxiway is a safety concern for airplane movement. Collision between airplanes is a frequent event.

Fuel-Savings Benefiting Airlines in Eco-Airport

On long-distance flights the amount of arrival taxi fuel saved on the ground represents significant savings on the flight plan, as you need to consume fuel to carry fuel to the destination. Therefore, at eco-airports, departure and arrival taxi fuels can be excluded from the flight plan fuel quantity calculation, resulting for each flight valuable fuel saving and providing the airline corresponding increases in payload and, hence, revenue. The fixed cost of such a towing system is insignificant compared to the variable costs of extra fuel burned on every single fight, as well as the extra maintenance costs of airplanes and their engines. Expensive airplane-towing vehicles will not be needed in eco-airports.

On departure, the airplane is towed back to the transit pad, where the engines will be started. As the airplane towing schedule is timed precisely and controlled by the control tower, there is no idle time on the taxiway caused by the lining up of airplanes awaiting takeoff, which happens frequently at busy conventional airports. This way fuel is saved, reducing costs. The new eco-airport designs and operations not only improve safety and reduce manpower; they save millions of gallons of fuel as well as conserve the longevity of engines, tires, and other components and systems. Airplane engine exhaust gases are also reduced.

Fog-Free Airports

Many airports suffer from heavy fog blanketing during winter periods in the northern part of China, reducing visibility to a few feet and causing lengthy flight delays. The eco-airport will not be affected by heavy fog as it incorporates a fog dispersal system that releases warm air into the atmosphere around the runway vicinity to prevent mists from forming.

Tire-Pressure Monitoring and Tire-Replacement System

An automatic tire pressure checking and charging system is installed at each airplane parking gate. The system is operated by a mechanic. Checking and inflation of the tires are done automatically in accordance with the airline specifications. This will eliminate the common and expensive problem of tires bursting during takeoff, caused by low tire pressure and human errors. Due to a variety of reasons, such as tire gauge being inoperative, manpower shortage, undetected low tire pressure, or tire being under-inflated, the tire temperature will rise on long taxi and take-off runs. If the temperature reaches a critical level, tire bursting can occur, with serious consequences.

With an automatic tire pressure monitoring system installed on the ground, the expensive computer-controlled system on board the airplane is unnecessary. This will save airlines millions in maintenance costs and assets, and unnecessary return of the airplane by the captain, who often receives false indications of low tire pressure. Every tire pressure reading on the ground will be automatically registered and forwarded to the airline central maintenance station at the headquarters for quality analysis and monitoring.

Tire-Replacement Process and Logistics

Landing gear hydraulic jacks for different types of airplane are available at each departure gate for ease of tire change, which occurs quite frequently. Tire suppliers have an inventory of spares at the gate. Such arrangements improve resource-management efficiency, significantly reducing costs to the airlines. Airlines do not need to spend capital upfront to buy the tires, or hire expensive staff to manage the logistics, storage, and movement of the tires between the airline and suppliers. Tires are leased and paid for each landing. This is a win-win formula for the airline and tire supplier.

Cargo and Airplane Services

Cargo-Handling System

When the airplane is parked at the arrival gate, a cargo loader will be raised from the underground tarmac to retrieve the containers from the airplane cargo holds. Baggage containers are then forwarded by an automatic conveyor-belt system to the assigned baggage belt according to the container's code number detected by the sensors on the conveyor. Commercial cargo containers will be forwarded to the airfreight terminal for further processing.

Catering Operation System

Flight kitchens and catering services utilize the underground automatic-delivery system, which delivers catering carts to the airplane galleys. Empty carts could be unloaded and returned to the flight kitchen by the same delivery system in a very short time. Such a system eliminates the need to use ground vehicles and manpower for delivery and retrieval of catering carts.

Logistics of Airplane Catering Equipment

Every catering cart is leased from the supplier in order to eliminate the traditional logistics problem of keeping track of and maintaining the required quantity of serviceable carts by each airline at every airport. A standard design specification for the cart is accepted by all the Chinese airlines and cart manufacturers. Coffee, tea, water, and fruit juice dispensers are also leased from a third-party supplier. With such a leasing scheme, the airlines benefit from reduction in manpower, operation, maintenance, and inventory costs.

Airplane Maintenance Services

The underground tarmac is equipped with automatic supply systems of electrical power, biofuel, fresh water, heated air, air-conditioning, firefighting, and pneumatic air for ease of airplane servicing and maintenance on the ground. Toilet waste is discharged into an underground sewage system. Cabin trash and waste are disposed of through an underground pneumatic system. Such systems dispense with the need of using traditional vehicles to transport wastes. Recycling plants are located in the vicinity of the airport to recycle waste from the airplane, airport, and commercial operations. All movements of cargo and airplane-servicing operations are performed by vehicles operated by battery power.

At every airport, a centralized spare-parts warehouse is managed by a consortium of airline operators who pool their spare parts to save inventory-holding and manpower costs. Airline mechanics would utilize an automatic delivery system connected between the centralized warehouse and various arrival gates to retrieve the parts or components they order via their Internet-connected notebook issued by the airline. Hence, there is no need for the mechanic to drive to the warehouse store to obtain replacement parts, which takes time and causes unnecessary delays to flight departures.

An individual airline not in the pool could suffer from long delays due to spares being unavailable. Long flight delays could affect airport curfew hours, resulting in flight cancellations. The central store is computerized so that any item can be quickly replaced by the vendor. Superseded parts or components can be promptly exchanged.

Airside Ground Traffic Control

To ease traffic flows at and around the airport, and to reduce traffic jams, passengers and airport workers are encouraged to take trains or buses connecting the city to the airport. Low-cost bike rentals at the airport train and bus stations are provided for workers to cycle under protective cover to their office. Parking fees at the airport are set at an expensive rate to discourage car owners from driving to the airport. Check-in services are available at designated downtown user-friendly train stations to attract passengers. Underground train service provides unimpeded journeys to and from the airport.

Eco-Friendly Infrastructures

Solar panels and wind turbines are erected throughout the airport vicinity and nearby fields. Power generators using biofuel are the main energy supply. All rainwater and snowmelt are collected and drained into a reservoir for water supply and firefighting. Biodegradable waste products and wastewater are collected and recycled by waste-processing plants near the airport. A sophisticated integrated waste-management system is implemented by the airport authority so

1. food waste from the airplane, airport catering kitchen, terminal, and restaurants are channeled into a waste system for final processing into electrical power and compost;
2. disused cooking oil is collected for processing into biofuel;
3. wastepaper products are recycled back into paper;
4. canals and reservoirs are built around the airport to prevent flooding and to ensure adequate water supply at all times; and
5. recycled water is used for firefighting systems and for washing airplanes, airport tarmacs, and terminal buildings.

Airfreight Terminal

A state-of-the-art airfreight terminal was built adjacent to the passenger terminal. At the dispatch terminal station, the dimensions of each piece of cargo are measured by a robotic system and stored on the computer database. The computer will then find the best fit of container for the various cargos. Such computerized systems maximize the volumetric carriage of cargo, thereby increasing the productivity of the airplane. Every container is electronically tagged with a Chinese BeiDou NavSat GPS system for ease of tracking. The system is supervised and managed by a remote-control center manned by mostly physically disabled persons on a 24/7 basis.

Once a container is fully loaded, it will be ready for transportation by electric conveyor belts to the departure gate of the cargo's flight. Some containers will be diverted to the passenger terminal. Loading of the containers is performed by a robotic system with minimal human intervention. The computerized airplane cargo loading system will evaluate the best loading configuration of the cargo holds. The container will be sealed once it is ready for shipment after it passes the scanning check for safety measures.

As the weight and center of gravity location of the containers is computer generated, and the weight of passengers and seating location are preloaded into the database, the airplane dispatcher can have his load sheet and airplane empty fuel weight rapidly and accurately prepared for airplane refueling purposes. In conjunction with the computer-generated flight-sector fuel quantity, refueling for each tank can commence quickly. Speed is of the essence in resource-management efficiency, and this is achievable with fully integrated computerized systems. Overall, the airline can improve its turnaround and flight crew time. Daily airplane utilization can be increased for higher productivity.

Maximizing Productivity and Safety of the Eco-Airport

The eco-airport authority will benefit substantially as airport gates are more efficiently utilized with higher turnover rates arising from shorter airplane transit times. Safety is enhanced as human errors in cargo loading and erroneous calculations of airplanes' center of gravity, which have resulted in airplane crashes and tail-planes scratching the runway, are eliminated.

Seamless Custom Clearance System

The passenger terminal is connected by a conveyor-belt system to the airfreight terminal. This is to cater to incoming and outgoing cargo being transported by passenger plane. A central customs clearance center embraces a one-stop office that deals with all matters concerning imports and exports of goods and compliance with all regulations and rules, taxation, and goods of a dangerous and expensive nature.

The customs department and all the airlines share the worldwide airfreight software database that tracks all incoming and outgoing cargo and the nature and contents of each container. After the cargo manifest has been cleared electronically by customs, the airfreight forwarders will be informed when their containers are ready for collection. Rapid loading takes only a few minutes by the computerized robotic operation, as the loading bay is managed by several robotic arms operating simultaneously. Time saving means better productivity of the airport operation and saving of resources. Heavy and chaotic traffic at airfreight terminals is a common sight at traditional airports.

The eco-friendly airfreight terminal operation and system, designed for minimal human intervention, manages to eliminate all the theft and smuggling of cargo, as well as missing cargo that plagues many airports around the world. An eco-friendly airport means saving human and material resources and reducing carbon footprints. Although robotic operations and computerized systems have reduced the number of manual workers, the net effect is that the economy of the local area will have a higher productivity and income because of more high-value-added services being introduced, and the skill of the people will increase correspondingly, as will their income.

Standardization of Cargo Containers

Keeping a high level of spares and maintaining real-time serviceability of cargo containers is a logistics nightmare for airline cargo management. To solve the problem of empty containers that have to be returned to their original stations, and to reduce operational costs of searching for missing containers, the airlines have decided to lease, instead of buying, the containers from suppliers that make them to standard specifications.

An independent logistics company would maintain 100 percent serviceability of containers at every airport. It will also help the airport authority to keep the tarmac free from idle containers scattered haphazardly around the airport. Using the Chinese BeiDou tracking system, the logistics company has real-time information about serviceable containers that are serialized in the inventory.

Air-freight operations are quickly expanding to cater to the global demand for rapid transportation of goods—for example, electronic parts and perishable foodstuff that have a short shelf life in the marketplace. Online shopping in China is increasing, and air shipments will increase correspondingly.

Firefighting System

The firefighting design on the runway is rather sophisticated. It is envisaged that airplane fires could be extinguished by a foam system within seconds. Such a foam system eradicates the potential danger of injured passengers being run over by firefighting truck. Such a tragedy occurred at one US airport in 2014 when an injured female passenger covered in foam was run over by a firefighting truck which is not needed in the new firefighting system.

Fuel spilling out of disabled fuel tanks could be immediately flushed and drained from the runway into a side-drainage system. Video cameras are installed along the runway for remote monitoring.

An emergency medical room next to the runway serves as the first-response rescue station for treatment of patients with burns and fracture. A helipad serves as an emergency landing for ambulance helicopter which is always on standby. Every airport has an Accident and Emergency medical clinic to satisfy the airport emergency requirements.

Airplane Salvage

The airport is equipped with several heavy-duty cranes that could lift a disabled airplane. Loaded on a huge platform, the disabled plane can be towed to a safe distance so the airport can resume operation as soon as possible.

The platform is a composite structure that allows joining as many mobile sections of smaller platforms together to suit the actual size of the disabled plane. With such a system the airlines would accrue substantial saving, as they will not need to provide and maintain expensive airbags at every airport. The airport operational capability would not be unduly compromised.

The airport authority could recoup its investment in equipment by levying an insurance fee on each airline for access to the cranes and towing operation. A heavy penalty will be imposed on an airline that has a disabled airplane obstructing the runway, resulting in airport closures affecting operations that could lead to staggering losses amounting to hundreds of millions of dollars.

Impression by VIP Visitors on the Eco-airport

The sophisticated integrated systems of operations with automation, the close cooperation between the airport and airlines, innovative ideas to increase productivity, the use of technology to enhance the safety and efficiency of airport operations, the seamless transportation of passengers and workers to and from the airport, and the efficient management of airfreight operation, have given the visitors a deep admiration.

The cost-effectiveness of the massive airport facilities is immeasurable. It also highlights one of the main objectives of creating an eco-city: to automate as much as possible the production of goods and services to achieve the desired goal of eliminating manual labor, which is not viable and is in short supply in future economic developments.

The important features of the new airport are eco-friendly and enhance safety, efficiency, cost effectiveness, and productivity. This eco-airport design will be the one for future airport construction and operations around the world.

Chapter 10

Expressway Traffic System

Landscape along the Expressways

On the expressway, driving from the airport to Meigui City, the VIP visitors are able to see rows upon row of eco-farm troughs neatly dotting the landscape and stretching to the horizon as far as the eyes can see. Installed in the midst of the farmlands are thousands of colorful wind turbines and trees planted in between. The visitors are told the land on both sides of the expressway used to be arid, and there was no vegetation due to lack of water. The land was not inhibited for decades but is now rejuvenated.

The landscape is now transformed, and the area has come alive with economic activities. Lakes and reservoirs have been built to provide fresh water to the eco-farms for crop productions and to the fish farms. Canals, served as a balancing system to prevent flooding, are dug alongside the raised expressway. Energy is available from power stations using renewable biodiesel produced by the eco-farms. Energy also comes from wind turbines and solar panels.

The solar panels installed over the expressway serve to prevent snow falling on the roads and allow unhindered traffic flow. Snowfalls on expressways have caused serious accidents in many parts of northern China, and road closures lead to transportation chaos and traffic standstills for days. Smog reduces visibility, which poses danger to drivers in northern China. Traffic comes to a snail's pace, and accidents frequently happen. To improve visibility, warm air is blown along the expressways via ducts.

Twenty percent of the world's fatal road accidents occur in China, a record China is not proud of. It must be rectified in the new Eco-World. The annual number of deaths and disabled persons arising from road accidents is estimated to exceed the population of Singapore. It is a significant loss of human lives and financial resources, a burden to the bereaved families, and a contributing factor to life and vehicle insurance premium increases. Many of these accidents can be avoided if the traffic system is improved, the human factors that cause the accidents are eliminated, more vehicle safety features are incorporated, and traffic infringement monitoring and enforcement are enhanced. Technology is widely used to enhance enforcement of rules and regulations and to provide evidence against traffic-rule violations.

Expressway Design Criteria

The constructions of modern expressways throughout China follows an ISO 9001-approved design specification, which is based on

1. past experience of designs and traffic problems;
2. human factors that result in road accidents, and remedial actions to prevent recurrence;
3. vehicle compliance with safety regulation and rules;
4. studying traffic environments;
5. adoption of latest technology; and
6. installation of all-weather expressways.

The specification adopts many best practices from around the world. The network of expressways aims to provide commuters with safety, speed, convenience, and improved capacity while helping the country with its economic and social developments. Every expressway is built with a bend every six miles to prevent drivers' tendency to fall asleep on a monotonous straight road, which subconsciously induces increased speed.

As all road transport vehicles in the future are powered by battery, many battery-charging stations are installed along the expressways. Charging may take a few minutes for a full charge. For vehicle owners who prefer to exchange their flat batteries with fully charged ones, they can lease the batteries from companies that provide this exchange service. All electric private vehicles are designed for ease of battery replacement within a time limit of two minutes. It is like a "plug-and-drive" process.

Along the expressways are signs reminding drivers to be attentive to road conditions, break up a long journey by resting at robot-operated restaurants or leisure parks located along the expressway, not recklessly overtaking and passing others, no tailgating, and swapping drivers with others in the car when feeling tired.

The following features are incorporated into the new eco-traffic system design:

Systems to detect traffic-rules violations: Speed sensors are installed on the expressway. Every vehicle is embedded with a computer chip installed in a transponder containing the driver's license number, type of vehicle, and name of registered owner. When a vehicle exceeds a speed limit, the license plate number and the name of the vehicle owner will flash automatically on an overhead electronic panel. The driver is required to stop at the nearest checkpoint to pay a fine and given a warning to stay within the speed limit. Failure to stop at the first checkpoint will result in an increased fine. After the third checkpoint is passed without paying the fine, the driver will be stopped and arrested at the expressway exit.

Every vehicle has to install an electronic yawing device that detects the swaying motion of the vehicle. If it exceeds a certain limit on a straight road, an alarm will sound, sending a signal to a traffic detection monitor. An electronic flashing warning will be displayed on a panel above the road to ask the driver to stop and rest at the first available rest area. The driver is obliged to call the traffic police for assistance. Failure to comply carries a stiff penalty. Such a system is essential to preventing fatigue-prone drivers who tend to drive long distances without taking a break. Installed on every long-distance running bus and transport vehicle is a trip meter that reminds the driver to stop and rest for at least fifteen minutes every three hours. The trip meter is automatically set at the entrance of the expressway. Any violation of this regulation will be flagged at the exit of the expressway. Such a system is also helpful for preventing fatigued drivers from causing traffic accidents.

Systems to detect goods-transport vehicle conditions: to prevent overloading, which is a common occurrence, a weighing platform is installed at the entrance of the expressway to weigh every vehicle transporting goods. Overloading carries a heavy fine and disallowed to be on the road. At the weigh station, an automatic tire thread inspection will be performed on all such vehicles. Any tire that fails to meet the minimum tread depth has to be replaced immediately, and the replaced tire is quarantined. A fine is imposed on the owner who fails to keep his vehicle in proper roadworthy condition. Tires with worn tread possess less friction on the road, increasing braking distance and potentially causing an accident from hydroplaning.

Traffic lane discipline: To prevent heavy and long-goods vehicles that hog the fast lane at great speeds from causing serious accidents, they are restricted to the slow-speed lane of the expressways. Road sensors can detect deviant drivers, and they will be flagged by the overhead electronic display panel and be fined on the spot.

Recalcitrant traffic offenders: To prevent recalcitrant driver with repeat traffic offenses from making more mistakes, he will be warned to be careful at the expressway entrance. After several repeat warnings without success, the driver will have his license suspended. When he shows up at the expressway exit, he will be arrested if caught with repeat offense.

To help drivers find their way, every entrance onto and exit from the expressway is allocated with GPS coordinates for ease of navigation. It is compulsory to install a GPS in every vehicle. When the vehicle approaches the input coordinate, a warning sound can be heard from the radio speaker for the driver to make preparations for exiting. This system is helpful to a novice using the expressway for the first time or to a new and long-distance driver driving at night. With such a system, making a U-turn will no longer be necessary.

Slip roads design and construction: The ISO 9001 design criteria for slip roads joining the expressway is to allow smooth merging of traffic during peak periods without causing traffic jams or bottlenecks. Extensive computer simulation is carried out to arrive at the final destination and to cater to a smooth traffic flow. The new design involves many three-lane slip roads, connecting the expressway to an overhead road that encircles the entire eco-city. The number of such three-lane slip road is the same as the number of exits and entrances needed to join the main arterial roads in the eco-city. Such design avoids piling up of traffic causing bottlenecks during peak periods.

Landscaping of expressway: Construction of expressways requires the approval of the state environment agency to ensure construction does not destroy the ecosystem and natural habitats. With more land made available for parks and tree planting, China's team of construction workers takes cues from landscape architects to plant trees and flowers of different species and color, to build small ponds, lakes, playgrounds, and parks along the expressways. Lookouts are built to allow picnickers to glance at the panoramic scenery of mountains, waterfalls, lakes, and streams.

Expressways to towns/cities and scenic places: Visitors are reminded that China is a huge country with a large population. It has the unique problem of moving two to three hundred million people in a span of a month during the lunar new year and national holiday periods. Expressways are always congested when masses of people travel to their hometown from the cities to visit their families and go to holiday resorts.

The sudden surge on the roads by commuters in such a short time requires ingenuity of mass transportation and control of traffic flow. The number of traffic lanes connecting the expressways to the entry points of towns and cities has to be carefully studied to provide sufficient space to simultaneously accommodate a large number of road users.

Traffic flow at scenic places: With more wealth, the general public can afford to buy private cars for leisure and work, and China has the highest car ownership rate in the world. Traffic congestion is inevitable during peak periods when many visitors converge toward the scenic places in droves. Parking facilities must be sufficient to cater to large numbers of private cars and tourist buses during holiday periods. Many robotic traffic wardens are required to direct traffic and allow smooth flow of vehicles at entrance and exit points, which have to be far apart to prevent bottlenecks. However, as long as the congestion is bearable for a short time, there is no perfect transportation system that can cater to sudden peak demands.

Parking lots at sports stadiums, concert halls, popular scenic places, or any other convention centers must be booked on the Internet in advance to avoid parking unavailability. A parking lot number is given after a reservation and payment are made. Every car lot is provided with a bicycle for the driver to cycle to the stadium, hall, or convention building.

Traffic news: For the benefits of motorists traveling to scenic places, CCTV cameras will show real-time images of the traffic conditions, which can be seen on the website of the Transport Ministry. Whenever there is a traffic accident on an expressway, a radio announcement will be made to alert all motorists. A message is also displayed on the electronic notice boards along the expressway, giving an estimate time of delay.

Unique expressway design with emergency bypass:

The center of every expressway incorporates a bypass section to allow drivers to continue their journey by crossing over to the opposite side of the expressway to avoid an accident area blocking traffic. This section is controlled by a barrier and traffic police. They are built at three-mile intervals. A bypass also allows drivers to make emergency U-turn on the expressways.

Chapter 11

Water Conservation and Resource Management

Freshwater Supply Woes

It was reported in the media that 60 percent of underground water in China was too polluted for drinking directly, 16 percent of the country's land area was polluted, and one-fifth of all farmland was tainted by inorganic elements such as cadmium These serious environmental pollution problems are a culmination of continuous defying by industries that discharge untreated waste products directly into the rivers, lakes, and streams. Lack of law enforcement by corrupt officials is another factor that promotes further escalation of water pollution. In addition, the archaic bureaucratic procedures of the local government involving too many departments do not lend a quick resolution to a pollution problem.

The water-supply problem is aggravated by having to use water in increasing volume to support factories that manufacture commodities for exports. There are profligate water users in the urban cities that do not help with water conservation. The dire situation will get worse and is detrimental to the health and safety of the entire country. Indeed, water sits on the nexus of grave issues of food shortage, diseases, and economic curtailment.

Years of application of fertilizers and insecticides by farmers have contributed to land pollution, making the soil unsuitable for further agricultural production. Water is in critical supply in China. With 20 percent of world population, China uses less than 6 percent of the world's water resources for food production. It is a tall order to expect China to produce more food in the future when water is getting scarcer and more polluted and the population is increasing. It is not a pretty sight. It was estimated that pollution to the environment and water reduce the economic value of GDP by 15 percent.

The two largest rivers in China, Yangtze and Yellow, provide water to hundreds of millions of people living along their banks. However, these rivers are heavily polluted. Out of 663 cities, 440 suffer from clean water shortage, and of these, 110 face severe water shortages. China relies on rivers and lakes for clean water. Its thirst for water has jumped significantly with increasing urbanization and a super-charged economy for the past three decades.

The shift to an animal protein diet by the affluent has added to the strain. It takes fifteen tons of water on average to produce about two pounds of beef, compared to six tons for poultry, and 1.5 tons for corn. As a result of water shortages, food prices rise. Inflation ultimately adds more pressure to the cost of living.

Shortage of Water Affects Health, Eco-Systems, Industries, and Agriculture

Protracting the water crisis will result in too prohibited and unbearable consequential social costs of disasters caused by food and water shortage, rising incidences of public health diseases from toxic chemical contaminants in the water, accelerating desertification, and curtailing of industrial and agricultural production and social development. Therefore, China cannot afford to put the crisis on a back burner until it reaches a point of no return.

A water crisis does not come with simple solutions, because of the complexity of the problem. However, the new pragmatic leadership of the central government takes the issue seriously and invites experts from around the world to study the crisis and offer innovative solutions.

The water crisis in China can be surmised as follows: uneven distribution, floods, droughts, and pollution. Due to its large and diverse geography, China has a wide spectrum of terrains and climate zones. The south and east provinces receive copious amounts of rain, whereas the north and west receive very little. Historical records reveal contrasting events of some southern provinces battling floods while others in the north suffer from prolonged drought.

Over the years, severe droughts in the north affected hundreds of millions of acres of farmland, millions of livestock, and countless humans. In 2009, the most severe droughts happened in five western provinces, affecting more than sixty-one million people. Drought has caused many important lakes and wetlands to become dry lands, affecting the ecosystem.

Industrial Pollution

As China gallops along with industrialization, many local governments, in their fervent desire to show the central government their achievement of industrial development and job creation and producing higher GDP at all costs, ignore the importance of keeping the water resources free from contamination. They permit industrial firms to discharge their untreated waste from the factories directly into rivers and lakes. Equally harmful chemical pollutants seep into groundwater. Harmful gases released from factory chimneys react with rain, producing harmful acid water that finds its way to rivers, lakes, and the seas.

Many of China's dirtiest factories (tens of thousands) are located along rivers or lakes, or in heavily populated areas. The Yellow River, China's "Mother River"—which supplies water to hundreds of millions of people in the country's parched north—is dying from pollution. Many polluting firms in the upper and middle reaches of the river treat it as a sewage channel. Although strict rules and regulations on chemical waste disposal and treatment are set by the central government, the local law enforcement is lax, and corrupt practices at the working levels prevent prosecution of lawbreakers. Some lakes are so polluted they are beyond redemption.

The Chinese are paying a heavy price for rapid urbanization, extensive exports, and economic development that ignore the importance of keeping water resources free from contamination. Polluted water also causes harm to aquatic lives. Farmers sometimes contribute to China's water scarcity and pollution problems by inefficient irrigation methods.

Meanwhile, groundwater faces contamination by pesticides, insecticides, fertilizers, and animal waste from the farmland runoffs as well as effluents from industries. Many vegetable farmers close to the urban cities use contaminated open drain water for irrigation. This raises the concern of health issues when contaminated water, containing carcinogens mixed with pesticides, is used in agriculture.

Uneconomic Use of Water

The problem with planting rice is that it requires lots of water to grow. Rice farming consumes 70 percent of the entire water resource for agriculture in China. Too much water could drown some rice plants, and too little could hamper growth. Nutrient and water loss are high due to ground seepage and vaporization. Inexperienced farmers did not realize over-irrigation and poor drainage could increase the soil alkalinity, which affects yield and quality of rice.

One thousand tons of water is used to produce one ton of wheat worth US$285, which is not a worthwhile economic investment if the farmer has to pay for the water. Many farmers switch from rice planting to corn for better economic returns, severely reducing rice output in China, the largest rice consuming nation in the world. Due to increase in wealth, people consume more meat than before. This has caused an overgrazing problem, turning grassland into semi-deserts that in turn cause the ecosystems to lose their capability to trap water, ultimately making the land even dryer.

Desertification, Deforestation, and Dust Storms—China Is Rapidly Losing Arable Land

China is severely affected by desertification, arid land now covering more than 30 percent of the total land mass (approximately 3.6 million square miles) and impacting the lives of more than four hundred million people.

The annual desertification rate reached three thousand square miles. Extrapolating this rate of desertification with greater intensity annually, in the next millennium more arable lands will transform to deserts, especially in the dryer parts of northern China. The chief culprits of desertification are overgrazing, exploitation of land, deforestation, urban sprawl, and droughts brought on by global warming.

Once a piece of land becomes a desert, it is hard to return to its original state. With unabated deforestation in the countryside, the topsoil will loosen and be easily washed away during rainy seasons. The annual quantity of topsoil flowing into the Yellow River totals 1.6 billion tons, which raises the riverbed in the lower reaches by four inches each year. Such a scenario creates the danger of the river overflowing during heavy-rain seasons.

Every year during springtime, dust storms are kicked up by strong surface winds in the north and spread to many cities, including Beijing. The dust originates in the deserts of Mongolia and the northern part of China. The dusts contain many harmful pollutants such as sulfur, soot, ash, and other toxic heavy metals, like mercury, cadmium, chromium, arsenic, lead, zinc, copper, and other carcinogens. These dust storms are harmful to human health, degrade the soil, and affect wildlife. Toxic metals propagate up the food chain from fish to humans. Therefore, there is an urgency to act on preventing further desertification and reducing dust-storm activities. Only with an adequate water supply can the problems of dust storms be resolved.

Impact of Contaminated Water on Human and Aquatic Lives

China's water pollution problems have a serious impact on national health. Pollutants such as pathogens can produce waterborne diseases like cholera, typhoid, and dysentery, which continue to harm millions of poor children in rural areas. About three hundred million people in China—a number equivalent to the entire US population—drink contaminated water every day. Almost two-thirds of these people fall ill. More than thirty thousand village children die from dysentery each year, an illness caused by contaminated water from living in poor sanitary conditions. In addition, China's water has been blamed for high rates of various health abnormalities like cancer, stunted growth, low IQs, miscarriages, and birth defects. The costs of polluted water causing diseases, mental distresses, and deaths are immeasurable. It is indeed a waste of human resource.

Pollution could also destroy the wetland habitats of ecosystems. This happens when algae in the wetlands die and decompose, thereby reducing the oxygen level in the water, in the end killing fish and other aquatic organisms. Such a scenario affects wildlife's existence. Pollution is extensive in the seas—so much so that aquatic lives are rapidly diminishing. The prices of seafood and freshwater fish have skyrocketed, and the trend is ominous. There is no pollution tax levied on companies that pollute the land or source of water. Not a cent of the money that is earned from exporting commodities produced by industries that pollute the water is used to combat the pollution problems. It is the taxpayers who have to bear the pollution consequence and foot the bill. This situation is not sustainable.

Unlimited Supply of Water Project

In order to ensure an unlimited supply of clean water in the future, Waratah has proposed the innovative idea of recycling water from all the rivers that flow into the sea. In addition, pollution control is to be implemented to keep all the rivers and water catchment areas free from contamination from industrial pollutants and run-off from farmlands. Such a water-conservation system ensures complete isolation of clean water from external contaminants. These projects will give perpetual returns on investments and eradicate the potential shortage of the clean water and food supply.

Water conservation and elimination of water pollution are two main water projects envisaged by the central government in conjunction with the creation of an Eco-World. Rainwater is a good source of clean water and should be harvested and retained. Water in various rivers can be diverted inland instead of being allowed to flow into the seas. It makes more sense to treat river water instead of desalinating seawater to get fresh water. To conserve surplus water, many reservoirs and lakes are being built, especially in western and northern parts of China, where water resources are grossly inadequate.

With determination, focus, and vigor to solve the nationwide water crisis, China would embark on the most remarkable river water redirection project ever taken on in human history to conserve the precious water resources for the sake of future generations. The Eco-World project team will carry out comprehensive research into the extent and severity of the damages over the past century caused by droughts and floods in various parts of China. Using the latest computerized weather-forecasting model, detailed studies of the topography of the weather-battered areas, population growth, and agriculture, forestry, and industrial needs, the scientists and engineers established the following programs:

Redirection of River Water Flow

Dams are built at river mouths for water to be pumped to inland reservoirs. The pumps are driven by power generated by tidal waves, wind power, and solar-energy generators. The volume of water being pumped is determined by the water usage in every eco-city and the requirements for eco-farms, rejuvenation of wetlands and dried lakes, reservoir replenishment, and replanting of trees. This is the most important project ever taken by any nation in history to recycle water. Water is essential for human life and all living things.

Building a Network of Canals and Reservoirs throughout the Country

This network ensures uninterrupted clean water supply to any eco-city in China at any time in the future. The levels of all the reservoirs that supply water to the eco-cities are monitored by a centralized computer system in Beijing in the north and duplicated in Guangzhou in the south. Ancient China built by hand the first of many canals in Kaifeng, a capital city of the Song Dynasty some two thousand years ago, linking the local river to the mighty Yellow River for transportation and control of floods.

Building many huge lakes and numerous channels in the rain-soaked regions is intended to catch and retain the sudden heavy downpour of rainwater that used to flow into the low-lying areas, resulting in heavy flooding. New canals connecting the lakes are built to allow excess water to flow into the reservoirs to prevent overflow problems.

Dredging the Riverbeds of Major Rivers

Sludge from river dredging is pumped to the deserts and arid lands to rejuvenate the lands for tree and grass planting. This program will help arrest the problem of deforestation and recovery of land due to desertification. On the recovered new land, Jatropha and other biodiesel plants are cultivated, which will then be used for making biodiesel. China is ambitious in making the deserts disappear. Many huge lakes are built on desert lands, creating oasis-like environments with lush vegetation suitable for habitation. This is also to influence precipitation formation, which encourages rain formation.

Bird's Eye-View of a Water Resource-Management System

All the VIP guests are shown a mockup of the entire water conservation and maintenance project involving the pumping of river water back to inland eco-cities and eco-farms; building of numerous reservoirs, lakes, and canals; pollution control measures; recycling of wastewaters; and how recycled water is used to grow trees across the entire countryside. In fact, water is an important component for producing biodiesel plants, which are used for power generation.

Water Pollution Control

In order to prevent further degradation of water quality due to pollution of rivers, lakes, and seas in the new Eco-World, the project team took the following steps:

1. Channels are to be built on both sides of rivers and around the perimeter of all lakes. This is to segregate river and lake waters from mixing with external sources of polluted water, such as sewage waste, factory industrial discharges, storm-water drains, and floodwaters that are considered contaminated and pesticide- and fertilizer-infected runoff from farms. The external waters will be channeled into treatment plants. The treated water will then flow into new reservoirs.
2. All eco-cities incorporate an automatic system of channeling wastewater from residential houses, condominiums, hotels, hospitals, offices, schools, restaurants, supermarkets, and entertainment centers into a centralized sewer-treatment system. The treated water will be analyzed to ensure it meets the required standard before being discharged into new reservoirs. With toxic substances removed, the residuals from the treatment plants will be used as fertilizers.

The design of wastewater treatment and recycling system complies with ISO 9001 standards. The system is reviewed yearly and continuous improvement is a built-in feature in the ISO 9001 approval process. All factory waste products will be channeled into holding tanks, which are collected and automatically forwarded to special treatment plants before they are discharged into new reservoirs.

Cattle farming will be restricted to specially constructed eco-farmhouses where animal wastes are contained in order not to cause contamination to the soil and underground streams. The same applies to poultry and pig eco-farms. Again, all animal eco-farms must comply with ISO 9001 pollution control and management measures.

Factory Pollution Control and Monitoring

Every factory is required to comply with ISO 9001 regulations. To ensure full containment of factory waste products without polluting the clean water supply, all factory locations are restricted to a particular locale. This is to prevent the repeat of the cancer village of Liu Kuai Zhuang, seventy-five miles from Beijing, where one in fifty residents suffer from cancer caused by many chemical factories discharging heavy-metal pollutant waste into the environment.

In case of industrial waste and chemical leakage, the entire industrial estate will be encircled by a wide channel to collect any chemical spillage and washing liquids. The quality assurance manager must file a monthly report on water quality control compliance test results on his company website. Road transport of flammable chemicals, liquids, or gasses must be accompanied by a police escort and a permit.

Management of Reservoirs

Reservoirs for Flood Control and Firefighting

All reservoirs are regularly checked for pH value and impurities. The results are public knowledge to highlight the danger of pollution. Special algae plants are grown in the reservoirs for biofuel and biomass production. All new reservoirs are interconnected by canals for flood control. An automatic chemical analysis laboratory is set up to test the water samples collected daily. Canals are built in the forests to fight forest fires with automatic fire alarm systems installed at strategic locations. Water for forest firefighting comes from the new reservoirs. The levels of all the reservoirs around the country is monitored and controlled by the Reservoir Control Center in Guangzhou in the southern part of China. There is an automatic level balancing mechanism to ensure the level of every reservoir is maintained at a safe limit.

Water Resource Conservation and Management

In the Eco-World, the quality of water in rivers, lakes, reservoirs, seas, and oceans are significantly improved after antipollution measures are firmly in place. To all the marine life and wildlife in the ecosystems, this is good news. Fishery industries will flourish with abundant supplies of fish and other aquatic products for the public. With sufficient water supplies from rivers, lakes, and reservoirs, subterranean waters will no longer be needed, and this should help keep the wetlands, marshes, and lakes from drying up. Many of the dried-up marshes and wetlands will be rejuvenated. The natural ecosystem will be restored.

Drought Has no Effect on River Water Levels with Resource Management

During the worst drought in 142 years, the Yangtze River experienced its lowest level, with many ships run aground midstream. Water shortage affected millions of people. The economy took a hard beating, amounting to 1 percent of the GDP.

With the new water resource-management system, such drought effect would have no bearing on any river as all the rivers and new reservoirs are interconnected by canals to balance out water distribution. Similarly, all economic and human activities are unfazed by flooding because of the flood control capabilities of the new water-resource management and control.

Bursting of Riverbanks Is under Control

Since the 1990s, China, on average, suffers from flooding, resulting in heavy financial losses amounting to 1.5 percent of the GDP. Many rivers, including the two mighty rivers, Yangtze and Yellow, used to burst their banks during heavy flooding, resulting in the death of millions of people and devastation of assets and properties. With the new water resource-management systems with interconnected rivers, canals, and reservoirs, the problem of flooding is eradicated, and the two mighty rivers will never overflow again.

Public Health Standard Improvement

Health standards are vastly improved with adequate supplies of clean water and prevention of polluted water coming into contact with human beings and farming. Health care costs will be drastically reduced. Premature deaths due to contact with contaminated waterborne diseases are eliminated. Streets in the eco-cities are so-designed to be washed every night by an automatic cleaning system, with runoff water and detergents flowing into the storm-water drains that are linked to water-treatment plants. Dust on the roads are also a source of health hazard pollutants.

Returns on Investment of Water Resource-Management Projects Are Incalculable

With the assurance of adequate clean water supplies for all consumers in the future, and the cost of water resource-management operation maintained at fairly constant values, inflation will be kept at an acceptably low rate as the once-off massive investments are amortized over decades, just like highway and railway construction investments. For reason of national security, there was no question asked of the returns on investment in human lives and resources to build the Great Wall of China. As a comparison of national security project, the water conservation and resource-management project costs are much below the combined aggregate of the wide spectrum of costs arising from

1. fighting continuous water pollution nationwide
2. relentless searching for various new sources of freshwater supplies
3. direct and indirect consequences of water and food shortages and the needs to import food
4. persistent increases in waterborne diseases and associated medical costs
5. continuous loss of crop production due to floods, droughts, and natural disasters
6. loss of human lives due to diseases caused by toxic water contaminants and floods
7. loss of economic value of land due to desertification and deforestation
8. loss of fishing revenues

Shipping Costs and Freight Movement Improvements

With a vast network of interconnected rivers and canals, shipping goods to all parts of China is made easy and helps ease congestion on the roads. The whole country's inland shipping routes are centrally controlled and managed to avoid congestion, just like the air-traffic control system. As riverboats and ships are automatically operated on 24/7 basis all year round and unaffected by inclement weather, shipping costs are minimized.

Shipping accidents like collisions in foul weather or foggy conditions caused by human errors would be history. Ships and boats that travel along the canals and rivers are powered by biodiesel-powered motors. Waste products are not allowed to discharge from the vessels into the canals and rivers. All internal combustion engines that used fossil fuel are banned.

The design of all commercial ships and boats in river transportation will incorporate automatic computerized operational and anti-collision control and navigation management systems just like those used on modern aircraft. This way they can be controlled by onshore operators on a 24/7 basis without the need of a pilot on board. Their positions are monitored by GPS. On docking, the ship is automatically connected to the onshore computerized shipping management system, which caters to waste discharge, refueling, and water replenishment. Cargo loading and unloading is also handled automatically by an automated all-weather remotely controlled cargo loading system. An electric freight-train station is built within the cargo consignment and dispatch holding center.

The shipping along the canals serves a valuable transportation backup for some of the four billion passenger-trips that happen during the long holiday period of Lunar New Year and National Day. Buying a train ticket to go home for a once-a-year holiday with their love ones during Lunar New Year is the hardest thing to do for a migrant worker working in the city. Even with the eco-cities established, travel between eco-cities will continue to be tight when Lunar New Year arrives. An exodus of millions of travelers happens with China's 1.36 billion people.

Eco-Farm Production

Across the vast expanse of China are hundreds of thousands of automated eco-farms that grow crops for food, animal feed, biofuel, and Chinese herbal medicine productions. These eco-farms are connected to the eco-water resource-management system, with thousands of manmade canals, lakes, and reservoirs for clean water supply. Nature is not always perfect in the provision of habitable and arable land for living. It is necessary for humans to adapt to the environment, not vice versa. We need to learn not to damage the environment beyond redemption.

The new water resource management guarantees there is no interruption of water supply to the eco-farms at any time now or in the future. It is, therefore, considered an integrated national defense system to safeguard the national interests of survival with self-sufficiency in food, energy, and water. Any fault in water resource management will have dire consequence of civil war within China or economic war with other countries. The cost of war will outweigh all the financial and human resources invested in water resource-management systems. War consumes natural resources with no benefit to mankind and is incompatible with the environment.

Rejuvenation of Dried Lakes and Desert Lands

Rejuvenation Needs a lot of Water

With the new water resource-management scheme in place, dried lakes and desert lands are now rejuvenated by vast amounts of recycled water being directed to the planting of trees and grasses and the creation of wetlands and shallow lakes. Thousands of oases will be built in the desert areas to bring back wildlife and wild vegetation. China has lost more than two thousand lakes over several decades due to increased water consumption and global warming. These lakes will be rehabilitated.

Jatropha plants and giant king grass are planted across the vast rejuvenated desert land as feedstock for producing biofuel. Many shallow lakes created in the old desert lands are used to grow algae for mass production of biofuel. Climate change and drought have no effect on the rejuvenation process.

Tree Planting across China's Desert and Arid Lands

Special tall trees are genetically modified to suit dry weather conditions. They are selected for replanting in the rejuvenated regions. Recycled water from the new reservoirs is piped to feed the trees at regular intervals. Hopefully, with an abundant supply of water in the rivers, lakes, and reservoirs, the water table could be raised sufficiently for more trees and grass to grow naturally.

It is envisaged that eventually, with eradication of deforestation and overgrazing, deserts will disappear. The hundreds of millions of people who live in the northern part of China, such as in Beijing, will be elated as the yearly sandstorms from the north would not recur due to replanting of hundreds of millions of trees.

Tree planting is accomplished by specialized remote-controlled robotic machineries. An automatic tree planting system is used, one similar in concept to that being used to lay tens of thousands of miles of railroad tracks across China for the high-speed rail network. An automatic water supply system is installed on the ground to maintain the flow of water for the trees. Tree planting continues until all the desert lands are covered with trees. It might take ten years or more to complete the operation. Deserts cover one-third of China's vast land expanse. It means China is able to recover huge desert landmasses into usable habitats. Special valuable woods such as teak and rosewood are planted in large quantities for furniture making. The government allocated an area in the southern part of China where the environment is conducive for creating a large rainforest.

Economic and Health Benefits of Water Resource Management for Future Generations

When water supplies in the Eco-World are plentiful and unlimited, it is envisioned that in the near future, China will be self-sufficient in food supplies, biofuels, and energy. With these accomplishments China will indefinitely save hundreds of billions of dollars in foreign exchange without the need to import oil and grain. With adequate domestic supply of foods, inflation is under control. Diseases related to lack of water and contaminated water affecting millions of children will also be eradicated, with great savings in medical costs and human suffering.

Although the initial investment in the water conservation and resource-management project is astronomical, it is a wise investment that can yield immeasurable benefits to mankind and help balance the ecosystem, on whose life wildlife depends. For survival, and to avoid astronomical costs, civilization cannot afford not to have an Eco-World with water conservation and resource-management measures.

The Waratah Organization is very impressed by the water conservation and resource-management project adopted by China. The success of this project will be replicated in other parts of the world to achieve similar benefits to mankind, to solve water scarcity problem and to help agricultural and aquacultural industries. Freshwater is essential for healthy living by all living things, for energy and food productions, and for industries. This should improve the social and economic development of all countries and to maintain an ecological balance and world peace.

Chapter 12

Eco-Farms for Agricultural Industries

Headquarter of Eco-Farm Industries

After arriving at the first eco-city of Meigui, the VIP visitors are taken to an eco-farm nearby. It is the first of many hundreds of thousands of eco-farms established around the country, and is the brainchild of Huang Long. She and Phil Kendall are partners in designing and building the eco-farms, which are really factories that produce agricultural products according to specifications.

Entering a massive building—the headquarters of Huang's center of research and development—the foreign visitors are welcomed with a tour of a huge laboratory and a nursery filled with all kinds of agricultural plants from around the world.

Huang's Agricultural Plant Laboratory

Many scientists and research scholars of different nationalities work on experiments of different species of food crops, agricultural plants for biodiesel fuel, and feedstock for animal husbandry. Herbal plants are also included in Huang's experiments for TCM (traditional Chinese medicine). The experimental farms contain tens of thousands of different kinds of plants grown in a controlled environment and in different mixtures of composts. Nutrients are supplied to the plants via capillary tubes buried in the compost, and CO_2 is released into the plant enclosures. Sunlight for the plants is controlled. Pictures are taken during the entire plant-growing process. Plant growth could be enhanced in a CO_2 environment.

Unlike traditional wetland rice fields, where methane is produced as the terminal process of the anaerobic breakdown of organic matter in the wetland soil, eco-farming for rice is methane-free, thereby reducing the effect of climate change in a significant way.

Experiments on Various Agricultural Products

Back to Fundamentals

In the laboratories, various plants grow in a controlled air temperature, pressure, and humidity environment. Water with soluble nutrients is conveyed to the roots via tiny biodegradable capillary tubes inserted in the compost and released from a central tank at preset intervals. CO_2 is pumped into the enclosure and released at a predetermined rate. The composition of compost, water and nutrients, temperature, pressure, humidity, and CO_2 are varied for different experiment troughs. The growth rates are recorded by cameras.

Meticulous Experiments

Selected plants are dissected each week for detailed examination under the electron microscope and by biological and chemical analyses. Experience shows that rice and wheat grown in different climatic and soil conditions produce different kinds of crops with different tastes and qualities. The scientists will endeavor to produce the best seedlings for a particular locale. Each type of rice plant absorbs different kinds of minerals and chemicals from the soil.

Experiments are conducted by scientists and engineers to vary the flow rates of nutrients and water for various plants, compost mixture and environmental conditions of temperature, humidity and sunlight to determine the best results for mass production. One of the important experiments involves restructuring the plant's roots, stem and panicle to increase the absorption rate of nutrients for faster growth. A comfortable stress-free home environment for the plants from seedlings to maturity is essential for its healthy growth.

Searching for the Best Plant

Every experimental plant has a genetic code to signify its genetic structure, growth rate, various parameters of temperature, pressure, humidity, sunlight exposure, CO_2 immersion rate, water flow rate, and compost constituents. It is a tedious process to go through each cycle of a single plant experiment with varying inputs of every influencing parameter to obtain the final best plant that has the optimum quality of nutritional values and benefits. With automation and computerized software program, such tedious processes are reduced to a routine. All the experimental results, including DNA mapping, are recorded and stored in a database housed in two separate remote sites for security reasons.

Reasons for Setting up Eco-Farms in China

Shrinking of Farmland and Farmer Population

The Agriculture Ministry officials give a presentation to the visitors explaining the background for setting up of hundreds of thousands of eco-farms around the country. The background would enable the visitors to appreciate that China has no option but to embark on the eco-farm project as it concerns national survival. China, despite its huge land size, has only 15 percent of total land mass suitable for crop cultivation, and unfortunately, it is shrinking due to desertification, soil contamination, and more land being used for industrial and social infrastructures.

Production of crops is also affected by shrinking clean water supplies and bad weather, and many farmers have called it quits to become industrial workers. These are domestic problems that have no foreseeable solutions. With increasing population and food demands, China has to depend on continuous imports to fill the shortfalls of food production. This dire situation is unsustainable for a country with a growing population. Food shortage becomes a national security issue.

Increasing Population and Decreasing Food Production

The Chinese government and the Waratah Organization did scenario planning of global food production and demand for the next millennium. Their conclusions are startling. Shortage of food worldwide is a distinct possibility, and war over food supplies is inevitable in the next two decades. They deduce:

1. world production of food crops lacking behind global demand
2. decreasing cultivatable farm land
3. shortage of water
4. decreasing population of farmers

5. increasing ferocity and frequency of inclement weather due to climate change affecting agricultural production
6. relentless escalating prices of fertilizer impacting production costs
7. relying on nature for sustainable crop production unreliable and risky

China's increasingly huge imports will have a considerable impact on price and supply in the commodities market. Wild fluctuations in food prices play havoc with the cost of living, inflation, business operations, and economic planning in China.

Food Shortage and National Security

China has been importing a lot of wheat, soybeans, and corn worth more than US$3 billion from the world market, and this amount is growing rapidly each passing year. There is a remote possibility that China's national security could be strangled by unpredictable international political opponents, uncontrollable terrorists applying undue pressures on food-exporting countries to stop food shipments to China, or food embargos by unfriendly foreign political leaders.

There is no permanent friendship in international relationships. The vagaries of global politics cast an uncertainty of oil supply that serves to add more complexity to the problem of food production and supply. Oil has an impact on food prices. Fear of oil supplies from the Middle East has led to wars that caused high oil prices and global inflation. War due to global food shortages could even spell greater threats to social order and world peace.

Causes of Food Production Decline

Clean water supply in China is dwindling, and it affects farm irrigation and production. Water contamination has reached an alarming level. Floods and droughts add further production pressures. Income derived from antiquated farming methods are dismal and cannot catch up with galloping inflation, and generations of farmers remain poor. With more farmers' children relinquishing farming and choosing urban life, food production precipitously declines. China, as the second-largest economy in the world, cannot afford to be a victim of a global food shortage that can cause social unrest with irreversible consequences.

Eco-Farm—A Knight in Shining Armor

In order to produce enough food to satisfy the demands of 1.36 billion consumers in China for the next millennium, it is a Hobson's choice that China has to build eco-farms around the country in conjunction with the creations of four hundred new eco-cities. Eco-farm projects are long-term investments, and only China under Communist Party rule can carry out such gargantuan projects without being hampered by the usual endless debates in a parliament controlled by polarized political parties. Eco-farms guarantee China with an adequate supply of food for the next millennium.

Eco-farming is not the usual traditional farming operation that depends on nature and hopes for good weather. It is really a manufacturing process that integrates the application of technology, plant biology, chemistry, photosynthesis, genetic engineering, nutrient technology, and metabolism. All the agricultural products are produced in accordance with scientific specifications. They are of persistent quality and are unadulterated. Eco-farms are environmental friendly and can be established anywhere and in any climatic conditions. Eco-farming is not bothered by climate change or unpredictable weather.

Eco-farming's initial investment outlay is astronomical, in the same league as the high-speed railway investment project that provides China the largest high-speed railway network in the world. However, compared to the high-speed railway project, eco-farms generate a host of annual returns from savings of billions of foreign exchange on food imports, reduction of emergency stocks of food grains, curbing inflation, stabilizing cost of living, increasing national security, and improving productivity of human resources. Eco-farm production has the highest quality and productivity of grain production in the world per capita. The whole production process is fully automated. With an eco-farming system, China can grow any quantity of grains of any kind for home consumption and exports for the next millennium.

In conjunction with other renewable energy resources, eco-farms that are used to produce crops for biodiesel production for energy generation could save China hundreds of billions of dollars of foreign currency annually on oil imports. The intimidation and threats by oil-exporting countries and oil cartels will become history. Moreover, eco-farming is eco-friendly without causing pollution to the environment, soil, and water resources. Rice planting in eco-farms produces no methane gas (CH_4).

Eco-farming is a green industry that helps reduce climate change detriments. It produces synergy of more downstream industries that offer increased economic benefits to China and its people. Eco-farms eradicate the perennial problem of inflation due to incessant increasing costs of imported grains caused by climate change and rising costs of fertilizers.

Eco-farms operation is fully automatic, so no human labor is needed. The redundant farmers will move to live in the new eco-cities. They would be retrained for job-specific skills so they could pursue higher-income jobs in the new eco-cities. The annual government relief aids to alleviate natural calamity problems suffered by the farmers to the tune of many billions of RMB will not be needed perpetually. In addition, the government will save a huge amount as it disbands the massive civil administration for the rural areas throughout the country. The century-old problem of poverty and the associated human miseries in the countryside will be consigned to history.

The Eco-Farm is a Game Changer for China and the World

Eco-farms are Perennial Cash Cow Industries

China will benefit from having higher GDP when the ex-farmers as skilled laborers are able to improve their annual income from the previous paltry amount of about US$400 per annum to US$8,000–10,000 in the eco-cities. They now become taxpayers. Century-old poverty affecting six hundred million people in the rural areas is hereby eliminated, and China can simultaneously attain 100 percent self-sufficiency in food supplies. China will become a middle-income society. It is a win-win situation.

Eco-farms are really solid cash cows and are ever-green industries. The synergistic effects and benefits of eco-farms are multifaceted and far reaching in the country. Eco-farms are a game changer for better human living conditions and ecosystems. The perennial crisis of foul weather affecting crop production and farmers' income is completely isolated. A new human history has begun.

Eco-Farms Characteristics

The first prototype eco-farm project is funded by Waratah. It is designed by Huang and her team of scientists and engineers, together with the expertise provided by Phil Kendall and his company in automation systems. To escape the adverse effects of rain, wind, drought, frost, snow, insects, weeds, poor quality of soil, lack of water, and intermittent supply of nutrients, food crops in the eco-farms are planted in specially prepared compost mixtures contained in enclosed troughs and grown in a controlled environment. Their growths are progressively monitored.

The compositions of composts that are suitable for healthy growth of each type of crops, such as rice, wheat, and corn, are carefully studied and selected so the final compost composition can produce the best-quality crops. Raw materials for the compost come from the eco-city's wastes treatment plant, the worm farms' vermicompost, and the residues after the crops have been processed. There is no manual labor in the operation of the eco-farm.

Water for eco-farming comes from the canals that are built around the eco-farms. The canals also serve as a waterway for transportation of grains and goods to the eco-city from the eco-farms, and are connected to the reservoirs with water being recycled from the eco-city and river outlets. From planting to harvesting, and from packaging to distribution, the entire process is accomplished by an automatic system in every factory. The number of factories built depends on the production of grains to meet the local eco-city demand and buffer stock.

There is no need to look for fertile land for eco-farming because the planting troughs are supported by a rail-system structure above ground. All the troughs are driven and anchored to their precise positions by a motorized chain system. Every trough is protected by a cover that seals the enclosure from the outside environment. Solar panels are attached to the covers to provide electricity to operate the eco-farms. Power is supplemented by power station using biomass fuel. Cameras are installed to monitor the plants' growth.

There is an automatic system to introduce scheduled amounts of water and nutrients to the plants. CO_2 gases are piped into the troughs regularly. An automatic environmental control system provides the appropriate temperature, pressure, and humidity of air into the enclosure via a pneumatic ducting system. All the monitoring parameters are recoded by a computerized system in a remote station. There will be no more contamination of the soil or underground water due to pesticide, fertilizer, and insecticide penetration.

During harvesting, the troughs are driven to the factory where the crops are automatically processed and the final products packed for sales and distribution. The packed grains are transported to the eco-city distribution center by canal barges that are pulled by tug boats driven by batteries. The factory's residues and compost materials are recycled and re-used. With full automation and a closed-loop eco-farming system with proper supply of sunlight, CO_2, water, and nutrients, the production of food crops is assured, and the supply chain for all food crops would be radically shortened, thus saving costs to the consumers.

Crop can be harvested four times a year. It takes days, not weeks, from harvesting to dispatching to consumers. The logistics are simplified. With eco-farming, waste due to ineffective processing and storage in the rural areas is completely eliminated, as are the grain losses due to traditional problems occurred in the pre-harvest, harvest, and post-harvest stages, as well as grain storage losses from infestation of insects and damages by mycotoxins, fungi, and rodents. With technology, eco-farms could achieve near-perfect output of grain production of the highest quality.

In eco-farms, crop planting is not season sensitive. Planting and harvesting can be more precise and tailored to suit various local demands and to minimize transportation and storage problems and related expenses, thereby saving costs for the consumers. Lead time for supply and delivery of grains is shortened. Various eco-farms are designed and established to produce various kinds of crops required for human consumption, production of animal feeds and biofuels. The most important safety aspect of eco-farming is that food productions are entirely safe from contamination. There is no GM (genetically modified) food in eco-cities.

Advantages of eco-farms include

1. no need to have fertile soil.
2. contamination-free crop production and processing
3. eliminating water waste
4. consistently high quality with highest nutrient values
5. growth that is unaffected by soil conditions, water contamination, climate change, blizzards, storms, floods, drought, or pests
6. unlimited production volume to meet future demands in any season
7. highest productivity
8. lowest production cost
9. unaffected by oil prices
10. crop residues that are recycled and reused
11. shortened food supply chains
12. grain processing and storage waste minimized
13. productions always on schedule
14. no need to apply insecticides and pesticides
15. no inflation
16. causing no harm to subterranean water resource and ecosystem
17. shorter growth cycles
18. no storage loss due to pests
19. unrestricted planting and harvesting seasons
20. reduction in grain stock piles
21. no production of methane

New Evolutionary Grain Production and Distribution

Using the current knowledge of science and technology, eco-farming instantly transforms China. It is very efficient as infertile and barren lands are fully utilized. Water utilization per ton of crops produced by eco-farming method drops significantly as water waste through ground seepage and evaporation is eliminated.

Eco-farming is eco-friendly. Crop planting, processing, packing and storage, and final transportation and distribution to nearby consumers in every eco-city are fully computer-controlled with maximum efficiency in a close-loop system. Hence, the cost to the consumers is minimal and is maintained at a fairly constant value without any external influence from foreign countries. Stable food prices keep inflation in check.

Eco-Farming Production Always on Schedule

The entire process, from plant seedling, growth, harvesting, packaging, and distribution to final destination to consumers runs on schedule and does not miss a beat because it does not depend on the weather or a human element. The invincible benefits of eco-farming, such as national security and protection against famine, are immeasurable.

The food chain and quality is automatically controlled with fewer commercial intermediaries. Stable supply of foods begets stable price. The infrastructures of eco-farms are durable and easily maintained. The traditional hard labor of back-bending of planting, weeding, and harvesting has to make way for the more advanced method of eco-farming to cater to a changing world and is in harmony with the environment. The eco-farming industry resembles that of the current apparel industry, embracing high technology and automation, producing dresses with high quality and quantity at relatively low prices. Gone are the days when the apparel industry was dominated by sweat shops with low-waged employees working in deplorable conditions. Time has changed. Technology helps social advancement.

Eco-Farm for Rice Production

Huang Long has several discoveries of hybrids of "miracle rice." She has experience with rice plant's historical evolution from the wild stocks that had been adapting and evolving to the current cultivated varieties planted in different geological regions. Help is extended by research engineers to find the best structural pattern of the rice plant for receiving maximum sunlight for photosynthesis during the entire growth period, and to analyze the weight of the grains bearing on the panicles without undue stress. The biologists and engineers study the rice plants from different regions, and genetically alter their body structure to support heavier weight for maximum grain production. Unlike wetland rice planting that produces methane (CH_4), eco-farming rice is methane free and reduces the effects of climate change.

The scientists study the structure of the compost mixture so that the roots of the plant have freedom to grow and attach to a firm foundation for healthy growth. They also study and examine the roots' propagation and the compost texture and property for proper root attachments. Their aims are to search for the optimum nutrient and water absorption rate for healthy growth, and to analyze the effects of all the negative factors on the plant's overall health. Every variety of rice plant has its own genetic characteristics and growth pattern, and, therefore, the eco-farm agriculture specialists will design different composts, nutrient compositions, and CO_2 and water flow rates for various rice strands.

Eco-Farm for Wheat Production

Similar research is performed by Huang's other research teams into other major staple food grains, like wheat, corn, barley, soybean, and others. Huang recognizes that wheat is a universal grain, accounting for more than 20 percent of the total food calories consumed by humans, giving more nutritive value than other grains like corn, rice, or barley. Therefore, she has been concentrating on research into various wheat varieties suitable for growing in different climatic conditions with different compositions of compost and nutrients.

Although China is the world's largest wheat producer, it continues to import from the United States and Australia to meets its shortfall. Wheat yield in China is relatively poor compared to other wheat-producing countries. Leading to poor harvests by the small farmers are lack of water, poor soil conditions, lack of technical knowledge of crop management, lack of funds to buy fertilizers and pesticides, shortage of good seeds, and bad weather conditions. Furthermore, there are many wheat diseases that destroy crops in addition to post-harvest losses caused by rodents and insects.

Eco-Farm Wheat Production to Ease World Shortage

There is an insatiable demand for wheat in the world market, and coupled with rising prosperity in many of the countries in Africa, the Middle East, Asia, and South America, China, with large-scale eco-farms, is poised to increase production of wheat not only to meet local demands but to help stabilize the price in the world market, with substantial profitable exports. The world has seen wild fluctuation and sudden jumps in wheat prices over the past decade, mainly due to oil price increases, climate change effects, and commodity speculators causing inflation and misery to many poor people around the world. With eco-farms, China not only averts its own crisis of its food supply but also provides relief to poor countries that are faced with relentless wheat price increase.

Eco-Farm for Corn Production

Corn is an important cash crop as human food. It possesses qualities that make it suitable for making feedstock for industrial cattle, pork, and poultry farming. Corn is also a major feedstock for ethanol biofuel production around the world, especially in the United States. As rising incomes in China continue with changes in eating habits from grains to more meat-based diets, more feedstock is required to produce more cattle, chickens, and pigs.

However, China is unable to produce enough corn to meet demands and has to import to fill the gap. It is nearly impossible to keep the price of corn low because the price paid for the US feedstock tends to mimic oil prices, which reach new heights in the oil producing countries whenever there is a sign of regional war, which seems to happen often. Demand for oil continues to rise and hence price of corn will fly north.

The increased production of ethanol in the United States to combat rising oil price stimulates higher demand for corn, pushing corn price higher than ever before. This, in turn, results in farm acreage being diverted from other food crops to corn production. This reduces the supply of the other food crops and increases their prices. Costs of transportation, production, marketing, storage, and distribution are a large portion of the price of food (about 80 percent) sold in the market, and these are closely related to oil prices. Higher energy costs due to high oil prices affect these costs, and in particular, transportation. So there is a chain reaction. When oil prices rise, ethanol prices do too.

When energy and food prices go up in tandem, there is a chain reaction with certainty that social crisis would erupt and hyperinflation would quickly set in. When more people chase the same stuff in limited supply, there is an inevitability that the price will increase. Therefore, the eco-farms in China would do the world a favor when they start to produce and export huge amounts of corn to countries that need it most at the lowest possible price. Eco-farming does not rely on oil-related fertilizer and transportation.

Eco-Farm for Soybean Production

Soybean is a cash crop that can be used as food like tofu, a low-cost source of protein for human consumption and animal feed, and is a source of cooking oil and biodiesel production. Soybean is a favorite crop for food, beverage, and sauce making in China and Asian countries. Production of soybean in China decreases significantly due to same reasons that befall wheat farming. The farmers in the northern part of China, where soybean production plays a major part, are often confronted by natural disasters. Volume of import of soybean represents about four times the total domestic production in China.

The price of soybeans is greatly affected by increasing demand in the world market. As Chinese production is decreasing, price of soybean naturally rises as there is insufficient supply in the world to fill the large drop of production capacity in China. With eco-farming systems, production of soybeans in China easily satisfies both local and world demand at a lower and steady price. Eco-farming is a game changer for agriculture and a welcome human ingenuity of averting a global food-shortage crisis and possibility of war.

TCM Herbal Plants

Huang and her scientists performed experiments on various herbal plants used in traditional Chinese medicine (TCM). The soil in which each of these plants grows in its natural habitat is analyzed. Experiments are conducted to grow the plants in containers with special compost mixture in conditions similar to their own natural habitat. According to TCM teaching, each plant has its unique intrinsic nutritional value to human health due to the plant's absorption of chemical elements that are not found in other common plants.

Some of the herbs are grown in the wild or in remote places in China that are difficult to reach and harvest. Severe climate change and air and water pollution have a detrimental effect on the growth of these hardy yet delicate plants. Unless they are protected and propagated, they might become extinct in the future. With successful research, these herbs can grow in a more suitable environment, their costs will be greatly reduced, and more patients will benefit.

Huang's ultimate aim is to produce herbs of all varieties to make TCM available to hospitals and private chemists to dispense in China and foreign countries. She would work with select universities and hospitals to prepare a standard reference and prescriptions book for dispensing TCM for treatment of various ailments. Sales of herbs are by prescription approved by physicians only. The herbal TCM are manufactured under strict government testing, approval, and licensing, eliminating the current open practice and laxity of government control. Production of medicinal herbs must pass ISO 9001 standards.

Grass for Animal Feeds

Another team of Huang's scientists and researchers perform research into various wild plants that grow on rock surface in cold, dry and arid climate in different parts of the world. Their aim is to find out how they could survive in such extreme harsh conditions, and whether it is possible to extract their hardy genes so that they could be crossbred with other plants to produce a better hybrid of grass as animal feeds.

Most pastoral lands in China are overgrazed, and the grass is of poor quality for animal feeds. Beef production cannot meet the demand in the present affluent society in China. Huang's research team look for different types of grass from different parts of the world and carry out experiments to develop the best crossbred grass that can help produce better-quality cattle. Relying on nature to produce good quality animal feeds is not sustainable in a world affected by climate change, lack of clean water, and overgrazing.

Production of Biofuel Plants

Biofuels are increasingly taking center stage in replacing fossil fuels as the source of fuel for vehicles, airplanes, and energy production. Massive scale of eco-farming of bio-crops like Camelina, Jatropha, giant king grass, rapeseeds, sunflower, and algae ensures the death knell of fossil fuels that have been blamed for causing climate change due to their greenhouse gas emissions. The residue from biofuel processing is a good source of compost materials for eco-farming.

As more climate changes occur in the future, releasing more greenhouse gases, medical research reveals human health conditions will deteriorate more rapidly with higher ambient and more subzero temperatures, causing more incidents of depression, anxiety, asthma attacks, and even suicidal tendencies. Hence, continuing use of fossil fuel is counterproductive to people's quality of life. Offshore exploration and extraction of oil damages the marine environment. Dredging stirs up the seabed and destroys the sea plants on which marine creatures need to survive.

Oil tankers and drilling platform accidents have caused untold environmental damage and deaths of marine life, causing irreversible damage to the fragile ecosystems all over the world. The cost of such damages are not factored into the price of fuel at the gas station and are paid by taxpayers. Fear of diminished oil supplies has been blamed for many proxy wars in the Middle East, and the costs of these wars with losses of human lives and property damages are borne by taxpayers. Piracy on the high seas has increased the premium of oil tankers' insurance.

Biofuel production processes are simpler compared to the cracking and distillation of crude oil to its final products. Biodiesel can be safely transported by underground pipes from the factory to the destined distribution center. Eco-farms can produce as much biofuel as required to meet local market demand at a relatively cheap price as transport cost is minimal as compared to the total transport cost of crude oil from the Middle East to the refinery and from the refinery to the destined customers in remote areas by special trucks. Added to these costs is insurance against accidents and piracy. There is no war to be fought to get sufficient energy from bio-crops, and there is no danger of inflated prices of bio-crops from the eco-farms. Renewable energy sources from biodiesel, solar, hydro, and wind power are the answer to the future survival of the human race.

Chapter 13
Supply of Fish

Diminishing Fish Supply in China

There is an insatiable demand for fish in China for the huge population of 1.36 billion; but the supply is diminishing from the seas and inland rivers and lakes due to incessant pollution from acid rain, runoff from farms, toxic industrial discharge, and sewage. Also, there is a danger of eating fish that is contaminated with toxic materials such as mercury, cyanide, and cadmium. Nature cannot provide edible food indefinitely when the environment is constantly being polluted and when the sea is overexploited.

The increasing stress on both the freshwater and marine ecosystems is causing the habitat irreversible damage due to the incessant attacks by the polluting chemicals that destroy the plankton and other tiny organisms that are food for the fish. Global over-fishing adds further catastrophe to the declining fish stock. With decreasing supply, the price of fish has skyrocketed beyond the reach of ordinary citizens. Such a situation is unsustainable.

Over-fishing

Another reason for fish stock decreasing worldwide is due to unscrupulous fishermen using large nets to catch fish, including the infant fish—so much so that the fish stock is depleting. China cannot hope to import fish from foreign countries to meet its shortfall. The effects of climate change resulting in extreme temperatures, floods and droughts, and air pollution add further stress to the quality of water in the rivers, lakes, and seas. Hence, the fish population plummets and the fishermen find the catch insufficient to afford a worthwhile investment.

China has imposed a temporary ban on fishing in certain areas in order to allow the fish to breed and multiply. Although there are ten million people engaged in the fishing industries, this number is dropping due to uneconomic operation from low catches, and the dire situation is deteriorating. The current fishing industry is traditional and fragmented, just like the traditional food-crop farming, which is a not sustainable as a viable industry to feed the vast population of China now or in the future.

Solutions for Increasing Fish Supply in China

Fish is an important source of protein, vitamins, omega-3 fatty acids, and minerals. The dwindling supply has had an effect on the quality of human life and health, and hence, the Chinese government cannot kick the can down the road by ignoring the grave consequence of fish shortages. The only solution to solving the fishing problem on a long-term basis is to isolate the sources of water pollution.

After many deliberations and consultations with the experts from Waratah, the Chinese government decides the only viable solution is to establish an Eco-World fishing system with modern technology and keeping water resources free from pollution as the first step. The new modern fishing industry needs to be sustainable for the next millennium and compatible with the marine ecosystem. It has to be a high-tech industry on a big scale.

Centralized National Fishing Industry

Self-sufficiency in the supply of uncontaminated and affordable fish is a long-term national goal. The project for increasing a huge supply of fish for the country involves massive investments and resources. Hence, only the state can afford to take up the challenge. The solution is to increase supply from the rivers, lakes, seas, and other aquaculture with fish farms. Large fish farms are established along the eastern coast of China and inland rivers, lakes, and ponds. In order to achieve a high standard in the fishing industry, all fishermen must pass a prescribed course on marine life, fishing techniques, maintenance of fish stock, water quality and pollution, and marine biology.

The idea of a new fishing industry follows the same principle of the agricultural eco-farming system in which science, technology, and automation are utilized to achieve a production with little human intervention, highest productivity, and lowest unit-production cost. Production will not be affected by inclement weather. The new eco-fishing system does not depend on nature but works within the confine of nature. The newly established National Fishery Department will spearhead the production of phytoplankton and fish fries of various species to be released regularly into inland waters and the seas. Seawater quality will be measured constantly to detect the presence of toxic chemicals.

Water Quality and Fishing Industry

With the establishment of the Eco-World in China, pollution of water resources is solved using the latest water resource-management measures. Fishing industries are helped by the creation of numerous canals, reservoirs, dams, lakes, and new systems of pollution controls on industrial discharge and sewage treatments. With pollution under control and the water quality reaching a high standard for marine life, fish stocks should multiply, and catches will be sufficient to satisfy local demand. Fish farm production will supplement any shortfall in daily catches from the wild and meet industrial food productions for the supermarkets or export.

Research on Fish Breeding and Fishing

To bolster the sustainable development of ecological fishery, the National Fishery Department will work closely with various universities in China and other countries specializing in marine biology, ecology, and oceanography. Research is carried out by the Chinese Academy of Fishery Science in all areas of aquaculture and marine and freshwater fisheries. In this respect, the Chinese authority will have a map of the population and density of various types of fish and their habitats. The seawater temperature and undercurrent, which affect aquatic life and fish migration patterns, are measured and recorded. Many fish migrate annually following temperature variations in the ocean. Endangered species are to be saved by artificially induced methods for spawning such as the Chinese sturgeon.

The academy does research into finding out the habitat of various types of fish and their local living environment. The latest fishing industry does not depend on nature alone. It is enhanced by R&D and application of science and technology. With continuous accumulation of information on marine life and their habitats, the National Fishery Department is able to provide comprehensive data to the fishing companies. In addition, the department encourages the academic world and fishing industry to apply new technology and invent new methods of catching fish. This includes designing a new sonar system to round up the fish into a holding area for easy catching.

Eco-World Fishing System

Modern Technology to Catch Fish

In the Eco-World of China, the fishing industry is considered a national priority for food production with self-sufficiency for the next millennium. Automation and technologically advanced systems are to be deployed in the fishing industry to maximize efficiency, productivity, and reduction of manual labor and costs. Safety is also an important factor to be considered in the fishing industry, especially fishing on the high seas and rivers during inclement weather conditions.

Many species of fish are adaptable only to local water habitats in every river, ponds, and streams. Due to pollution and over-fishing, many such species seem to become extinct. The government has decided to set up a special research department to look for such species and hope they can be found and multiplied.

With intimate knowledge of the living conditions and their rates of reproduction of various species of fish, the government is able to devise various methods of catching certain species of fish at the opportune time for maximum harvest without depleting the stocks.

Fishing boats with advanced sonar fishing gear and computer-controlled equipment to locate schools of fish have been designed by the academy and research laboratories in conjunction with other universities. Solar-powered pilotless airplanes are used to locate school of fish by special sonar instrument. In addition, numerous robotic fish, programmed to swim with schools of fish in the sea, send signals to the surface to be captured by radar on the fishing boats. After the fish are caught, accompanying ferryboats with special features for keeping the fish fresh will bring the catches to the shore for distribution. The entire load will be sorted and recorded. The stored information will be used for future fishing trips and for replenishment with fish fries if necessary.

To ensure the fish that is caught is devoid of contamination, selected samples will be taken at random and sent for laboratory examination and analysis. The fishing boats are equipped with computers for global coordinate locations using the Chinese BeiDou GPS and mapping of previous catches.

Operating around the clock, the boats can be automatically dispatched to the next location for continuous operation. The daily catch of various species of fish is recorded and analyzed for future reference and research for more productive fishing.

Automatic System for Inland Fish Harvesting

Special inland fully automatic fishing boats are designed to catch fish in reservoirs, rivers, lakes, and canals. These boats can operate even during inclement weather conditions, especially in the winter when heavy fog and strong winds are prevalent. They are operated 24/7 and controlled by experienced pilots stationed onshore. All the fish are kept alive on board the boats and delivered to specific ports that are connected to a rail network across the country. Maintenance of all types of boats is scheduled regularly and monitored by the Fishery Department. Certificate of maintenance and compliance with the national regulations and rules is necessary for continuing operations. It is necessary to implement and enforce strict rules and regulations to prevent accidents as China is too huge a country to micromanage the industry.

Chapter 14
Production of Meat

Meat Production Problems

Despite China being the largest meat producer in the world, demand for meat exceeds supply. Consumption of meats, such as pork, poultry, beef, and mutton, is on the rise as the wealth of the Chinese population grows in tandem with the rising GDP. With urbanization on a fast track, demand by more urbanites will further aggravate the meat shortage crisis. Such scarcity of meat, especially during an outbreak of animal diseases likes mad cow disease and swine flu, pushed up the meat prices over the years to new heights. Such a dire situation has to be solved to prevent potential social unrest. Once the prices have escalated, they do not fall; even the problem of animal diseases is solved.

Problems of Meat Production

With unabated price increases of meat and other foods affecting daily lives, the monthly CPI (Consumer Price Index) has relentlessly shot up. Loud protests by citizens and the media have constantly been aired, with the loudest cries from the poor in the cities. Salary increases do not keep up with galloping inflation. The government has been trying hard to put in fiscal measures to suppress price increases but to no avail. It is futile to lock the barn door after the inflation horse has bolted.

The Chinese meat production industry, especially pork, which has the highest demand, is too fragmented and uncontrolled. There are many small-scale livestock farmers with low productivity due to lack of knowledge of animal feeds. Coupled with high price of feeds due to high prices of corn and soybean, low profitability, and animal diseases, the profit margin is too small to attract farmers to produce meat on a large scale.

There is an economic trade-off for the able-bodied farmers who can earn more money by being a migrant worker in the city than being a meat producer in the rural areas. The local rural governments have limited resources to help the small-scale farmers.

According to reports from the US's *National Science* magazine, the costs of production of meat from beef are the highest when compared to production of meat from fowls and pigs. Land for cattle is twenty-eight times more than other animals, and water consumption is eleven times more. Environmental contamination by methane gas is five times higher. For each calorie of protein from the cows, one needs to feed them with ten calories of fodder. Beef is not really an effective economic meat transformer.

Animal Diseases and Effect on Consumers

Swine flu, bird flu, and mad cow disease are common in all countries. They affect animals and humans with fatal consequence. When these diseases strike, all the suspect animals are culled by law, causing the owners to lose everything, often bankrupting them. Hence, with lack of finance, technical competence on disease control, and facility management, marginal farmers would find difficulty earning a decent living. Consumers have been apprehensive about buying lean pork being sold in the market due to unscrupulous farmers feeding pigs with chemicals in order to produce leaner meat instead of fat.

Defying government regulations, some pork merchants slaughter diseased or dead pigs for sale to the public and food processors. Hence, confidence in locally produced pigs nosedived, and innocent farmers suffered financial losses. Lack of law enforcement actions and control of private illegal slaughtering of pigs, especially in rural areas, continues to instill fear in the country about disease-infected pork from swine flu or chicken meat from bird flu being sold on the market. China is too huge a country to micromanage the fragmented pork industry.

Unsafe Food Processing Production—Health Hazards and Dangers

Unsafe food produced in China for local and export markets have been a controversial topic for many years in the national and international media.

Despite the central government's effort in promulgating laws prohibiting the use of unauthorized additives and chemicals in food manufacturing, many unscrupulous merchants continue to flout the laws. There are too many government agencies dealing with food matters, and the buck does not seem to stop anywhere to solve common problems. However, the newly restructured China's Food and Drug Administration has helped streamline the operation and monitoring functions of the previous different departments. Heavy fines and jail sentences for serious offenses will be imposed as deterrents.

Past unsafe food-processing productions involved the following:

1. unsafe pork treated with steroids and sodium borate
2. pigs given feeds containing Clenbuterol, a fat-burning drug used by anabolic steroid users, to make meat leaner
3. rotten peaches spiked with sodium metabisulfite, a toxic food preservative used to mask rotten food
4. baby formula adulterated with melamine
5. rice contaminated with cadmium
6. noodles flavored with ink and paraffin
7. mushrooms treated with fluorescent bleach
8. cooking oil recycled from waste gutters

Eradication of Unsafe Meat and Food Production

The Chinese government decided it was in the best interest of national security that China be self-sufficient in production of all foods, including grains, meats, fish, and vegetables at the lowest possible costs and the highest quality and safest standard. Hence, large-scale fully integrated and automated state-owned animal eco-farms are established for beef, pork, mutton, poultry, and fish production across the country. The government possesses adequate resources in finance, technical expertise, and R&D to develop and operate numerous massive animal eco-farms across the nation and to maintain the quality and quantity expected by the consumers and export markets.

Eco-Farms for Meat Production

Specification for Meat Production and Processing

All eco-farms for meat production and meat processing companies are ISO 9001 approved. Quality control managers and veterinary doctors are employed full time to ensure complete compliance of rules and regulations for meat production, processing, and marketing. To ensure complete accountability, as in the aviation industry of aircraft manufacturing and production, documents for the origin of all raw materials used in the production, packaging, and storage of food products must be transparent and accessible for checking and proofing, and authorized and approved by competent people empowered by the appropriate authority. No deviation is allowed unless it is accepted and approved by officials.

Safety of consumption begets an acceptable standard of safe production. Eco-farms, once established and operating profitably, would be sold to the public through an IPO on the stock exchange. One golden share would be held by the government to ensure full compliance of food-safety regulations by the IPO company. The quality control manager would report to the company's CEO and health authority directly and daily. The CEO is ultimately responsible for the safety of meat production in the company.

Animal Eco-Farms

In the past, swine flu, bird flu, and mad cow disease caused panic to the health authority and consumers. Prevention of disease begins with cleanliness of animals, proper ventilation, and ambient control. At the animal experimental eco-farms, the animal husbandry scientists conduct experiments on cows, pigs, sheep, chickens, and ducks, breeding them with leaner species, resulting in less fat and leaner meat.

Crossbreeding with different species from different parts of the world is conducted for best breeding. At the farms, the veterinarians examine the animals for cholesterol levels, blood pressure, and disease-resistant capabilities. They will conduct experiments to see how these animals can be made happier in their living environment, hence promoting healthier growth. They have scheduled time for feeding, relaxing, and exercise. Their daily food intakes are monitored and varied and their growth measured. The central animal eco-farm employs artificial insemination and embryo transfer methods to produce high-quality offspring for all the animal eco-farms around the country.

China Offers Humanity Bailout to Countries Encumbered by Trade Sanctions

Russia is faced with an economic sanction imposed by Western countries due to the Ukraine's political crisis. In retaliation, Russia bans imports of dairy products from these countries, including the United States. A one hundred thousand-cow dairy farm, the largest in the world, is being constructed in

China to supply milk and cheese to Russia to relieve the pressure of shortages of dairy products. It is estimated that the US exporters would lose $1.0–1.4 billion and the EU countries $2.7 billion in dairy trade with Russia. China could do the same with other food products to abate hardship due to economic sanctions imposed by other countries because of political differences.

Largest Animal Husbandry University

China establishes the largest animal husbandry university in the world, employing local and foreign academicians and research scholars. The university campuses are spread over the entire country. Each campus specializes in animals adaptable to their locale. Their research papers are published in the *World Journal of Animal Science* and in other eminent publications. Quarterly reports are published on the health conditions of all livestock populations, similar to that for the city's population. Any pandemic disease found on the eco-farms will be promptly reported by the veterinarian and quality control manager, who report directly to the health authority. The scale of R&D on animal husbandry by the central government is unprecedented in Chinese history or in the world.

Animal Eco-Farm Operation and Maintenance

In the Eco-World, animal hygiene is considered on par with human. Legislation and ISO 9001 standards are imposed on all animal farming. Veterinarian quality control inspectors are employed to ensure every animal farm operation complies with the law and regulations. Their reports will be submitted every quarter using standard electronic format to the authority for approval. Licenses will be immediately revoked when discrepancies are discovered or when the animals suffer from any disease. Robots are employed to keep the farms sanitized and clean.

Waste Disposal for Animals in the Eco-Farms

To prevent methane gases released by animals into the atmosphere causing greenhouse effects, and to facilitate cleaning at the farms, the animals are housed in specially built facilities that are environmentally controlled. Animal fodders are carried along automatic conveyors to feed the animals at specified intervals. Animal droppings and urine are collected along a trough that flows into a collector tank. The waste tanks are connected and the waste is allowed to flow to a processing plant where the droppings and urine are treated. The final slurry becomes fertilizers for eco-farms' food crop production. The methane gases are led to a power generator plant to operate steam turbines. Wastewater from the eco-farms are collected and treated before being recycled for consumption at the farms.

Congenial Living Conditions

Solar panels installed atop the facility buildings provide power to keep the buildings ventilated and temperature controlled at a comfortable level. Supplemental power supply comes from the wind turbines erected in eco-farm fields. All the animals are required to walk around the building facility regularly to maintain a healthy lifestyle. To prevent the spread of disease, the facility is compartmentalized to accommodate a fixed number of animals in each compartment to avoid overcrowding and stress. Video cameras are installed inside the facility to monitor the animals' movements, behavior, and living conditions. The farms are equipped with shower facilities to wash the animals and to disinfect the living quarters regularly. There is no shortage of water around the eco-farms to ensure the strict hygienic conditions are met.

Quality Control of Meat Production and Processing

All slaughtering processes and slaughterhouse operations and maintenance are ISO 9001 approved. A freight station is built next to each massive slaughter house and is connected to the central city railway network, with connections to various main food-distribution stations. All meat-processing companies are to be located near the slaughterhouses to save on transportation costs and time. Every meat processing company must get a Seal of Approval of Quality (SAQ) from the quality organization.

Every fully air-conditioned slaughterhouse is managed and controlled by a state-of-the-art computer-controlled operating system employing smart robots and operating in an ultra-clean and sterilized environment on a 24/7 basis. Surprise checks are carried out regularly on meats that are sold in supermarkets and to retailers to ensure no expired or tainted meats are sold. Licenses will be withdrawn from those merchants selling inedible foods, and a heavy fine will be imposed on the company. The company's CEO would be summoned to court. Jail sentences would be imposed for serious law infringements.

Chapter 15

Power Generation

Current Background

China is the second largest economy in the world, with more than US$10 trillion GDP in 2014, producing multitudes of consumer and industrial products to satisfy the enormous local and global markets. China's power consumption in 2014 was about 5.53 trillion kWh and is growing rapidly. As China is the "factory of the world," its total energy consumption represents partial requirement for manufacturing goods for the export markets.

China—the World Largest Coal Producer and User

Burning Coal for Energy Production

In China, more than two-thirds of the electric supply comes from coal-fired power stations, with the rest from oil, hydro, gas, and nuclear powers, as well as other renewable energy sources such as wind energy, solar energy, and biofuels. Its energy consumption has surpassed that of the United States. China, the largest coal producer in the world, uses about 45 percent of the global total production. China is also the largest oil importer in the world to satisfy the world's largest car market. In 2014, China signed a US$400 billion contract with Russia for the supply of gas for thirty years.

With a projected annual economic growth of about 7 percent for future years, consumption of coal and oil will rise proportionately. The government is keen on accelerating the urbanization program for the remaining six hundred million poor residents still living in the rural areas. Hence, more energy is required to build housing and infrastructures to cater to these rural migrants as well as future increase in population and export markets. Where does the energy come from? Should China continue to use coal as the primary source of energy or should it go for other resources? Coal is a curse because it liberates greenhouse gases that affect human health and climate change.

Sustainable Economic Development without Pollution

There is plethora of issues that have to be considered carefully before selecting any particular source for future energy production. Emphasis will be on national safety that cannot be compromised under any circumstances, real economy, total net and opportunity costs, employment, impact on the environment and human health, compatibility with international politics, social and industrial development, and sustainability for the next millennium. Hence, experts on energy around the world are engaged to formulate a sustainable policy on energy production to achieve the desired targets without relying on fuel imports or causing pollution to the environment.

China will pull out all the stops to implement a new energy-production scheme to obtain clean energy and be proactive to avoid future unpleasant consequences that can be too prohibitive in cost to bear if the present situation continues unabated.

Coal-Burning Effect

Greenhouse Gases from Coal Burning

What is the real cost to humans by using coal? The answer is indeterminate. It could be hundred times more than the retail price of coal in the market. Coal burning generates greenhouse gases that cause climate change with resulting abnormal weather patterns. Flash floods, droughts, snowstorms, and extreme cold and heat waves now happen more frequently, and with record-breaking severity, causing widespread havoc to farm production, disrupting daily lives, curtailing economic activities, damaging properties, causing loss of lives, and causing many billions of dollars of damage due to recurring catastrophes. Coal burning ruins ecosystems and wildlife.

In addition, coal burning releases toxic chemicals that can cause arsenic and selenium poisoning, chronic obstructive pulmonary disease (COPD), and esophageal and lung cancers. It also releases sulfur dioxide, which forms acid rain that damages the ecosystem. Smog and haze occur more frequently than before and is serious when toxic pollutants in the air are trapped in the atmosphere and are blocked from dispersion. Tiny particulates could enter human lungs and bloodstreams with resultant poisoning. Many infants and aged people suffer from respiratory ailments during winter when the atmosphere is fogbound.

Costs of Using Coal as an Energy Source

In China, coal mining accidents often happen and have resulted in deaths of a few thousand every year. China pays a hefty price for the use of coal to produce energy. Unfortunately, the price of coal does not incorporate the costs of harmful side effects inflicted on society. However, reductions in coal-fired power stations will strangle the economic growth destined to eradicate poverty problems that are still besetting the six hundred million poor rural residents. The situation is paradoxical but in need of urgent resolution. China is the world's largest CO_2 emitter, and about one-third of the emissions are due to manufacturing goods for export. One can imagine what would happen to human beings living on planet Earth with thick clouds of CO_2 and toxic elements encircling the planet surface in the future. It will not be a pretty scene. Hence, the ultimate cost of burning coal is astronomical.

Effect of Using Petroleum

China is the world's biggest car market. With 120 million vehicles on the road, exhausting greenhouse gases like CO_2 into the atmosphere further aggravates the precarious problem of climate change. In mega-cities like Shanghai, Chongqing, and Beijing, each with more than fifteen million people, serious traffic congestion is a daily event. Extra fuel is burned when vehicles are caught in slow-moving traffic at busy junctions on century-old narrow roads. Commuting time on the roads could stretch to many hours between work and residence on the tightly-packed public buses. Beijing recently suffered from unprecedented winter smog problem, resulting in a surge of patients seeking hospital treatment, and paralyzing air and road traffic operations. Such pathetic scenes will repeat in the future.

China is the world's second-largest oil consumer. China's import of seven million barrels of oil per day in 2014 costs US$0.49 billion per day at US$70/

barrel or US$178.9 billion per year, a staggering amount that is the annual budget of many countries. With a rapid rise in car registrations each year, coupled with declining oil reserves, prices of crude oil will soar in the future, and this will cause widespread inflation and disruption to economic expansion. At the same time, increasing use of oil will increase the liberation of toxic gases into the atmosphere and the generation of greenhouse gases that will further exacerbate climate change.

The twin effects of exorbitant oil price increases and climate change will only deteriorate with time. Hence, the cost of using petroleum is more than the price charged by the gas station. We need to pay for higher medical bills and ill-effects of climate change. This is an inevitable consequence of using fossil fuels. One effective way of eliminating the use of fossil fuel for vehicles is to build electric cars, which will be the ultimate car in China and perhaps the world. Biodiesel will be used in heavy mechanical transporters with internal combustion engines. Transportation systems will be drastically revamped to reduce the use of private cars in urban centers, and the new eco-city design will emphasize the ease of public transportation for daily commuters.

Volatility of External Crude Oil Supplies

More than half the oil imported into China depends on the Persian Gulf countries. Future demand for energy will escalate as economic development continues unabated. Increasing oil import entails depletion of national foreign reserves. The amount of foreign currency for import oil bill will escalate sharply when oil price continues to rise until the production exceeds demand with price reduction. Using this amount of money to develop domestic renewable energy industries every year makes economic sense for China. It would more than offset the higher price paid for the imported petroleum and the attendant consequent costs of air pollution and public health.

Recurring international political conflicts and threat of terrorism have raised the bar of supply insecurity to the highest level. Piracy on the shipping lanes has become a lucrative business in the wild-wild west of East African countries, with demand of ransoms in the hundreds of millions of US dollars. Frequent threat of curtailing oil production by the OPEC oil exporting countries use oil as a political weapon, and this always looms in the minds of the officials in charge of national security.

The flashpoints in the Middle East and North Africa have been around for decades and will not disappear anytime soon. Political turmoil, volatility, uncertainty, and threat of war that entangle the oil producing countries in the

Middle East make future supply of oil precarious, unreliable, and interruptive. Such a situation is detrimental to the global and Chinese economy and creates uncertainty to business planning and economic and national development.

Oil Supply and International Politics

China is aware of the fact that the major western oil companies that control the global oil exploration and production of petroleum products wield immense political power that could derail the supply of petroleum products. China is a new player in the international oil politics in the Middle East and Africa. The African oil producers are beginning to play hardball, having tasted the power of oil. The Chinese government is apprehensive about unfriendly countries blocking the Straits of Malacca, through which all the super-oil tankers will need to pass from the Middle East to reach China.

All these unsavory factors make the Chinese policymakers jittery, realizing the future oil dependency on these exporting countries is vulnerable and carries high risks. Furthermore, there is no significant alternate source for crude oil supply to meet China's huge appetite. China is stuck between a rock and a hard place. China has to depend on herself to be self-sufficient in energy supplies in the long run, and the sooner the better. Investing money on domestic energy supplies and avoiding unnecessary expensive and unpredictable international politics is a wise decision, especially concerning the well-being of future generations.

Real Oil Price and Inflation

The OPEC members, oil speculators, and major Western oil companies that control exploration, production, and marketing wield immense power to manipulate the price of oil in the world market. Any war that flares up in the Middle East or elsewhere is a pretext for oil prices to rise. Price increases have a significant ripple effect on cost of living. Fluctuating oil prices have caused chaos on international trades and global inflation. In the past, every time there was a sudden increase in oil price, it triggered a rise in fertilizer prices that in turn caused a corresponding sharp rise in food prices globally, thereby raising the cost of living to new heights. Transportation costs also rose in tandem.

Rising inflation is a devil that casts a fear on many common people who see their life saving for retirement significantly losing its buying power. The vagary of oil price fluctuation considerably hurts business operations and the livelihood of low-income people.

Unfortunately, the US dollar is used as an international currency for trade in the present unstable global financial pandemonium. With the US government credit rating being downgraded for the first time in history since 1860, together with excessive sovereign debt, it could be envisaged that more crises and instability in energy prices would emerge. Unless the US government cleans up its act on debt problems soon, the world community could be at the mercy of an unstable dollar, which is also used as a political weapon. It is a financially explosive mixture of oil politics and an unstable US dollar.

If another big-scale war were to flare up with massive US military forces involved, the US dollar would definitely slither down the slippery road, bleeding dry the US treasury, which is already faced with a national debt of $18 trillion, an amount larger than its GDP. Massive global inflation would occur, especially when the US Treasury is fond of printing fiat money in their favorite quantitative easing policy, letting loose many billions of cheap dollars with a near-bottom interest rate in the international money market. Cheap money would entice people to borrow and invest with a frenzy in the property market, which would reach a bubble in no time, creating a financial crisis and subsequently creating global inflation. Unless there is an international organization to curb the excessive printing of US dollars beyond their true value, the world can expect to experience more financial crises in the future or a collapse of the US dollar, whose value is based on trust without real asset–backing, like gold.

The net cost of using fossil oil is not just the price of oil quoted in the stock market. There is a social cost to be paid when obnoxious gases and particulate matters are released relentlessly into the atmosphere, causing climate change and damage to human health and properties. Factored into the curse of oil spillage were cost of US$33 billion paid by BP to clean up the oil spillage in the Gulf of Mexico on April 2010 due to an explosion of an oil rig, and the consequence of irreparable environmental damage to the ecosystem and the loss of livelihood of many fishermen and marine lives.

In March 1989, the oil tanker *Exxon Valdez* struck the Prince William Sound's Bligh Reef, spilling between 260,000 and 750,000 barrels of crude oil into the sea, affecting a huge area of fishing ground and wildlife and causing irreparable ecosystem damage. In addition, there are the costs of keeping many navy ships to safeguard the safe passage of oil tankers on the high seas, the costs of payment of ransom money to sea pirates, and increased insurance premiums. There is no guarantee another oil tanker disaster or oil rig fire will not recur. Human error is always present.

Nuclear Energy

Although nuclear power is a so-called "clean energy," the costs of nuclear meltdown are enormous. There have been three serious accidents at nuclear power stations: in 2011 at Fukushima, Japan, with many deaths and widespread spills of radioactive materials; in 1979 at Three Mile Island in New York in the United States; and in 1986 at Chernobyl (Ukraine), Russia. The radiation from these accidents still lingers in the affected areas and might remain for decades. Many people suggest the town in Fukushima where the nuclear meltdown occurred would become a ghost town. Many refugees still live in relief centers. Several European countries have decided to ban nuclear power plants in the wake of the event at Fukushima.

Nuclear power stations are expensive to build and have a long lead time before completion. The location requires lots of water for cooling, and during a prolonged heat wave, the nuclear reactor might need shutting down due to lack of water. Nuclear reactors located near the sea could face the same fate as that in Fukushima. Maintenance of nuclear power stations requires meticulous planning, dedicated and experienced personnel, zero-tolerance for mistakes, and generous budgeting and training. Spare parts are expensive and require long lead time for repair and replacement. (It seems every nuclear reactor plant is custom made.) Disposal of radioactive waste is still a dangerous problem. Decommissioning of a nuclear reactor is time-consuming, dangerous, and expensive.

The advantage of a nuclear power plant is that it has a large capacity to produce electricity. The disadvantage is that once shut down for any reason, there is little hope of quick restoration of power from backup sources. The Chinese leadership is wise to forgo nuclear energy because having just clean energy at the risk of a serious nuclear mishap is not worth the sacrifice in loss of lives and properties, consequential nuclear radiation catastrophe, and expensive investments that can be put into better and safer alternate renewable energy sources.

Nuclear power is not an equitable trade-off for safe energy supply. There is no economic equation for payback of a nuclear power plant when the safety factor is indeterminate. Terrorist attack on nuclear power plants is a favorite topic of the security personnel in every country. It would be a nightmare to all citizens when terrorist attacks on a nuclear power plant were to occur. Human error is forever present to cause a mishap.

Reasons for Ending Coal as an Energy Source

China has taken more than three decades of hardship and sacrifices to build up its economy to become the second largest in the world. Such success is no mean feat. The Chinese leaders created miracles to improve the living standards of more than two hundred million poor people within one generation. More work has yet to be done to uplift the rest of the poor population of six hundred million. The tasks ahead are arduous and replete with uncertainty, social and political obstacles, grave global financial crises, and challenges in the interconnected world of the twenty-first century.

The present leaders are fully aware of the fact that with more toxic gases and particulate matters being continuously released by burning of coal and oil, the pollution problem could reach a point of no return where the human race would be devastated by clouds of toxic gases blanketing the cities, overwhelmed by natural disasters and cancerous diseases.

What would the future generations expect present government leaders do so they do not need to wear masks to filter all the toxic gases and particulates in the atmosphere to conduct their daily lives? Would they have endemic lung cancer deaths at a young age? What is the point of living, of having wealth without good health, spending hard-earned money on expensive medicines and long-term health care services? These serious questions require soul searching and cannot be put on a back burner.

The cost is just too astronomical to bear by future generations when the cumulative effects of greenhouse gases and toxic elements become too overwhelming for amenable solutions. There are no quick fixes except with resolute commitment to forgo the use of fossil fuels. Kicking the can down the road does not usher better future solutions.

Clean Energy in the Eco-World

With the establishment of an Eco-World, it is an opportune time for China to take an effective proactive action to implement a comprehensive project of investing in the industrial upgrading and restructuring covering energy saving, environment protection, emission reduction, recycling economy, and ecological environment construction. The country spares no effort in searching for new technology in renewable and clean energy, and low-carbon energy, making carbon reduction a new source of economic growth.

With success in these endeavors comes the long-term sustainable economic and peaceful social development for future generations. Progressively, with eco-farms producing sufficient biofuels together with solar, wind, hydro, and tidal wave power, China will cease to import oil. The Chinese government will henceforth breathe a sigh of relief for not having to deal with the dirty multinational oil politics that is time-devouring, irritable, explosive, dangerous, antagonistic, and harmful to national security and human lives.

The economic payback equation for renewable clean and green energy compared to fossil fuels will encompass the costs of climate change, diseases on a massive scale, loss of productive labor due to sickness inflicted by fossil fuel and coal burning, and loss of foreign exchange. The government is aware of the immense savings on reduction on the annual government budget for manpower and resources dealing with erratic foreign oil supply and the vagaries of price fluctuation and inflation, and the incalculable savings on reduction of national health care and medical services.

The grave problem with fossil fuel is the dreadful inflation imposed by the ever increasing oil price, affecting a wide spectrum of economic activities and hardship that could derail many worthwhile national projects. With greater ferocity of climate change, the unabated use of oil and coal could herald the gradual demise of planet Earth.

Benefits of Renewable Energy

Using locally produced renewable energy sources provides large-scale employment with multiplier effects on the entire national economy. It saves immense amounts of foreign reserves, eliminates the danger of international frictions, and circumvents embroiling in potential oil-related battles on foreign lands. The production of renewable biofuels is fully integrated with the creation of an Eco-World in China. The good synergy of having a self-reliant renewable energy industry is to cease importing inflation, and to provide stable energy production. Inflation exacerbates social divide between the rich and poor, which is evident in present Chinese society.

In the new Eco-World, China seizes the opportunity to establish a unified national super-smart electrical grid that is important to supply backup power to regions suffering from energy shortages, which happens often as China is a vast country with unpredictable inclement weather and seismic disasters. The economic equation for renewable energy projects is not a simple linear equation. It contains many variables, some of which are indeterminate and unidentifiable, such as those concerning national safety and security and climate change consequences.

If China can spend US$26 billion to build the massive Three Gorges Dam and displace 1.3 million people to generate 22.5GW electricity, there is no reason not to invest in renewable energy sources to produce the same electrical output. In fact, the cumulative annual savings from not importing oil is more than sufficient to offset the investment costs of renewable energy projects.

Electrification of Transport Vehicles

Battery-Powered, Environmentally Friendly Vehicles

The eco-city design and infrastructures will significantly improve energy efficiency as well as reduction of carbon emission. The theme of eco-city design is to minimize unnecessary commuting traffic using private cars during working hours, and staggering of working hours for all government departments and large commercial firms in the city centers. Electric trains and buses are the main public transport vehicles, and the power comes from renewable energy sources.

The city design would incorporate specific areas for different types of industries, commercial establishments, entertainment centers, and other community facilities. All of these areas will be efficiently served by public vehicles in a fully integrated transport system. There will be a new system of energy savings for consumers. Discounts on tariffs would be given to consumers during periods of low power utilization. China will invest heavily in inventing a system of storing excess energy as a backup.

Power Generation in Eco-World China

With the establishment of an Eco-World, China will spare no effort in carrying out the following energy production projects.

Wind Power

Wind roses of various parts of the country have been thoroughly studied in order to build wind farms for effective power generation. China follows the examples in Demark, where more than 39 percent of its energy came from wind turbines in 2015 and is expected to reach 50 percent by 2020. Nuclear power stations are banned in Demark.

Wind turbine energy is reliable and demands little maintenance, and it is easily installed. China is the world's largest wind turbine manufacturer. The government has plans to exponentially increase the wind-power energy supply to offset the reduction of coal-fired power supply. Wind power is used as a main supply for the national grid and standby power.

Tidal wave power and wind farms are built at the river mouths near the sea to power the pumps that transport the river water back to the inland for recycling. For coastal eco-cities, offshore wind turbines will be installed to take advantage of the natural relatively large temperature differentiation between the ocean and land mass, resulting in high velocity wind along the coast.

Wind speeds in desert areas are relatively high and are therefore suitable for large wind farm installation to supply power to convert deserts to useful pasture lands and to arrest desertification. China intends to turn all the deserts that are one-fifth the size of its land mass, into useful arable land in conjunction with the gigantic project of river water recycling and creation of thousands of canals, reservoirs, lakes, and marshlands.

Solar energy

The sun promises to be an important endless source of solar energy for mankind. It has been estimated that the Sahara Desert (about the size of China) holds enough solar power to satisfy Europe's energy needs many times over. China has many deserts, about eight hundred thousand square miles in total, about one-fifth the size of the Sahara. The deserts provide opportunities for both solar and wind power developments. To achieve diversification of energy production from renewable sources, China commits unlimited resources to developing solar energy industries that include photo-voltaic cells, concentrated solar power systems, and solar power towers.

China produces half the world's solar photo-voltaic panels. Solar water heaters are ubiquitous on the roof tops of many high rise buildings in Chinese cities for hot water production. Solar power helps China not only stop desertification, but also reverts deserts into ecologically and economically viable land replete with trees, grass, vegetation, oases and wildlife. The perennial severe sand storms that blanket Beijing and other northern cities annually will forever be eradicated. Blue skies and clean air will prevail for better living and a healthier environment.

Hydropower

China is the world's largest hydroelectricity producer, which supplies about 20 percent of domestic power demand, and is the second-biggest energy source after coal. China boasts more dams than the rest of the world combined. Hundreds of new dams are being planned for the middle and upper reaches of Yangtze River and more dams are planned for the Yellow River in the Eco-World. The massive US$4.17 billion Yellow River dam built near Xiaolangdi in central China is the nation's second largest dam project after the Three Gorges Dam, the world's largest. Hydropower station requires little maintenance, is reliable and leaves no waste behind.

Tidal Wave Power

A new tidal wave power generator is designed to continuously generate energy using the principle of the gyroscopic effect. A flywheel, coupled to a motor, is installed inside a gyroscopic generator and is kept in continuous motion by the forces of the tidal waves, which constantly rock the generator in the ocean. Strong tidal waves are available along the eastern shores of China, where giant tidal generators can be used to incessantly generate electrical energy.

Saving Energy: The Super-Smart Electrical Grid

An electrical grid is an interconnected network for delivering electricity from the power stations to the consumers. When supply and demand are in synchronized mode, the electrical distribution system would be balanced. The grid would kick in when the demand exceeds the current supply so that the backup supply could be connected. Or when there is a malfunction in one supply system, the grid would look for a standby system to take over. In an antiquated grid, power transfer could be tricky, and brownouts could occur.

Where power generation is erratic is typical for many renewable energy sources, for example, wind and solar, and consumers' demand fluctuates, so matching the supply and demand of energy becomes a complex engineering work. The higher the share of renewable energy in a power grid, the more complex it becomes to match supply and demand. A conventional power grid would incur energy waste. In order to reduce transmission losses in a modern eco-city, a super-smart grid is built and would link up various energy sources and combine them in an intelligent way, adapting to changing demand. Standby renewable sources and backup batteries could be turned on to meet peak demand from a remote distance.

Future Private Car and Energy Production

China will invest heavily in R&D to seek better ways of producing energy from renewable energy sources with lowest costs and highest efficiency. Private cars using battery power will be the ultimate car for individual transportation. Taxes will be imposed on private cars based on utilization on the road. A breakthrough in carbon storage and capture (CSC) technologies could turn coal power plants, currently the cheapest but most carbon-intensive way of generating electricity, into a climate-friendly viable alternative source of energy supply. China, as the largest coal producer in the world, would continue to research into the CSC with a view that CO_2 emission would be reduced to an acceptable level.

Outlook for China on Energy Production

China has taken the opportunity to build an Eco-World where renewable energy production would generate immense economic activities with synergic benefits of enhanced national security, self-sufficiency in energy, savings of massive amount of foreign exchange, elimination of greenhouse gas emission, improved healthy living conditions, taming of imported inflation, and circumvention of international political conflicts and stress related to oil. China will enjoy a peaceful environment for the next millennia.

Chapter 16

The E-Education System

Present Education System: Rote Learning

Education plays a pivotal role in nation building and economic advancement. There is no payback period calculation to judge the actual value of an education budget. On the contrary, without investing in education, there is no hope of raising the living standard of the people. The old Chinese way of rote learning teaches students to be conformists. Deviation in thoughts is frowned upon and considered rebellious. Such rote learning has no relevance in today's modern world as it is only good for reciting poems, not for creating new ideas.

Social Problems Facing Urban Children

The one-child policy that has prevailed in the last two decades has changed the manner of raising a child in China. Many urban parents and grandparents tend to spoil the only child, who grows up to be selfish, demanding, and antisocial. Such children do not learn well in school, and they grow up to be a misfit in society. Because many parents are too busy making a living or too tired to spend time with their children after a hard day's work, many children are left to their own device to while away their time playing computer games and become addicted to them. China cannot afford to let young children go astray and become a burden to society. The government will need to find a solution before the social problems become too ominous to handle.

Education in Rural Areas

Although China has attained accolades by being the second-largest economy in the world, it may not reveal to the outside world that living in the rural areas are more than six hundred million people who have little money for their children's education. The schools in the villages are bare-bone structures with earthen floors and are equipped with dilapidated wooden desks and chairs. In winter, the classrooms are freezing, and in summer they are sizzling hot. The poorly paid and under-qualified teachers lack proper professional training and the latest teaching skills. School books are many editions behind.

There are more than 250 million children in rural and remote areas. Many students are malnourished and suffer emotional stress and psychological problems due to absentee parents being away from home as migrant workers for long periods of time. Under such living condition many students become delinquents. Some thirty million village children are sent by their parents to boarding schools, some of which can only be reached after traveling for days from the remote mountainous villages, traversing dangerous mountainous paths. Some of these schools do not have qualified teachers, and ill-treatment of students is alleged to have happened. For such village students to pass the national high school examination to gain a place to study at a university remains a dream. Poverty in the villages perpetuates for generations. Indeed, it is a waste of human resources. Such pathetic situations will be rectified in the Eco-World of China.

Education in the Urban Cities

It the cities, primary and high school classes are bursting at the seams due to increasing intake of new students from rural migrants' families that have a local residence permit. Old schools in the cities cannot expand due to lack of space. Many migrant workers face obstacles created by the local governments that refuse to enroll their children into the public schools. Some public schools in defiance of the central government's policy impose additional fees on immigrant children if they want to accept enrollment offers.

Many migrant children encounter discrimination and prejudice in schools because of their different social backgrounds and inability to speak the local dialect. Some private schools accept these children, who are excluded from the public schools, but the standards of these schools are low due to the teachers being paid little. This unfair treatment affecting more than twenty million children in the cities will create resentment against society.

Enrollment to good schools requires connections with the appropriate school administrators plus a payment of gratitude. To get good grades, it is imperative for parents to engage school teachers as tutors. Compared to Western countries, it is an expensive investment to educate a child in China through primary and high schools just to get an experience of rote learning. This education system is not cost effective to society or the nation and is potentially a waste of human resources. Many parents send their children overseas for better education and, hence, a source of lost foreign currency and a potential loss of talent due to emigration.

High School Examination—A Turning Point in One's Life

High school national or university entrance examination is an important event in China because it determines a child's future. The threshold of eligibility of entering a university is high. Entrance to the few prestigious universities in the major cities is keenly contested especially when the population of high school graduates increases each year, but the number of vacancies for popular university courses remain fairly constant. Migrant children have a distinct disadvantage if they have to go back to their hometown to sit for the examination after studying in an urban public school. This is because each region sets its own curriculum.

Many students pursue their course of study based on allocation by the university. After graduation, many find difficulty in obtaining jobs that suit their interests. Hence, millions of university graduates remain unemployed for a few years. Such dichotomy of supply and demand of university graduates is a waste of human resources. Many students are forced to take a course of study not of their choice because their preferred courses are not available. After graduation, they feel frustrated as they cannot find the right job of their liking. Such an education system creates not only disgruntled youngsters but is a waste of human resource. The current education system does not yield satisfactory productivity of resources of man, material and money.

Overseas Higher Education

Many parents are willing to sacrifice in order to send their children overseas for further education, often at great expense. After graduation, these students may choose to remain overseas to seek employment. Foreign countries benefit immensely from these migrant Chinese students who have good academic qualifications. China cannot afford such magnanimous talent exports for free caused by archaic education policies. Since the government's liberalization of foreign travel by citizens in the 1980s, more than a million students have gone overseas to study, ultimately draining hundreds of millions of dollars out of China. Such money can be utilized in the new Eco-World education system, which will offer courses to meet the demand of all the students.

New Approach to the Education System

If China wants to move up the value chain, and to become the strongest economy of the world, a new education system is needed. With variable standards of teaching, a human-based education system in China with a huge student population is not cost effective. Value for money is not attainable. The archaic rote-learning process that is good for reciting and regurgitating poems and literature cannot produce thinkers, innovators, and entrepreneurs like Apple's Steve Jobs, who was a mover in technology application and produces high value-added products like iPhones and iPods for sale around the world.

Where possible, China goes beyond its national boundaries to attract foreign talents with a world vision to teach in local universities. Current modern industries demand not only thinkers and innovators, but also ingenious system integrators who can assemble and produce a high value product from components made by specialist companies from around the world. An example is the manufacture of modern commercial airplane that has tens of thousands of sub-components designed and made by many foreign OEMs, original equipment manufacturers. Even the United States' latest submarine incorporates a silent propeller made by a Japanese company. A military stealth jet in the United States is sprayed with a paint that cannot be detected by radar—this paint was made in Japan. A manufacturing company that has an efficient global supply chain system that supplies all the necessary components will have a good chance to produce a product that meets the global customers quickly. This is essential in a global market when the lifecycle of a consumer product is getting shorter by the day.

China's export economy of the past three decades could not have achieved sterling results without the adoption of many modern industrial and management practices and quality standards from the West. An open mind in learning is a prerequisite to producing innovation and discovery. That is the reason Deng Xiaoping opening up China, which had been closed for six hundred years to the outside world. In the interim, China benefits from the overseas returned scholars to help filled the vacuum of the latest thinking and developments on science and technology, management, and social science.

China should open its door wide to accept foreign talents to work in China. Acquiring a ready-made foreign talent pays great dividend in national economic development. This is one of the reasons that the United States is a powerful country for such a long time because of its generous immigration policy of attracting foreign talents to become citizens. The United States has nothing to lose to increases its pool of imported talents.

Chinese leaders realize that the stakes are high and the opportunity costs astronomical if the old rote learning method is not replaced. A paradigm shift in the current education policy is needed for the Eco-World of China. The new education will not be a make-over of the current education system or having bells and whistles attachments, but an entire new concept that dovetails with the prevailing digital, fast changing, and highly competitive, interconnected and interdependent cyber-world. There is a need to redefine the purpose of education and the desired return on investments for the benefit of the country and society to last another millennium.

Constantly moving up the value chain is the national aspiration and compassion. This is the new Chinese dream. Students should be more confident and creative after graduating from the new Eco-World education system. The new education is to be fair and affordable to every student irrespective of financial background. Every promising student is a rough diamond ready for polishing. There is no one-size-fits-all education template that is suitable for developing students of varied emotion inclination, inspiration, personal interests, talents, and intellectual capability to their fullest potential. The new education first teaches principles and fundamental knowledge of the universe to students. Freedom of choice of school subjects is to suit the individual student's preference. The school should produce thinkers and not copycats. Creative ideas that generate quality and useful products are the new paradigm in education.

China hopes to encourage more students to do R&D so as to help industries manufacture higher value-added products for sale around the world. Now is the golden opportunity for China to sprint ahead when so many Western countries are mired in financial difficulties. Now is the golden opportunity not to be missed. Talented foreign professionals and academicians should be encouraged to migrate to China, just like what the United States did after WW2 with attracting talent from Germany, Russia, and other Asian and European countries.

To achieve the objective of effective education for future generations, the new Chinese leaders have no reservations in introducing a revolutionary education system using digital media and humanoid robotic teachers. Already, mass media and the Internet have gathered a lot of information ready for anyone to retrieve 24/7. China needs to feel technologically proactive and superior. The rate of human progress depends on the rate of application of technology in everyday life. A manual system of education is too cumbersome and slow to impart the latest knowledge to students of various backgrounds and capabilities.

Training and upgrading the standards of teaching of human teachers is time consuming and costly and resources are not readily available in every school throughout the country. Quality of teaching varies widely according to individual teacher, whereas humanoid teacher provides consistent quality. The children of today live in a digital, multimedia world, and they should have no problem using the Internet to search for information and knowledge. Many older generations of teachers are not computer savvy.

Eco-World Internet-based Education System

In every eco-city ordinary human teachers will be replaced by robotic teachers. The textbook materials will be loaded in school portals that can be downloaded into special I-Pads or similar device of the latest design that suits primary and secondary education. Curriculum changes are centralized and standardized nationally. Teaching materials are the culmination of intense discussions among educationists, industrialists, various professional bodies, and social scientists. The curriculum will be uniform throughout the country and can be updated anytime. The online assessment tests provide instantaneous feedback on the student's rate of progress of knowledge absorption and positive remedial action to guide the student to improve his test results.

This new education system achieves tremendous savings in money, labor, and time with attendant benefits of teaching children with the latest information, knowledge and technology. It eliminates duplication of work and administration that prevail throughout the country in every province in the past where curriculum varies in different provinces.

Self-Learning and Teaching Standard

It will be a relief to parents and students alike that no heavy school bags need to be carried on students' backs. There is a great opportunity for students to explore and search for information on the Internet and in school portals. Every school has an e-library with millions of reference books that can be downloaded from the national library. Online teaching and research materials offer immense scope and depth of knowledge for individual student and group learning in a contemporary environment. The new education system is a fun thing for both the students and the school. The robotic teachers are constantly reprogrammed with the latest information and teaching skill.

The advantage of using robotic teacher is that it never gets tired, takes sick or vacation leave, and always retains its composure, enthusiasm, and friendliness toward its students. Its teaching quality never wanes. Some human teachers have biases against slow-learning students, but this will not happen with robotic teachers, which are programmed with standardized pronunciations so it wouldn't matter which province the schools were located in, and all the students are taught using the same pronunciations. Presently, the teachers in every province speak non-uniform Mandarin with a local accent. Unlike humans, robotic teachers never lose their temper or memory of teaching materials.

Costs of New Education System

The new computerized education system would incur a substantial initial outlay of capital costs in developing robotic teachers, computerized course materials and curriculum, and total revamp of intellectual assessment tests and examination system. However, amortizing the initial outlay costs of IT software over a period of thirty to forty years, the costs are acceptable. Such cost amortization method is used for building high-cost expressways and high-speed railways. With the advent of IT, the airlines adopt a very expensive computerized reservation system to streamline its entire operation in sales and marketing throughout their global network, resulting in enhanced ticket sales, passenger yields, flexible ticket pricing, and elimination of double-booking by travel agents for ticket sales. Reservation and ticketing can be done online 24/7, including interline tickets.

In the "old days" one could buy a ticket only during office hours, and for interline ticket, one had to wait many days for confirmation. With computerized ticketing, the airline does not need to issue a hard copy ticket. Technology has revolutionized the airline industry with much improved productivity and cost reduction. Similarly, the net value of education system enhanced by IT application will be immeasurable for years to come. IT is already a necessity in modern living.

The entire e-learning software system will be developed by Waratah Organization in conjunction with Phil's Robot Company and local software and hardware manufacturers. Its running costs would be significantly lower than the prevailing manual system of education that encompasses hundreds of thousands of schools with duplication of duties, administration and training, manually revising obsolete teaching material and information, and high overhead costs of employing hundreds of thousands of temporary teachers and administrators with varying standards and quality.

The government is mindful of the escalating payment of pensions to retired staff of several million and the ever-increasing contribution of medical insurance for all the staff. Technology will lighten the financial burden of the government once the eco-education system is in place. China will take the lead to revolutionize education systems for mankind.

Eco-Education System Fair to All Students

The old education system is biased against the poor and favors the rich. Slow-learning students are disadvantaged because they cannot catch up with lessons. This new education system is universally fair to all students of any financial and social background. There will be no pent-up pressures on the parents and students during the yearly high school examinations across the country.

Students are encouraged to offer new ideas and ways of learning. Progressive school assessment and tests are based on the student's ability to comprehend and their analytical skill. This is no more examination subject based on regurgitating textbook materials. There will not be necessary for parents to engage tuition teachers. Tuition fees take their toll on parents' financial resource in the present environment. The new eco-education system can identify students with special learning skills and potential for higher education in a particular discipline, thereby helping the students select the appropriate course of university or technical college education.

More Creative Thinkers Graduating from New Universities

New university education system will be reformed entirely. University entrance is based on a computer-based test that evaluates a student's ability to think and excel in original ideas. University courses will be offered based on the aptitude and intellectual capability of the student and his or her extracurricular activities in sports and social activities. The prospective student needs to pass a test at an interview panel. The universities allow students to change course after the first year of study.

University teaching staff would adopt US and UK university teaching methods, which encourages students to search for knowledge and expound their findings and present original ideas. They are taught to have a helicopter view in solving problems. Such a system of education allows students to think for themselves and be creative. Students are encouraged to do research projects in their post graduate courses. China hopes, with the reformed education system, there will be more outstanding graduates who can push China to the frontier of scientific and technological arena comparable to or even surpass the United States.

Using robotic teaching and online course materials, young students are inquisitive enough to search for information to learn on their own, whether in the fields of arts, science, and technology or other disciplines, which will give them a head start to develop their potential at an early age. Generous grants are given by the government and industries to students who do research. Business incubators together with government agencies would provide funding and business support assistance to start-up companies with new innovations created by students. Scholarships will be given to students of excellence in academic and sporting fields.

Open-Minded Education System

The new national education system will be introduced progressively in stages during the creation of new eco-cities that are being built across China. It aims to produce new generations of thinkers. It emphasizes creative, innovative, participative, communicative, and interactive skills and collaborative learning processes. Problem solving, understanding first principles, engaging all students with different dispositions and family backgrounds, and sharing of knowledge are the hallmarks of the new eco-education system, opening the minds of pupils to a wider view and horizon.

The school will assist the students in their university course selection with several options based on their scholastic achievements, personalities, interests, extracurricular activities, and aspirations. Emphasis will be on using technology to replace manual workers, of whose population will decrease with each passing year.

Parents Participations

In the new eco-education system, the quality of teaching and the status of every school is the same throughout the country. There are no more elite or mediocre schools. Every student will be developed to his or her fullest potential. Parents are to be involved in the new system in educating their children starting from the tender age of attending primary school, helping build character foundation, and nurturing their children to appreciate social graces and etiquette. Parents' firm support and passion in educating their primary school children are the drivers of enriching their children with good academic results and confidence.

Participative Learning

Parents and school supervisors meet regularly to discuss the student's progress and remedial actions if required at the primary school age. Continuous assessment of the students is through computerized, multiple, selective test questions and assignments. The results will reveal how well the students perform progressively and the depth of their intellectual capability and their scholastic liking.

The students could choose the high school subjects either in the science or arts stream with advice from the parents and school supervisors. Polytechnic will form an important part of the new eco-education system that serves as a venue for students who prefer to seek practical experience and venture into doing own business.

Main Features of New Education Systems

Emphasis on First Principle and Practical Application

The new education system embraces stimulation of the student's brain to search for the truth of nature, the meaning of living things, and ecosystem subsistence. The students are encouraged to be resourceful when faced with ambiguity, as there are options to fix a problem on short or long-term basis, to gain interim or long-term benefit. They shall not be insulated from the outside world. They must understand nothing is permanent, and every system diminishes in value with a time expiry date. Every student is encouraged to have a mutual friend from a foreign country, and a chance to stay with the foreign friend during summer vacation.

The course materials encourage students to develop inquisitive minds and seek practical solutions to problems encountered in daily life. The senior students will learn the significance of inventions, discoveries and new technologies, computer software development, and 3-D printing. Continuous school tests and assignments would help the students apply their knowledge and understanding of what they have learned from school, and from the Internet research materials. Every high school student learns traditional Chinese medicine and the common diseases that affect health, and they are taught to be mindful of the harmful effects of smoking, sedentary living, compulsive eating, drug abuse, and excessive drinking. Indulgence in computer games is discouraged. Outdoor activities are encouraged.

There will be lots of field trips and experiments for students to put their knowledge into positive actions. Such system of education encourages and motivates students to become more open minded and try out new way of learning and discovery. Commendable scientific innovations will be shown in city's exhibition halls, and annual competitions will be staged for the best invention.

The government will help any student who would like to commercialize their invention. In addition to study, every student is required to take up a sport to keep fit, and to understand the importance of healthy lifestyle and maintaining a balanced dietary food intake. Every primary student is required to take up an arts subject like singing, playing a musical instrument, painting, or chess. Every student must participate in scouting activities to develop community spirit and mutual help to one another.

Vacation Training and Job Counseling

During school vacations the senior students are to attend workshop talks on how things are manufactured, how the economy functions, and how the interconnected world affects one another, especially in the stock and financial markets, and how the parity of cost of manufacturing affects every country, and the concept of value of money. These workshop talks are to empower students to think, learn, and understand the new interconnected world order, climate change, technology, IT systems, globalization of finance and industries, and the short lifecycles of consumer products. It is about the future survival of the human race relative to the future production of energy and food, and supply of clean water to meet the ever-increasing population.

The university students are encouraged by the government and industries to take up part-time jobs during vacations to gain practical experience and a feel for working life. A tripartite group consisting of career counselors from the government, industrial organization and universities would give career guidance and advice to all graduate students from colleges and universities to prepare them for their future career. Postgraduates with one or two years of industrial work experience are invited to give a talk to the fresh graduates on working life in the real world.

Classroom Setup

The classroom is fully equipped with computers, a large computer screen, a video system, and robotic teachers who resemble good-looking human beings pleasantly dressed. Such a setup is standard in all primary and secondary schools in the eco-city. Every student uses a tablet to study and do homework. Audio-video presentations are liberally used to supplement the subjects in science, history, chemistry, geography, arts, music, and mathematics. A large LCD screen hung on the classroom wall will show pictures of pertinent subject matters to catch the attention of the students.

Supervising teachers will stimulate lots of discussions among students and create an atmosphere of fun learning and being inquisitive. They encourage students to produce answers from fresh ideas. Students are given assignments on the school Internet portal and tests of various difficulty levels are conducted weekly to examine the students' progress. Students are given group project on topics to be selected by the students, and the students will present their reports at the end of the school year to the class. Students could contact their class supervisor using social media like Skype or Chinese media websites to discuss any problem. The whole atmosphere of learning is enlightening and being creative.

New Primary and High Schools

In view of the new teaching system of using robotic teachers and online materials, the Education Ministry decides to shrink the size of primary and secondary schools to accommodate students from residences within a radius of 1.25 miles. The primary and high schools are relatively small, each accommodating not more than four hundred children, as compared to the old type of school that could accommodate more than a thousand children. Many old schools are located in crowded city centers and subject to traffic jams.

The main objective of designing the eco-school of small size is to cater to students who do not need to travel long distances to and from school. All the schools are connected to underground train stations with covered walkway so that the students are protected from inclement weather during winter and rainy seasons.

E-Learning and Libraries

The digital libraries of all the eco-schools are linked to the mammoth main national library computer center in Beijing. This center stores and updates all the primary and high school teaching materials and educational video programs. School curriculum is standardized and streamlined, and updated every year for all schools in China. This eliminates duplication of efforts in all provinces. This saves time by individual schools that need to prepare a syllabus and reference materials.

Experienced teachers are deployed in every eco-city's District Education Department to offer assistance during teaching sessions. Overseas teachers are engaged to teach foreign languages online using websites. It helps students communicate with the foreign teachers to learn the correct pronunciation and their culture.

The e-learning program is particularly welcome by parents who work in overseas countries. The government will set up overseas schools for their children to attend classes similar to those at home. They will learn from the same syllabus and sit for the same tests. In the past, these children will need to stay back in China to attend schooling. Family life is now more pleasant with children by the side of their parents.

Public Invention Exhibition Centers

Every eco-city has a public invention center where students can exhibit their inventions. Each center caters to different types of inventions and is open to the public. These centers are administered by the Ministry of Science and Technology, which has a website to show all the national and international inventions displayed in the centers. To stimulate an interest in invention, all high school students are to participate in an annual competition. Annual national competitions are held for the best 3-D printing object, robots, and IT software. A handsome prize will be awarded to the winner.

The Chinese Dream

The new education system promises to be a game changer in opening up the potential of future young Chinese to be creative, entrepreneurial, and receptive to new ideas especially when the students are more exposed to the outside world through e-education. This should herald a new era of advancement in socio-industrial-economic development in China. The opportunities generated by the new found contemporary knowledge would help propel China to climb higher in the technical field.

Although China is now the largest trading nation in the world, its net income from the exports is small relative to the profits made by the foreign firms that own the exporting goods and intellectual property. According to industry observers, such situation will change when China's new crops of students graduate from the e-education system. The Chinese government will encourage students and research scholars to spend time on developing more inventions using 3-D printing, robots, IT, and manmade materials.

Together with eco-farming, the e-education system will help China eradicate poverty of six hundred million people that has persisted for millenniums. The investments of financial and human resources on the e-education system pay off handsomely in terms of greater human productivity and value-add by all future generations of ex-rural families. These are wise investments that have a lasting effect on the prosperity of China. The Chinese government is indebted to Waratah for its contribution.

Chapter 17

Public Housing

China Was a Basket Case in 1949

When PRC (People's Republic of China) was born in 1949 under Communist Party administration led by Mao Zedong, there was no foreign currency left behind by the previous administration of Chiang Kai-shek. The country was in financial ruins due to many years of fighting against foreign aggressors and civil war. Many buildings, factories, transport systems, facilities, and houses were destroyed during WW2. Unable to accept Communist ideology, many industrialists, professionals, and businessmen left town for other countries, leaving PRC short of drivers of economic developments. It was a one-man show for Mao to revive China from a foundation of hopelessness.

Inheriting an economically battered country with nearly one billion rural residents living from hand to mouth in the rural areas and millions of disgruntled unemployed workers in the cities, the battle-fatigued revolutionary Mao Zedong had the herculean task of building a new social order that could provide a home and sufficient food for everyone in the country. In 1951, the government initiated a policy of registering every family with a residency permit that placed a restriction on individual freedom of migration to the cities. It was designed to obviate severe food and housing shortages, unemployment and inadequacy of social infrastructure if too many farmers were to migrate to the cities in droves. Mao had no choice but to implement this restriction.

Under Mao's regime, the urban citizens did not need to worry about not having a roof over their heads. Every government department and state-owned company in towns and cities would provide housing to every worker's family for a nominal rent. Farmers were free to build a house on their plot of land. Their houses had no title and could not be mortgaged or sold to another person.

In the early years of communist rule, food rationing was introduced and people queued up for hours to get daily necessities. At that time China could claim to be the cleanest place on earth because nobody could afford to waste or had trash to discard. There were no traffic jams because people commuted by public buses and bicycles. Although living conditions were harsh, life was simple and peaceful. Petty crime was rare. One could leave the door open at night without fear of robbery. There was no corruption.

Kudos must be given to Mao for such an achievement in China. It was pure Communism the Chinese people became familiar with for the first time. There was no warlord to harass the farmers. Gangsters seemed to fear for their lives and disappeared from Communist China.

Relaxation of Residence Permits and Housing Market

In 1984, after Deng Xiaoping introduced a market economy, the government began to gradually relax the residence restriction by allowing migrant farmers, who had the means to support themselves, to transfer their residency permit to towns and cities. China began to introduce urbanization program for the hundreds of millions of migrant workers to live and work in the coastal cities. Private and foreign enterprises did not provide housing for their workers, who had to find their own accommodation. Pure Communism began to fade away.

With swelling of population, increasing wealth in the cities, and limited land supply, private housing prices skyrocketed by leaps and bounds, so much so that newlywed couples with university degrees could not save enough in their lifetime to buy an apartment. The real estate industry is the biggest capital investment in the Chinese economy. The relentless run-up in land costs pushed the housing prices to new heights.

Expansion of city boundaries requires farmland acquisition that incurs the wrath of some farmers who use self-immolation to protest forceful eviction with little compensation. Daily outcry from the public to put a cap on the runaway prices forces the government to introduce restrictions on property purchases and bank loans. Such measures dampen the economic activities of the housing industries, and the GDP dips as a result.

Effects of Poor Housing Policy on Social Developments

With hyperinflation, high apartment rental costs, stagnant salaries, and expensive living standard, many older migrant workers found it not worth their while to work in the cities. They began to return to their farms and worked spare time in nearby towns. The Chinese government cannot continue to play the catch-up game forever with the migrant worker numbers being so fluid and unpredictable, and the economic environment changing rapidly. There must be an end game to stop the price of an apartment skyrocketing that is detrimental to the social order. Many young people elect to remain single as they cannot afford to get married and start a family. Hence, the Chinese leaders have a lot of homework to do to quickly fix the housing problem.

The government had used the land as a commodity to derive an income. However, it should have treated the land as an investment vehicle to help promote a multitude of economic activities as had been evident in Singapore and elsewhere in other countries. China has injected capitalism into communism without a full comprehension of the downside of using state land as a commodity in a private housing project without a firm control of runaway housing prices that affect the social development, and generate inflation and hardship on the lower echelon of its citizens. Allowing speculative housing purchases by corrupt officials adds to the woe of price escalating relentlessly. Such policy suppresses the opportunity of raising the living standards of the lower income echelon and favors the higher income people who have a chance of making a profit from housing speculation. It is no wonder that the general public is unhappy with the government.

Borrowing Ideas from Singapore to Alleviate Housing Woes

With much deliberation and advice from experts of various disciplines, the final solution to the housing problem lies with creating an Eco-World in which the public housing policy emulates the Singapore government's Housing and Development Board (HDB) policy in principle and with modifications. With 82 percent of population living in the HDB apartments, the Singapore government is able to provide a roof over the heads of all eligible Singaporeans even with very low income. For the rest of the population, with income exceeding the top income ceiling for HDB housing qualification, they are free to build and live in privately built houses and apartments. Those who are single and too poor to buy can rent apartments from the government at low rental. Old folk's homes are available to cater to the special needs of the destitute. Such caring housing policy is fair, and welcome by all citizens.

Successful Singapore Housing Policy

This prudent land use policy helps Singapore in its economic and social development. Despite increasing population, there is never a shortage of housing for new buyers, bearing in mind that Singapore has a small land area of 720km^2 (Greater London has 1,572 km^2) for a population of six million, including foreign residents. Re-sale HDB units are available instantly in the open market. Although the population density is one of the highest in the world and with an impressive GDP per capita of US$64,000 in 2013, Singapore is acclaimed to be a garden city and a livable city by foreigners. With an upgrade program in place, old HDB units are refurbished or demolished for higher-quality design and construction.

The design features of the latest build-to-order HDB housing are comparable to the style of a private apartment. Although the Singapore HDB policy is admirable in helping Singapore's economic development, it has to be modified to meet China's desire and standard to suit the latest environment in China for the next millennium. The new Chinese low-cost housing will incorporate many new features and designs that are environmentally friendly not found anywhere in the world.

Eco-apartment Designs and Constructions

In the eco-city, every registered married couple is entitled to buy an apartment for a seventy-year lease from the government at the prevailing price based on the development charges and building costs. The size of an apartment available for lease depends on the couple's income and age. Upgrading to a larger apartment unit is possible when their combined income increases to the next level of higher income bracket.

Every couple, before marriage, would need to make a one-year advanced booking for a unit. They can utilize their compulsory pension fund saving to pay off their monthly mortgage. No one is allowed to sell or rent out the apartment to others except with the permission of the authority. They can upgrade to a bigger unit later by selling the old one. Such housing policy would lessen financial burden and stress on young couples who want to start a family. The government makes available an apartment to the parents of the couples who live in the same block.

The government reckons that with this policy in place, shortage of housing and price increases will be under control. This policy will help newlywed couples to start a family and have more children under the new two-child policy introduced in 2016 to obviate the population from falling. The great benefit of this housing policy to a young family is to allow them to have spare money to spend on daily living.

The new eco-apartments are designed to be eco-friendly. Every apartment has a built-in waste disposal system to collect wastewater from washing machine, kitchen sink, toilet bowl, floor traps, and solid waste. These waste products are treated by dedicated treatment plants for recycling. Biodegradable waste would be processed to produce methane gas for power generation and the residues are used for compost in the eco-farms. Solid waste materials would be recycled.

All high-rise apartments are built with two important features. One is to generate power from solar panels that are attached to the building facades. The buildings are designed to generate a tunnel effect such that wind turbines could be installed to generate power. The other new feature is for every apartment having a refrigerated unit in the wall next to the main entrance door for storage of food items ordered online and delivered by the merchants. Another dry box accepts dry goods purchased online. Every block of apartments will have a community club located on the ground floor to cater to social interactions, group activities and functions organized by the residents in the block. Every block has ample parking space for bicycles that are rented out to commuters who travel by trains or buses.

3-D Printing Construction to Save Costs and Time

The interiors of every apartment are designed to be in modular form so standard furnishing modules designed for various sizes of bedrooms, toilets, kitchens, lounges, and pantries can be installed easily. All the standard modules of furnishing could be ordered from the approved factories that produce them. Module installations take a day. They can be replaced easily. All the module materials are fire resistant.

Flexible locations of electrical power points, which are new inventions by Chinese manufacturers, can be changed easily when needed at any location in the home. Such invention eliminates the common problems of long electrical wires running on the floor or table tops when power points are permanently set at one location. All the power points are childproof.

Using 3-D construction methods onsite, the apartments can be built cheaply and at a rapid rate. The lead time for building an apartment for the market is much shortened compared to the traditional building method that uses a lot of manual labor. Technology helps social development at a faster rate and generates higher productivity.

The apartments are built to the specifications of a master plan of the eco-city for seventy years with expansion for the next seventy years to cater to population expansion until a limit is reached. Too large a city is too difficult to manage and the traffic situation and infrastructure becomes unmanageable. New eco-cities will continue to be built to accommodate future population increase. The apartments can be used as a retirement investment when the lessee sells to and rent back from the government. All the apartments can be refurbished to suit the prevailing building standards and market requirements.

Eco-Housing Estate Design

The town planning design team takes a cue from the Singapore HDB experiences in building many dozens of HDB estates in the history of Singapore. Every housing estate is self-contained and fully integrated with respect to the provisions of schools, medical clinics, shopping malls, entertainment centers, commercial buildings, public transportation hubs, arts centers, community centers, and office buildings. All these buildings will have eco-friendly design features that accommodate the principles of green living and in harmony with nature.

The residential areas will have plenty of parks, gardens and recreational facilities that are enhanced by the water features provided by the bountiful supply of water from the canals that flow through the eco-city. Every housing estate is served by a fully integrated traffic system incorporating an underground mass transit system and bus network.

Eco-Friendly Civil Service

The town center of every housing estate has next to the train and bus stations a building that houses branches of the civil service as a one-stop station for citizens to visit and conduct official business. This is to avoid inconvenience of citizens having to make multiple trips to various civil service departments at different locations. The government has a special website for citizens to make enquiries on any matter dealing with official business. If no satisfactory answer is received, the citizen could bring it to the attention of the local monthly meet-the-people session conducted by the Communist Party organization and its grassroots committee members for assistance until a satisfactory answer is received. These meet-the-people sessions also serve as a training program for young members of the Communist Party.

Effects of Good Housing Policy on National Developments

With the new housing policy in place, the government offers all the eco-city residents an affordable apartment to live in and an incentive for a married couple to start a family early. China begins to enjoy economic contributions of the new six hundred million ex-rural residents who will have a living standard comparable to those who now live in the urban cities like Beijing or Guangzhou. They will get well-paid jobs and begin to pay taxes to the government instead of receiving handouts when they were in the rural areas.

Once the children of the destitute farmers from the rural areas receive good education and start to work, the Chinese economy will rebound to double-digit GDP growth because of the huge increase in size of the domestic market and wealth creation contributed by the six hundred million residents with high salary jobs.

The central government will save hundreds of billions in having an efficient public administration throughout the country, improvement in social and economic developments and recycling of reusable materials from the new apartments. Moreover, inflation caused by high housing prices will be curbed. Previous common corruption by government officials on housing allocation will be consigned to history. Eco-city encourages community living with mutual help from neighbors. There is a strong connection between the government officials and the local citizens. Eco-housing is a game changer for all the Chinese citizens to enjoy a peaceful and happy life.

Chapter 18
Health Care Service

Present Health Care System

The eco-city design team together with medical care experts from the World Health Organization, Waratah Organization, and from around the world, analyses the statistics, historical hospital data, and feedback from the public. They surmise that the present health care system in China is archaic, wasteful, and inefficient, a legacy system from the past.

The prevailing dichotomous trend of rising cost of health care and diminishing quality of health care service has generated resentment against the government's lack of remedial action of rectifying the dire situation. It is intolerable to the general public that, on a purchasing power parity basis, the costs of local hospital surgical operations are higher than those in the western countries by a big margin. Such conditions cannot be sustained for too long to maintain a healthy population.

Common Grievances against the Hospitals

There was plethora of complaints against the urban hospitals and their substandard services. Excessive corruption, short consultation time, exorbitant hospital charges, expensive medicines, over-crowding, unwarranted prescriptions of drugs, and superfluous tests are the common ground for grievances against the hospitals.

The financially strapped rural governments do not have the means to support a fully integrated medical service to serve the six hundred million poor rural residents. The central government provides too meagre a sum to even establish a decent outpatient clinic for rural families.

Monopolistic High Cost Medicare Care Services

Healthcare System Not Keeping Abreast with Social Progress

With increasing population and longevity, the costs of healthcare escalate faster than the income increase. The crucial problem faced by all the hospitals in China is the low subsidy of 10 percent by the central government to cover the hospital expenditures, the other 90 percent being self-funded, thereby forcing the public hospitals to operate on a commercial and independent basis. Hence, the hospitals have no choice but to make profits to maintain its monopolistic business to serve both the community and its staff. This is not in line with the spirit of true communism. With a global purchasing power parity adjusted, a patient pays more for a hospital visit in China than in Singapore for a similar treatment.

It is no wonder that under such an environment hospital admissions and medical treatment charges are self-imposed. There are no standard charges for consultations and surgeries, and under such a monopolistic business environment, the public would not have a fair deal in healthcare services.

Having a monopolistic license to operate a public hospital does not lend itself any incentive to improve its quality and value of service. Its business is based on a cost-plus formula. However, there is every reason to blame the official healthcare system and not the service provider. Until such a system is revamped, the general public will continue to suffer. In fact, the situation will get worse with increasing population of all ages and when the daily consultation of patients increases without corresponding increase in medical staff and equipment and expansions of facilities.

There is discrimination of medical service in China, one serving the government officials and civil servants for free and the other the public for a fee. Government officials have priority over the public for hospital admission. Such medical system is not in harmony with Mao Zedong's idea of pure communism, and is definitely not fair to the public who has to foot the medical bills for the privileged. Some patients have to sell their homes to pay for the expensive medical and surgical fees. Such unfair treatment of the general patients cannot sustain for long in any society under any type of political system.

In 2012, China spent CNY2.9 trillion on healthcare services, which represent 5.15 percent of GDP as compared to average of 10 percent in Western countries. As the six hundred million rural residents hardly receive any basic medical service, the bulk of the national health care expenditure goes to the urban population of seven hundred million people. Moreover, the hundreds of millions of migrant workers who have shifted to the cities without changing to the local residency permit and without medical insurance do not benefit from any government subsidy that is given to the local residents.

The current healthcare policy lacks fairness and is discriminatory against the migrant workers who do contribute to the local economy but getting no equitable social benefits like others. This is not communism in true spirit and action. Lack of medical insurance coverage by the hundreds of millions of rural residents is another worrisome social problem that the government has to rectify swiftly. A country with many sick people is not a progressive society and is a waste of human resources.

Current Problems Facing Urban Hospital Administration

With rising income and better information through personal travel and the Internet, the public demand for better quality medical services increases. Meanwhile, the urban hospitals face pressure of overcrowding and shortage of doctors and nurses. This problem is exacerbated by the influx of large numbers of migrant workers from the rural areas flogging to the cities for medical treatment.

Every day many patients, after waiting in line for hours to get a number, are turned away because of the hospital's closing time. These irate patients, with obvious bitter complaints, have no choice but to line up again the next day. This scenario has persisted for years under the present system of hospital operations. The government has been under intense social pressure to curtail the hospital's staff heavy work and duties but to no avail under the present government policies and political structures.

The current operation problems are compounded by the increasing aging population and escalating costs of operations. The aged population of sixty years or older has increased to two hundred million in 2013, and the trend is rising. Increasing numbers of people suffer from coronary heart disease, and kidney and liver diseases due to the high pressure urban living and indulgence in late-night socializing involving alcohol, smoking, and irregular food intake. China has a quarter of world's diabetic patients, amounting to one hundred million. Sedentary lifestyle, unhealthy diets, environmental pollution, and lack of exercise exacerbate the health problems.

Another critical problem that affects hospital operations is that many people with common ailments like coughs and colds seek treatment in the hospital. Every winter, when the sky is blanketed with smog in the northern cities like Beijing, many people, especially the aged and the infants who suffer from respiratory ailments, flock to the hospitals for treatment. Indeed, the hospitals are bursting at the seams treating extra thousands of patients a day. This is an annual recurring event. More outpatient clinics are in dire need of setting up to serve outpatients with minor ailments. Hospitals are meant to serve inpatients who need specialists' attention.

Dilemma of Hospital Administration

There are never sufficient specialists in the hospitals due to increasing demands for specialist services. Training of specialist doctors is hampered by a shortage of qualified teachers and time. To the trainee doctors, free choice of specialist training courses is often denied. Deterring many promising university students from taking up the medical professions are the daily long arduous hours of working and heavy responsibilities in providing acceptable health care services in crowded hospitals.

It is no joy having to face every day many difficult patients and complaints that are beyond the doctor's control. Nursing staff are frequently abused by abrasive patients who are impatient to wait for consultation by doctors. As such, the hospital is not a pleasant place to work in. Unless the working conditions and pay scales are improved for doctors and health care givers, there will be fewer students taking medical and nursing professions in the future. Such conditions will exacerbate the current dire situation.

When a hospital has to stand on its feet to earn an income for survival, it is inevitable that it has to operate on a commercial basis. It is a constant struggle just to keep up with the excessive high number of in- and outpatients daily, and the situation does not seem to improve in the future. Under increasing pressures of more patients and without corresponding increase in staff and facilities, the doctors find it difficult to dispense proper medical care to all patients.

Many doctors and medical staff are fatigued with overwork. In some hospitals, doctors need to see more than one hundred patients a day, which means, in fact, spending two or three minutes per patient, giving insufficient time for doctors to explain causes of illness to patients. Quite often patients, after seeing the doctor, are asked to queue again for a blood test or X-ray and then return another day with the blood test report. Multiple trips to the hospital to get a proper medical consultation add further pressure on the doctor's time. In many cases, to increase the hospital revenue, doctors order unnecessary blood tests for the patients.

The current hospital management has encountered many unsavory events when unhappy patients or their relatives inflict the doctors with violence and even fatal attacks. Such scenario is a product of an antiquated system that is out of synchronization with the real world. Allowing doctors more time for medical consultation with patients would help reduce misunderstanding or miscommunication that leads to patient's unhappiness with the medical staff.

Rural Medical Services

Geriatric rural patients, who have toiled for years in the field and are under the weather suffer from multitude of illnesses, will have a hard time to consult a specialist geriatric doctor in a rural hospital, which is generally a dilapidated building. Lack of complete chemical laboratory for full range of blood tests, CAT scan and special X-ray machines hamper proper diagnosis and treatment of serious illness and disease. Needless to say, there will be no intensive surgical ward with comprehensive equipment and qualified medical staff to perform difficult and prolong operations that require blood transfusion and specialist anesthetist.

Definitely the rural people, numbering over six hundred million, will not have a hope of having a coronary by-pass operation that is so commonly performed in the urban hospitals. When they have high blood pressure, they just lived with it, and would see a doctor only if they have a stroke. They would live with their diabetes without seeing a doctor until they get gangrene in the foot. More diseases will occur due to water pollution and an unhygienic living environment.

Ignorance of basic knowledge of common diseases by many rural patients leads to many patients applying erroneous self-medications that worsen their conditions. The mediocre medical standards and facilities of the rural hospitals with poorly paid and under-trained doctors and nurses in the vast rural areas do not lend themselves to giving the best medical diagnosis and advice to patients. Such poor healthcare service is unacceptable to the rural citizens.

Pathetic Medical Service Conditions in Rural Regions

Lack of adequate funding by the local hospital administration to purchase the best medicines for the patients prolongs the healing of illness resulting in more repeat visits to the doctors. Coupled with unhygienic public health conditions, the low personal hygiene standard would aggravate the problems of disease prevention in the rural areas. As expected, rural doctors will not have the opportunities to attend medical conferences or refresher courses to upgrade their knowledge and skill.

As hospital operations are self-funded with little government subsidy, rural hospitals can only afford to pay low salaries to staff and buy cheap generic medicines. Healthcare services for the farmers and villagers are far from ideal. When patients need specialist treatments, they have to travel long distances to urban hospital for treatment and covalence, much to the inconvenience of the patient's spouse and children who have to stay in the city's hotels and guesthouse that are expensive to the rural residents.

None of the villages has a night clinic or an A&E ward for emergency treatment. Medicine supplies are limited. Medical equipment and instruments are obsolete and lack maintenance. The poor farmers indeed do not benefit from the wealth of the nation. The only way to get better health care service is to raise the income of the farmers. Communism is supposed to provide equal standard of treatment to everyone in the country. However, the second largest economy of the world has adopted the capitalist ideology in the medical health care system that favors the patients who can afford to pay.

Health Care Cost and Inflation

The economic situation in China is accelerating toward hyper-inflation as evident by the exorbitant prices of housing that are beyond the means of young wage earners. The annual compounded increase in food prices hit deeply the public's purse. Real interest rate is less than inflation. It is a wrenching experience in life to find one's whole life hard-earned saving in cash diminishing in purchasing power with time. Inflation will induce higher costs of medical treatment. With income not keeping pace with inflation, patients will find the rising medical costs unbearable.

Aging Population, High Health Care Costs, and Decreasing Workforce

Every social problem in China takes on a gigantic dimension because of its huge population. There are three immense social problems facing the Chinese government: rapid aging population, escalating health care costs and decreasing workforce. By 2020, it is estimated that 23 percent of the population of 1.4 billion will be sixty-five years of age or older, and the figure increases every year.

Meanwhile, because of the one-child policy, China's workforce decreases every year. Such divergent trend means that China is approaching the "Lewis turning point" and China would go from having an abundant supply of cheap labor to one with a labor shortage, and this is expected around 2025. This is being experienced by the rich Western countries that are beset with high numbers of aging population, a declining population of workers, and increasing inflation.

Inflation in the past decade has exceeded the real interest rate of saving. This is not helpful to people who have saved money for retirement. The government will be burdened by increasing health care budget to keep happy the increasing numbers of pensioners swelled by longevity. How to get more money from the treasury in the future when the working population is shrinking?

The current public pension system comprises an urban and a rural system. Both systems have flaws that would impact the pensioner's ability to live a healthy retirement life because of escalating inflation. Very low percentages of people from the rural areas participate in the medical insurance scheme.

Eco-World Project Offers Solutions to Healthcare Woes

The future social welfare funds will be enhanced substantially due to higher value-added goods and services output generated by the eco-cities and higher tax revenue to the government. With the abolishment of the one-child policy in the eco-cities and a congenial living environment with domestic robots for hire and low-cost housing and education, married couples will be inclined to have more children. The government will provide incentives for couples to raise more children who will become future working population.

Eco-World Health Care Services

Examining the health care cost of advanced countries around the world reveals three common problems: aged population growth, inflation, and more demand for treatments. The hospitals will be burdened by insatiable demand for medical treatments of diabetes, cardiovascular disease, hypertension, obesity, and high blood pressure. Causal factors of health-damaging lifestyles like tobacco and alcohol consumption, sedentary behavior, pollutions, and poor dietary intake in modern living conditions exacerbate the health problems.

Patients complain about overcrowding and long wait time to see a doctor in hospitals. Doctors and nurses are overworked and fatigued. Hospital administration faces lack of medical specialist training and patient to doctor ratio increasing. It takes twelve to fifteen years to produce a specialist from medical school, and such long periods deter students from taking the courses. Remuneration given to doctors and nurses does not compensate for the high pressure of work and prolonged mental fatigue. Relentless inflationary pressure increases costs of managing medical care services, insurance and litigation without compensatory increase in government budget.

Such dichotomy of increasing demand for medical services and the inadequacy of government budget to meet the public demand would create animosity against the government. There is no end to the demand for higher standard and quality of medical care and services but there is a limit as to the amount of budget that the government could afford to approve especially when the national income fluctuates from year to year.

The government cannot afford to give away welfare money to those who are bankrupt due to addiction to gambling and those who ruin their health by taking illicit drugs, excessive drinking and smoking, and living an unhealthy lifestyle. People should understand that keeping their body healthy is their personal responsibility and is an effective way of maintaining low health care costs.

Health Care System Revamp

After lengthy deliberations by the eco-city team members on the projected solutions to the current health care problems based on the current policy and root-cause analysis, the government finally decides to reform the present health care system in totality. It approves the blueprint for the new medical services, which will differ from the traditional system and policy. The entire medical care services will be revamped, making it the best and the most cost-effective and efficient system in the world, adopting the best practices from around the world.

The team members, using the latest computer simulation and the demands for better health care services by the population in the future, reveal that the future government cannot afford to continue the present health care system, which is labor intensive. Moreover, the government cannot afford to continue using taxpayer's money to shoulder the expenses for patients who abuse their body and ignore their health by unhealthy lifestyle. The whole of medical service can collapse when the aging population increases with decreasing birth rate. Therefore, the new health care system will incorporate three new ideas: decentralization of hospital services, applying technology, and change of lifestyle.

The new medical hospitals will be decentralized into three categories to facilitate more efficient use of human resources and expensive medical equipment and to offer dedicated services to inpatients who need medical specialists for treatments. Outpatients who have minor ailments such as cough and colds, bacterial infections, and minor cuts, and those who do not require overnight hospitalization would go to general hospital's outpatient clinics, some of which are located in various housing estates. The clinic's general physicians would provide patients primary health care services and referrals to specialist physicians in a general hospital for chronic problems that require specialist care, such as heart or kidney disease or chronic pain.

The next category is the general hospital that provides multi-specialty medical services including overnight hospitalization that need special medical equipment and facilities such as ICU and operating theaters. There are other general hospitals that specifically cater to children, maternity, ENT (ear, nose, and throat), cancer, geriatrics, psychiatry, and rehabilitation patients. Every general hospital is affiliated with the local university medical school as a teaching hospital for undergraduate and postgraduate students. Every medical student who passes the national examination can practice in any general hospital throughout the country.

The revamped hospital administration derives from the best practices in many foreign countries but with modification to adapt to local environment and demand. The third category is a hospital that provides traditional Chinese medicine such as acupuncture and massage. Doctors are paid commensurate with the years of study and salary rating established by the public service commission that evaluates the duties and responsibilities of every graduate profession.

The government believes that free medical service will be abused and not cost effective. The new policy does not advocate universal welfare dependency. It does enforce disincentive to people who insist on allowing their body to suffer from unhealthy lifestyle and abuses. The revamped health care system does not deal with the present issues in a piecemeal manner, nor would the government take incremental steps to rectify the current multifaceted problems that are legacy problems from an archaic policy of the past.

Complete dependency on the government for social welfare leads to erosion of social responsibilities of the people and reduces their motivation to improve their healthy lifestyle. It also results in escalating costs of meeting a never-ending demand for better services without considering that there is a finite limit of human and financial resources. It could lead to chaos and unmanageable health care problems affecting the rich and poor alike. Every person living in the Eco-World is insured. There is no free lunch.

Technology is to be utilized to help increase the productivity of hospital operations, and to provide value for money to patients, especially utilizations of hospital beds and operating theaters. Government departments cannot have priority of hospital beds for their staff, but they can book permanently a block of beds for their own staff at an agreed cost payable to the hospital, and their admission is to follow the hospital's operating procedure similar to the public system without any favor and dispensation. However, empty government-booked hospital beds can be rented out to the public on an as-needed basis to prevent waste.

Health care cost is a big ticket item in any country's budget. To keep the cost of health care down to a minimum, it is essential to remind people that it is their responsibility to keep their health in good shape, using similar logic as in maintaining their cars in good condition. It is ironic that many people do not mind spending many thousands of dollars on name-brand items and expensive car but are unwilling to spend even a small amount on keeping healthy.

People must realize that the government cannot endlessly increase annual budgets to build more operating theatres and employ more specialists to fix broken bones and repair disfigured faces that result from road accidents involving vehicle drivers who are reckless, drunk, inconsiderate, and defiant of traffic rules. They must pay for their selfish acts of causing harm to others. The annual number of fatal accidents and injured persons arising from road accidents in China are estimated to exceed the entire population of Singaporean citizens. The fatal accident rate represents roughly 20 percent of the world's fatal accident figure. Such waste of human lives and medical expenses cannot be tolerated forever.

Keeping the Body Healthy to Depress Health Care Costs

Health care costs must be shouldered partially by citizens rather than entirely by the government using money from taxpayers. This is the central theme of the revamped health care system. Keeping good health must start from young. Maintaining the mind and body healthy goes a long way to preventing the onset of preventable illness and diseases in later life. Early education is part of the preventive scheme introduced in the primary and secondary schools with visits to hospitals and drug rehabilitation centers to gain firsthand knowledge of chronic and preventable diseases.

The schools will instill in the young minds that life is more than just the pursuit of making money. Every person, before being issued a driving license, must visit the hospitals to see patients who were disfigured or critically injured from road accidents. Errant drivers must bear partially for the accident victim's medical costs for their mistakes and to prevent recurrence. Every driver needs to renew his driving license every four years after passing a proficiency test in a simulator to ensure his driving skill meets acceptable standards and his mental health is in good order.

School Curriculum to Include Healthy Lifestyle and Common Medical Knowledge

There is a common belief that a healthy, simple life is more enjoyable than a bedridden life with great wealth. Every student from primary to secondary school must partake in a sport. The nutritional values of different foods and the importance of balanced diet are taught in schools. Traditional Chinese medicines including herbs, acupuncture, and massages are included in the science subjects that are compulsory for both primary and secondary students. Secondary school students during long summer vacations are to spend certain hours during the days to do volunteer work in hospitals as nursing assistants. They will familiarize themselves with the hospital administration, procedures, and equipment. They are to visit the elderly patients in the rehabilitation centers and old folks' homes.

How to Keep the Body Healthy

Spending "good" money in small sums early to achieve a healthier body and a better quality life is superior to spending "bad" money in bigger sums later to fix a sick body with pain and suffering. Also a healthier person can enjoy life to the fullest, any time better than one lying on a sick bed with a rapid bleeding bank account and the associated opportunity cost of loss of employment and stresses to the family. Understanding the causes of diseases and maintaining a healthy lifestyle are the core values of the new health care system.

It is necessary to imbue the young in schools with the knowledge of common preventable diseases like diabetes, hypertension, emotional instability, alcoholic and drug abuses, and the associated encumbrances of contracting such diseases in terms of costs and mental anguish that could be daunting to the family. Children are encouraged to oppose parents who smoke at home. All government officers are forbidden to consume alcohol and smoke at all official functions. Movies and plays are forbidden to show smoking and heavy drinking.

Private Medical Services

The new Eco-World will allow private hospitals and family doctor clinics to supplement the public clinics and hospitals medical services. It allows the public the freedom of seeking medical treatment of his choice and affordability, and also offers competition between public and private hospitals and clinics. Competition offers differentiation of quality of services and value for money. Those who can afford better quality and standards of services can go to private hospitals that offer more personal care and attention. Every clinic and hospital needs an ISO 9001 certificate to operate. Every district with more than ten thousand residents will have a government out-patient clinic to cater to general consultations.

Eco-World Health Care Services and Procedures

The outpatient clinic or family doctor in the private clinics will refer the patient to the specialist doctors in the government or private hospitals for advice on difficult medical cases. Medical history, including laboratory test results, X-ray, and MRI films of every patient will be stored in the national medical archive so the patient's medical history can be followed up by any doctor around the country 24/7. This should help the doctor have a better understanding of the patient's medical prognosis and effectiveness of treatment, especially in A&E wards and emergency operations when the patients are outside their normal domicile.

Every patient must pay a fee for treatment in the out-patient clinic and government hospital, the fee being calculated in accordance with the patient's income tax and financial capability outlined in a formula. There is a tendency for people to waste medical resources when the treatment is free. Also, from experience of the countries that practice free medical service, the wait time to consult a doctor is very long, and for surgery, the time can stretch to more than a year. According to World Health Organization experts, it is more rational for patient to co-pay 20–30 percent for the medical services. Charity organization will help the needy who cannot pay for whatever reason.

All the public clinics and hospitals are built next to under-ground train stations and bus stops with wheel-chairs available for rental. All of them have an internet portal to indicate available consultation time slots for reservation. Every patient must fill up a comprehensive medical history form online. A general doctor will review the history and inform the patient if he needs to have a blood test, X-ray, CAT scan, or MRI before meeting the recommended specialist doctor or general physician on the appointment date. This procedure allows both the doctor and patient more time to discuss the illness and treatment, and more importantly, eliminates the need for a repeat visit to the hospital. Outpatient clinic visit and hospital admission is by on-line registration, and a queue number is given after a payment of admission fee. The new online registration system with prerecorded medical history ensures valuable hospital resources are maximized and effectively utilized.

Every smoker in China must be registered and given a card that allows him to buy cigarettes. The vendor will record the quantity of cigarettes sold to the smoker and the information is passed to the Health Authority. This information will be stored in the smoker's medical history. The smoker has to pay double the amount of normal medical fees at the government out-patient clinic and hospital for treatment. Cigarette or liquor advertisement is banned and movies must not have smoking or alcohol drinking scene. Cigarette and alcohol advertisement is banned.

Revamped Hospital Setup and Operations

All the public hospitals and outpatient clinics, with ISO 9001 certificate, are fully subsidized by the government. Each hospital administration is governed by a tripartite committee, comprising representatives from the Health Ministry, Medical Professional Board to whom all medical doctors belong as members, and a central charity organization that represents the donors of individuals and companies. Representatives from the medical Insurance companies and consumer association are co-opted to represent the general public.

The committee publishes an annual report on the financial income and expenditure, patient visits, hospital bed occupancy, types of sickness and diseases, medicine-dispensing quantities, equipment and operating theatre utilization, and patient compliments and complaints. Future projects and expansion plan are included in the report. There is a report card that shows the performance of the hospital as determined by an independent consulting firm that interviews selected patients for their comments.

Every hospital has reserved land for expansion for the next fifty years, beyond which a new hospital will be built. Every person is required to register online in the government medical portal as a potential patient, and is advised to update personal information every year. Every government hospital and clinic can have access to the patient's medical histories for follow up. Payment for consultation and medicines is done by patient using Internet banking account or through the medical insurance company. No cash is involved.

Every hospital's manpower requirements are reviewed by a panel of committee members who would ensure the hospital is adequately staffed and every staff is properly trained. Vacancies for doctors in every department are advertised on the website of the hospital. Latest medical equipment is to be purchased to replace the outdated model based on the recommendation of an evaluation committee. Hospital doctors are encouraged to explore new techniques of surgery procedures. Independent external audit report on every hospital and clinic is published openly and transparently, especially on the types of drugs used and their quantity. Every doctor is to attend medical conferences to update his knowledge and the latest discovery.

Like in the airline industry where pilots and cabin crews are not permitted to work beyond a stipulated period per week, similar restriction is imposed on doctors and nurses. Every patient must be given at least twenty minutes of consultation. Occupancy rate of hospital beds reaching 80 percent rate would trigger a signal that expansion of the hospital is necessary to avoid overcrowding and dropping of medical care quality, standards, and effectiveness.

Each hospital has a rating system that compares with the best hospital in the world for the same services provided to the public. No matter how poor the local resident is, the best medical treatment will be provided at affordable fees. Every specialist hospital is affiliated to other specialist hospitals in the country and patient transfer is possible without additional expense so that the patient can receive the best available medical care. Hospital staff will receive incentive payment for receiving compliments from the public. The Health Ministry and every hospital will conduct an annual review of the quantity of medicines dispensed for each type of illness treatment to detect if there is any abnormal trend and consumption rate.

A charity drive is conducted yearly. All large industrial organizations, government departments, schools, multimedia, and entertainment circles actively participate in getting as much donation as possible for the hospital administration and improvement programs. Volunteer organizations help out in the donation drive, making it the biggest social event in the city. It becomes a local city culture. The citizens feel proud to be active participants. To them, the hospital is theirs wholeheartedly. Many rich patients donate generously and regularly. Every local citizen from school age on receives a free annual medical check-up. Blood pressure and urine tests are conducted freely at every housing estate community center. Test results are recorded in the patient's medical history.

New Hospital Facility and Administration

Internet and Technology-Based Hospital Administration and Operation

Hospital administration is fully computerized. Patients must make an appointment on the Internet, thereby cutting down all the unnecessary long waiting time. Non-booking patients have to wait at the end of the line. With such Internet operation systems, a lot of manual administrative functions can be dispensed with. Pre-booked appointments attract a discount on consultation fees. A surcharge is payable by walk-in patients who have to wait in line. Late arrivals for appointments will be posted to the end of the line. Cancellation of an appointment attracts a fine. Such strict procedures are to ensure the valuable hospital and clinic services are not wasted.

Medicines that are dispensed are recorded in the patient's record and are collected at the consultation station. The medicines are sent by an automatic pneumatic delivery system from the air-conditioned and humidity controlled central drugstore that is fully computerized in its inventory and retrieval system. There is no one working in the store. All the medicines for each patient are retrieved from special container with the dispatched medicines sealed in packages. Dosage and the patient's name are coded and printed on a special sticker that is glued to the packages. A receipt is attached to the medicine pouch. The total cost of consultation and medicine is deducted automatically from the patient's bank account. Cash transactions are prohibited. Any patient who offers a bribe to the hospital staff will receive severe punishment, and the incident will be recorded in the patient's medical record.

Inventory control and management for drugs and medicines is managed by the Health Authority. Daily, weekly, and monthly consumptions of various medicines and drugs are published statistically for various government agencies dealing with medical care services. A report of expired drugs will be presented for review and prevention of waste. An anti-corruption agency will monitor and investigate any abnormal consumption rate of a particular drug.

X-rays, CAT scans, and MRI images are recorded on a computer and can be retrieved in the doctor's consultation room for review on a big screen. No physical film is required to be brought along by the patients, thereby saving time and resources. The advantage of these new computerized images is that they can be viewed inside or outside the country by distant doctors who can be called upon for assistance or opinion in diagnosing unusual or unfamiliar medical conditions. To assist many patients who have a tendency to forget to take their medicines, all medicines are packed in packages stamped with days of the week and color-coded for each day.

Every hospital publishes an annual report of all the different illnesses and diseases treated by the doctors, with highlights on unusual medical cases that warrant further medical study, research and better method of treatment in the future. The surgeons would work with robot manufacturers to make special robots for physically handicapped or disabled patients. The hospital would call a meeting with the patient's relatives on how to provide home care to the patient and if need be, to contact the hospital for further advice. Home nursing care is available for patients without any attendant relative at home. Humanoid robots are available for hire for any incapacitated patient who needs 24/7 care at home.

Surgical Wards and Procedures

The operating theatres of the various specialist hospitals are equipped with the latest computer-control operating instruments, tools and equipment. General surgeries, microsurgeries, and organ transplants using remote-control techniques are managed by surgeons either in-house, in another part of the country, or even in a foreign country with prior arrangement.

Surgeries using computer-control technique offers significant advantage over the traditional method as doctor's fatigue and patient's anesthetic effect is greatly reduced. Consequently, surgeons have better concentration and longer endurance resulting in superior surgery results. Many of these specialist hospitals oblige requests from foreign countries to perform remote surgeries on patients in emergency. All the specialist hospitals are teaching hospitals, and are adjunct medical faculties to the local university's medical schools.

Every teaching hospital receives grants from Waratah Charity Foundation and other Chinese charity organizations to do research on various medical sciences in both the Western and traditional Chinese medicine (TCM) treatments. All the teaching faculties have twinning programs with selected medical schools in foreign countries. Teaching professors and specialist doctors are regularly exchanged with foreign universities. Traditional Chinese medicine is rapidly being accepted by other countries for treatments of many diseases and sickness that require invasive surgeries. TCM does not involve surgical operation. Acupuncture is now a specialty subject taught in every medical school around the country.

All teaching hospitals are equipped with video, cameras, and voice recording setups to record every surgical operation for teaching purposes. The video can be played instantly for teaching of undergraduate and postgraduate students in universities and doctors in other hospitals around the country. Such a system of training improves standard of surgical operation, reduces time of specialist training, and increases output of medical professions at cheaper costs. Additionally, the doctor using Chinese Internet social media communication can see and talk to the home patient on scheduled time to review the progress of recovery. This system can be recorded for teaching purposes.

Post-surgery patients are encouraged to return home early to recuperate as they will not feel lonely and could recover earlier with familiar surroundings. Specially programmed robotic nurse would accompany them home to perform any function that is required, for example, taking the patient for a walk, to the toilet, to bathe, to take medicine or physiotherapy exercises. Relatives and family members can help intimately by being with the patient at home without having to travel to the hospital and waste time traveling on the road or taking time off from work.

Robotic Humanoids

In China, there are more than ten million disabled people. These people need help for mobility and employment opportunity to lead a normal life. In each eco-city, there is a special hospital for disabled patients. The orthopedic hospital would assist the patient in acquiring a personalized robotic suit. The suit would allow the patient full freedom of movement of arms and legs. With the robotic suits, all these disabled persons can lead a normal life. Robots will be a ubiquitous worker of the eco-city life as they are to fill the vacancy created by the decreasing number of workers in China caused by the one-child policy that began in 1979 until 2016 when it is abolished.

In a virtual office, the handicapped people can work just like anyone else, controlling the movements of robots. They can be employed in various industries. They can be remote baby sitters, office administrators like bookkeepers and accountants, telephone operators, and do Internet sales and marketing, material inventory control, travel agency telephone sales, security surveillance, teaching, and government office jobs. Phil Kendall foresees the future demand in China for robotic workers would rise exponentially, especially in the field of health care for the rapidly increasing aging and disabled population.

Humanoid robots play a significant role in hospital operations. Different robots are trained or rather programmed to do specific functions thereby relieving the pressure of the nurses. Robots are now utilized to turn patients to prevent bedsore, helping patients to go to the toilet, taking body temperature and blood pressure, changing sheets, cleaning and mopping the floor and toilet, emptying trash bins, and delivering foods to and retrieving trays from patient beds. The hospitals are designed such that the robots could wheel the patients to various parts of the hospitals to take X-rays, go to physiotherapy, and take physical walks.

If required, special robots can be hired and programmed to look after the patient 24/7. The robot that serves an individual patient possesses the ability to take verbal commands from the patient (for example, "take me to the toilet," "play a piece of music or song," or "sing a song or narrate a story"). The vocal voice can be programmed to simulate a voice that is familiar to the patient (for example, his wife, her husband, or a member of the family).

The attractive feature of the robot is that it can be made to look identical to any person that the patient wants. Its dress could be designed to be fashionable or identical to those that are familiar to the patient. It does look like a human being when it is fully dressed up. A special robot can be hired to accompany the patient home or to the rehabilitation center.

Hospital Kitchens Staffed by Robots

Varieties of Foods Easily Prepared by Robots in Hospital Kitchens 24/7

The hospital kitchens are entirely operated by robots. Meats, vegetables, and other foods have been cleaned prior to delivery to the hospital and packed in standardized containers of various sizes and weights. They are then placed in the refrigerators in different compartments known to the robotic cooks. The robots will retrieve the containers to prepare dishes in accordance with input from the kitchen manager, who has a panoramic view of the entire kitchen on his huge computer screen.

The daily meals of each patient have been coded and sent to the kitchen's central computer database. The meals are prepared by the hospital nutritionists who would program each robot to prepare all the foods for the day. The cooking process for each dish has been programmed by experienced cooks and the robots just need to follow the process automatically as if he is the human cook. Once the meals are ready, they are placed in a mobile cart and transported by conveyors to various parts of the hospital. The ward robot would deliver the trays of foods to individual patients.

Rehabilitation Center and Community Club

A rehab center is built in each apartment block for a community of one thousand residents. It is fully furnished with equipment and aids for patients who have recovered from surgery and stroke. Professional caregivers with robotic nurses are available to help patients on personal needs in showering, dressing and toilet movements, exercising, walking, eating and drinking, massaging, speech therapy, and other personal needs.

A community club, supported financially by the local council, is managed by volunteers from the estate. Apart from many other social activities they organize, the volunteers would look after those lonely aged or sick persons who are unable to take medicine on schedule because of physical handicap or just being forgetful. These volunteers with the help of robots would assist these people in taking medicine, doing physiotherapy, checking blood pressure, taking insulin jabs, and general physical exercise. If medical conditions are found to be abnormal, the patient will be immediately taken to the hospital.

Many parents are now living on their own because their children have found jobs in other parts of China and do not have time for frequent home visits. The club provides an opportunity for these parents to mingle with their neighbors and participate in social activities, helping them lead a healthy and graceful retirement life. Activities like social dancing, mahjong and card games, morning exercise, taiji (martial art), and karaoke, are organized for the club members. The club members can have a communal dining hall where members can have meals prepared for them by the consenting neighbors. Such clubs help the local residents lead a healthier life.

The club could arrange robots to do house cleaning, washing, and act as companion that can sing and tell stories and jokes, programmed with a vocal voice to one's preference. Such an arrangement is better than living in an old folks' home that is alien and unfamiliar to many. They may end up living in a lonely environment with despair and self-pity. When the aged person needs financial assistance, the volunteers will help him apply for sale and lease back agreement of his apartment unit with the government. The government will buy back the unit at market price and the proceeds will be used as the ex-owner's old age expenditure spread over a period of time of his choice.

The new health care system is well suited to solving the universal problem of aging that demands a lot of medical services. With a self-help social system, there is no need for the aged to feel depressed and demand more medical care from the government. When the citizens are well educated from early on how to keep a good healthy lifestyle, there is no reason to believe that they cannot live to their ripe old age without much complaint of sickness and ill health. Coupled with new community spirit of living and mutual cooperation amongst residents in the same estate, people should have less stress which is a major contributing factor of developing mental problem and related illness.

The Best Health Care System in the World

Living in the eco-city with the latest state-of-the-art hospital facility staffed by well-trained health care service providers and adequate funding is a joy and blessing that has eluded many people who live in other affluent countries. The old system of health care services was not only expensive but also wasteful and ineffective. The government and Waratah Organization are pleased with the results of the revamped health care services in China for the benefits of 1.36 billion people.

With the new emphasis on having personal responsibility of maintaining a good health and a balanced diet, and a good understanding of the causes of common diseases, the future generations will lead a better life than their predecessors. The final verdict from the medical fraternity of various countries is that the Eco-World health care services offer good value and quality for money, are efficient, effective and affordable. The government has finally achieved its aim of universal health care service for the people. Once people passionately participate in the health care system, they will understand the basic principle that keeping good health is the best policy for leading a healthy and enjoyable life.

Chapter 19

Eco-Transport System

Present Transport System—Congestion and High Fatal Traffic Accident Rate

Conventional surface traffic systems involves traffic crossing for slow-speed pedestrians and high-speed vehicles. This system immensely slows down vehicular traffic flows, especially during peak periods, and is a major cause of traffic jams and accidents involving car and pedestrian collisions. Certain irate or road-rage drivers caught in traffic jams feel a compulsion toward other road users by reckless driving. Impatient drivers develop high blood pressure because of anxiety of being late for appointments or work.

Constant stopping and starting caused by traffic jams can accelerate wear and tear on vehicle engines and brakes and lead to higher fuel consumption. The net result is owners having to pay more to maintain a car. Frequent road users like drivers of buses and taxis, delivery drivers, and salespeople, who are caught in daily traffic jams, could develop health problems leading to absenteeism and higher medical expenses. Traffic jams drive up costs and reduce the fun of living. In China, ignoring traffic rules and regulations by pedestrians and vehicle drivers is a common occurrence. Such an antiquated transport system cannot continue in a modern city, as traffic accidents cause human deaths and miseries. In China, road traffic accidents and death tolls are among the highest incidence rates in the world. When road space is fixed and road users are increasing every year, the inevitability of road accidents will occur.

Transport Woes in Beijing

One evening during the winter of 2010, Beijing, according to a media report, with a car population of 4.5 million and fourteen million residents, experienced 140 serious jams. The jams were worsened by the rain and an increase in road users due to the approaching public holiday, the Lunar New Year. One taxi driver complained he took half an hour to go through one set of traffic lights that normally took three minutes, resulting in high opportunity costs to him. During the peak periods in the morning and evening, the average vehicle speed on the congested roads is slower than that of a cyclist. Many workers complain that they spend too much time every day on the road commuting by bus to and from work.

Parents complain bitterly that it was a nightmare to take their children to school in the mornings. Logistics companies faced constant problems of inability to punctually deliver goods to customers. Farmers were finding easy-traffic time slots getting squeezed during the night to bring their produce from the outskirt farms to the central markets when traffic congestion extended deeper into the night. Some farmers brought one extra driver to relieve the first driver who often faced extended period of traffic jam. Even ambulance drivers found traffic congestion unbearable to attend to emergency calls. Delays in traveling time raised the cost living in a congested city. Traffic jams caused temper to flare and road rage was a cause of traffic accident. There is no fun living in a traffic congested city.

In August 2010, a traffic jam measuring more than sixty-two miles was reported to have been at a standstill for more than a week on a highway linking Beijing with Inner Mongolia. Prolonged traffic jam situations are a familiar event when Beijing faces problems of heavy snow, flooding, and smog, followed by increasing car population and traffic accidents.

There are annually hundreds of thousands of deaths on the roads, and the number increases each year. Such situations cannot continue unabated in a civilized society. During traffic jams, extra amount of CO_2 and other toxic gases spew from the idling cars, buses, and trucks. These greenhouse gases take a heavy toll on the inhabitants, causing respiratory and lung diseases. They also contribute to climate change. Obviously, such contaminated environment cannot sustain healthy human life and is one of the reasons that drive people to migrate to other countries with clean environment.

Eco-Transport System

Transport is one of the four basic necessities of life, as the Chinese proverb says, the other three being clothing, food, and shelter. Transport transcends all the fabrics of society. It has to facilitate without undue impediment, the movement of people, goods and services, enabling the smooth functioning of public and administrative services, and commercial and industrial activities. It has to cater to the safeguarding of public and national security at any instant.

Although the infrastructures of a transport system are costly in investment, complex in nature of construction and operation, and unpredictable in the future demand, the design team of the Chinese Transport Ministry and Waratah Organization would endeavor to design an eco-friendly transport system to satisfy the demand of the people in the eco-city for decades. It is easier to start from a clean slate than to modify an existing transport system that has many constraints of space and costs.

To live in a more conducive environment that is devoid of air pollution and unsafe traffic conditions, innovative programs and eco-friendly transport system are required. In order to succeed, it requires drastic change in the social environment of living and working style from the past habitual pattern. This can be achieved by judicious commitments of human and financial resources in an Eco-World.

The new traffic system is a culmination of intense discussions, studies and experiments conducted by Waratah, the Chinese Transport Ministry, and several universities in China and the United States. The design team establishes many computer-simulated models based on the design criteria provided by various government departments, and inputs from various public and commercial organizations, including tourist and entertainment industries. Every member of the design team is tasked to take into account that a smooth and safe public transport system is a prerequisite of the eco-city that exemplifies the quality of life that is compatible with the environment, free from air and noise pollution that affect health. Technology is widely used in the design of the eco-friendly transport system.

The new traffic system must create an atmosphere of safe and pleasurable driving without the feeling of stress created by traffic jams, accidents, and road rage that are commonly encountered by the traveling public. Travelers are to feel a new experience of a transport system that is busy yet orderly and silent, fast, and safe. All vehicles must run on either renewable biofuel or batteries. Heavy fines are imposed on drunk driving, speeding, and inconsiderate driving, and mandatory jail sentence on drivers who cause fatal accidents due to drunk driving or speeding. Driving licenses are to be renewed every four years. The driver has to pass a test on emotion stability and driving skill on a simulator.

New Public and Private Transport Systems

The new eco-transport system will incorporate the following features:

1. Underground Traffic for Buses

Separation of roads for bus operation and private vehicles is essential because of speed and safety consideration. There are more fast-speed private vehicles on the road than slow-speed buses, and therefore, they cannot share the same roads without causing traffic jam especially during peak periods. During peak periods, it is stressful to drive a bus with a full load of passengers, and negotiating tight corners and narrow lanes and especially during inclement weather conditions in the old cities. Stress and fatigue are two causal factors for road accidents.

Underground bus lanes in the eco-city will be constructed for the sole use by electric, driverless public buses. All the city buses will start from and end at the central station. The system operates on a hub-and-spoke fashion. The buses will traverse in the directions of east-west and north-south, allowing the buses to cover all the streets in the city. They will stop at every bus stop along the way when signaled by the commuters on the bus or flagged at the bus stop.

Rental bicycles at cheap rental fee are provided at every bus stop. Information of arrival times of all bus numbers will be displayed on electronic display boards installed at all bus stops which are individually identified by an identification code. The same information is also available on mobile phones. Every building and residential apartment is given a GPS coordinate to facilitate easy identification by commuters and the nearest bus stop.

Passenger boarding numbers are automatically transmitted to the bus central station which will release more buses to the bus routes where passenger loads are heavy. Underground bus system is operable in all weather conditions. This is good news to all commuters during snowy winters or rainy days. Electric, driverless buses are relatively cheap to operate, and the bus fare is also cheap. Every bus is equipped with accommodation for a wheelchair-bound passenger. All outskirt express buses and the MRT trains from the residential areas will connect to the central bus station.

2. Surface Roads for all Private Vehicles

A multilane city ring road encircling the city will be constructed for the surface traffic of private vehicles coming from and going to the expressways. The ring road has slip roads to join up all the arterial roads in the city. The slip roads have long wide lanes to merge with the expressways and arterial roads to avoid congestion. The entrance to and exit from the city ring road will be monitored and controlled electronically so that heavy traffic on a particular arterial road will be directed to others where traffic is lighter.

All the traffic in the city follows a one-way street pattern, and there is no traffic light at any cross-junction where a roundabout is built. Hence, the traffic flow is continuous. If a particular traffic roundabout is heavy, an automatic traffic signal will appear on the overhead traffic sign to direct the traffic from the busy street to an alternate route where the traffic is lighter. Every street has CCTV cameras and electronic sensors to detect errant motorists violating traffic rules such as speeding, tailgating, passing without signaling, and reckless driving. As future private vehicles would be battery operated in the eco-cities, many battery charging points are provided at strategic locations in the city. Battery shops along the highway and expressway would provide battery replacement, charging and loan services.

3. Mass Rapid Transport (MRT) System

A mass rapid transport (MRT) system is an absolute necessity in the eco-city as it provides an unimpeded, fast, smooth, and comfortable ride without the effect of inclement weather. It allows mass transportation of passengers during peak periods every day in a populous city at a relatively affordable price. People can seldom have the opportunity to live near the place of work, and, hence, daily commuting is necessary. Every commuter wants to spend minimal amounts of time traveling to and from work every day.

To facilitate commuters living in different parts of the eco-city's residential areas, five trunk lines are built, one line each in directions of east, south, west and north and the circle line around the city center. Every transit station has space provisions to cater for expansion of extra train carriages for future increase in passenger loads. Electric and driverless feeder buses in various housing estates will feed passengers to the MRT stations. MRT is an environment-friendly transportation tool and is sustainable to the next millennium. Train timetables for every station are displaced on the train platform and are available on mobile phones.

Passengers alighting every station are monitored and controlled by the central station, which would dispatch extra trains to busy stations. To encourage commuters to stagger their traveling time to ease congestion, peak period has a higher charge than non-peak. Senior citizens pay concession rate for traveling during non-peak periods.

4. Separation of pedestrians and vehicular traffic

One of the common causal factors of fatal road accidents is that pedestrians are often knocked down by cars, trucks, buses, and motorcyclists on the surface roads and at pedestrian crossing. Reckless drivers, drunk drivers, and drivers who do not abide by traffic regulations are the causes of many accidents. In China, pedestrians frequently and habitually ignore traffic rules and regulations by crossing against traffic lights or jumping over the road fences. Hence, to cut down on accidents, it is necessary to separate pedestrians from surface road vehicles in the eco-city to prevent their collision.

Pedestrian walkways are constructed on the same underground level as for the buses and MRT. This would facilitate commuters taking buses or trains. Installed on every bus is a proximity sensor that would cause the bus to stop when an obstacle is sensed in close proximity. All the pedestrian walkways are covered to protect them from inclement weather, especially during snowy and rainy days.

5. Bicycle lanes

Bicycle lanes next to the pedestrian walkways are provided for people who like to cycle to work from home, bus and train stations. Ubiquitous automatic bicycle kiosks provide bicycle rental service to pedestrians at various bus and train stations, commercial and office buildings. Separation of cyclists from private motorized vehicles in this transportation scheme eliminates potential accidents.

Bicycle rental fee by way of a pre-charge card is very low to encourage high usage by residents. The rental bicycles are simple to manufacture and easily identifiable if it is lost. Hence there is no problem concerning theft of the bicycles as no one can buy or possess such a bicycle. The manufacture and design of the bicycle is done locally and is owned by the state.

Electrical Power Supply for Transport Operations

Above the surface, roads are covered with solar panels for power generation with enough transparency to filter sunlight to shine on the roads. Night time lighting is provided by power generated by wind turbines around the city. Power can be supplemented by power generated by the eco-city steam turbine generators using biodiesel. Display panels are installed to indicate traffic flow conditions on all roads and highways. Motorists are advised to take alternate routes whenever there is any traffic jam.

Battery charging stations are provided at the car park of every block of building and also along certain locations of the expressways. Exchange service for car batteries of various capacities is available at petrol stations. Every electric vehicle is designed to have a quick change of battery pack that can be removed and reinstalled within minutes. Every electric car is designed to specifications that ensure all batteries are made interchangeable regardless of brand or model made by different manufacturers. All retired batteries can be disposed of at these battery charging stations.

Changes in the Social Environment of Living and Working

Expensive roads are not meant to be used indiscriminately and without control, as they are utilized as economic conduits to move people, goods, and transport vehicles without obstruction or hindrance. In order to maximize the economic value of the roads, the roads must not be blocked at any time. Therefore, road users must stagger their time of the usage so that the demand for road space does not concentrate on a short period of time in order to avoid creating traffic congestion that induces potential road accidents. Buildings are designed to minimize the need for people to drive their cars.

Government Office Buildings

Government office buildings tend to have high occupancy density, which means there would be a large concentration of office commuters taking public transport simultaneously, causing traffic congestion during peak period if they compete with other commuters going to work in the same locale. Therefore, it is prudent to build government offices outside the city center. To help ease traffic congestion further, all government office workers would stagger their hours of working in order to avoid rushing for transport simultaneously. MRT and bus stations are located adjacent to the government buildings to facilitate convenient movement of commuters.

Commercial Buildings

The density of occupants in the commercial buildings would determine the number of such buildings that can congregate in a specific location along the city streets. Such design scheme would cap excessive transport demand during peak periods. Factories are not permitted in the city center. Commercial firms' operating hours must also stagger.

The city administration imposes a limit on the number of supermarkets that could be built in the city center where traffic is heavy. A decentralized policy of building integrated shopping malls in the housing estates with supermarkets, retail and departmental stores, eateries, restaurants, cinemas, and other commercial services is a national policy of diluting traffic into and out of the city center.

Site of Eco-Schools, Universities, and Colleges

No schools are allowed to build in the city center as school children are vulnerable near and on busy roads or streets. Schools located in the old city always cause traffic jams when parents go to fetch their children from schools by cars that are parked on the streets. New eco-schools are to be built in the residential areas and located next to MRT and bus stations, and hence, problem of transport would not be an issue especially eco-schools have small classes and only a few hundred students compared to over a thousand in the old traditional education system. The access roads from the MRT station to the schools are covered to provide shelter against inclement weather.

Universities and colleges would be built outside the residential and city areas and would have large expanses of space for lakes, gardens, and recreational facilities for the thousands of students and teachers on the campus to mix and spend time together. There would be hostels for stay-in students and lecturers, and the campus would look more like a small community with a shopping mall. MRT trains and express buses would operate to and from the universities and colleges. The campus would provide free use of bicycles. Robotic workers are employed in as many menial trades as possible to maintain a 24/7 operation and to reduce manpower requirement in the campus and administration buildings.

Entertainment Centers and Sports Stadiums

Mass entertainment centers, such as concert or music halls and large sports stadium attract big crowds and, hence, to prevent traffic congestion, they are to be built near expressways and far from residential areas. All the MRT trunk and circle lines and various express buses from the housing estates would operate to these centers and stadiums. Ample car parks are also built to cater to the demand for parking. Car parking is to be booked online in advance and space is allocated with pre-payment of fees. This is to facilitate easy location of parking lot by drivers. Booking would stop when the car park is full. Carpooling is encouraged for people living in the neighboring estates to go to the same entertainment center. A carpooling website is available for interested parties to connect.

Hospitals and Outpatient Clinics

Hospitals and the outpatient clinics are decentralized to different housing estates and city center depending on the population density. Arterial roads are to connect to hospitals and clinics together with MRT and express buses. To ease crowding at the hospitals and clinics during morning rush hours, all hospitals and clinics have a website to encourage patients to login to register and pre-pay for an appointment with a doctor. Such procedure reduces the time spent waiting in the hospital and thus reducing congestion at the car park. Staggering of visit time by patients to the hospital and clinic reduces stresses on the road at morning peak period.

Change of Habit of Working Hours

It is a foregone conclusion that when every worker in the city goes to and leave their work place at the same time, not only the public buses and trains are unduly crowded, traffic jam on the roads would lengthen the journey time significantly by as much as three hours on an inbound and outbound journey in congested cities such as Beijing or Shanghai. To avoid congestion, the prudent solution is to stagger working hours of office staff.

All the commercial firms in the city must comply with the city administration rules and regulations on the requirements of staggering time for their workers. The workers who must start work at a specific time have priority to pick the starting time of work, with the rest working on flextime. Convenient time of work must be balloted to avoid unfair allocation. Compliance of this regulation is a prerequisite of obtaining a business operating license. Violation of this rule attracts a heavy fine and a suspension of license for the recalcitrant company. All heavy vehicles are banned on specific streets and roads during peak periods.

Employing Internet Technology to Improve Living Conditions and Lessen Road Trips

In the eco-city, all government departments are to employ Internet technology to communicate with the citizens not only to increase service efficiency but also to eliminate the need for citizens to make road trips to the department.

Incentives are given to all civil service workers who could suggest innovative ideas to improve Internet service efficiency. Visits to government department are to be by online appointment to reduce wait time and traffic congestion.

Road Sensors and Cameras

Installed on the streetlight posts are surveillance cameras and electronic sensors to capture information of vehicle speeds and identification. This makes stolen vehicles and speed violators easily traced. A speed warning sign will be displayed on the electronic display panel above the road to inform the oncoming motorist of his traffic violation. A computer system will automatically issue the car owner a composition fine for speeding. Repeat violators will have his insurance premium increased, and the driver may face a possible suspension of his license for exceeding a certain number of violations. The traffic offender will need to sit for a test of theory and driving skills. A pass is necessary to have his license renewed.

Every car must install a GPS, electronic box in-vehicle unit (IU), a transponder, and a 360-degree video camera in the car to record traffic violation and accidents for evidence in court cases. The IU, together with a cash card system, allows the motorists to pay parking fees, speed violation fines, and to serve as a location detector. Real-time information on road traffic conditions can be downloaded to the mobile phone. Where roads are congested or blocked, alert information would be sent out by the Transport Authority (TA) to all road users via radio stations, the TA website, and electronic display panels. Passenger can also login their query to find the best route to go home or other destination in the shortest time or cheapest fare by public transport.

Chapter 20

Banking and Financial Institutions

Current Global Financial Debacle

Cause of the Property Bubble Burst

The aftermaths of the economic debacles created by the tumultuous 1985 Japanese land price bubble, the Asian financial crisis in 1997, the 2008 subprime mortgage crisis in the United States, and the EU Great Recession of 2008–12 have taught many government leaders valuable lessons of being mindful of the easy credit availability for investors to indulge in speculation in the real estate and stock markets. China went through some social uproar during the early 2000s when property prices went berserk. Only with tough cooling measures could the government rein in the galloping housing prices that are beyond the ability of many young couples to purchase a modest home.

It seems the cycle of foreign liquidity of hot money for easy borrowing moves around the world once every few years. As has happened in many countries, using short-term hot money by investors to chase up the stock and property markets does not create real wealth in the economy but misery when the bubble burst. Many foreign governments were happy with the Chinese government for not devaluating its currency during the 1997 Asia financial crisis in order to maintain stability in the Asian money market. The Greek national debt crisis in 2015 is a lesson to be learned by government leaders not to overindulge in borrowing money beyond its means of repayment.

Lessons Learned by China about Pitfall of Easy Money

Sudden and abnormal surges in land, property, and stock prices disturb the normal rhythm of business cycles and could induce a herd mentality in people to invest in frenzied moods. When the market collapses, many people are left penniless. Only the punters and the financing bankers with insight information would reap a bumper crop. The leftovers would be massive unemployment and bankruptcies, which might take years to solve and which could derail the smooth running of a government.

Such economic dislocation creates sociopolitical problems that could shake the confidence of the local and foreign industrial investors. The situation is exacerbated by currency devaluation followed by high inflation. This economic malaise seems to be a recurring event happening around the world, and it plays out without any warning to the innocent citizens of the affected countries, making their hard earned savings depreciated considerably.

Laxity of Government Financial Control

Histories reveal that in all cases of financial crises, the incumbent governments in the affected countries are always behind the curve of monitoring and controlling the financial activities of the banks and financial institutions. This situation has to change to prevent recurrence. Many hedge-fund managers are eager to earn a quick profit in a short period by the use of high frequency trading, which focuses on the immediate and general direction of the market and not the economic fundamentals. This leads to market volatility, which is unhealthy for stock market operations.

The banks and financial institutions seem always at the front line of creating opportunities of reaping quick profits from selling Ponzi-scheme products in the shadow banking system that avoid the watchful eyes of the regulators. Fortunately, with its conservative banking policy, China escaped from the vagaries of such Ponzi products in the past.

Effect of the US Subprime Mortgage Crisis—Global Recession

The US Housing Market Collapse and its Reverberation

The crisis of 2007 subprime mortgage in the United States, valued at US$1.3 trillion in March 2007, was characterized by rising subprime mortgage delinquencies and foreclosures when the borrowers could not meet loan repayment. The virtual housing market collapsed like a house of cards when no more punters came to the market to buy. Home prices plummeted precipitously, and the financial institutions like Lehman Brothers that sold the mortgage-backed security (MBS) in the United States and worldwide ended up with foreclosed houses worth less than the mortgage loan. Those who hold the MBS certificates suffered heavy losses around the world. Lehman Brothers, which had never lost a cent in its entire one hundred years of operation, went bankrupt.

The housing bubble crisis expanded to other parts of the economy when banks were too terrified even to lend to other banks for fear of default on repayment. Total losses due to the subprime crisis were estimated to be in the trillions of dollars worldwide. Hundreds of banks went belly up in the United States and around the world. Many depositors had a run on the precarious banks. Economic activities took a nosedive. The global financial system was hit by a tsunami of no-confidence.

Downgrading of Credit Rating of the US Government

A Slew of Economic Crises arose from Financial Meltdown

The stock markets around the world took a beating. US stock owners suffered $8 trillion in losses in 2008. Stock markets in other countries lost 40 percent of their value. The central banks of many countries affected by the crisis went overdrive to implement quantity easing packages, or economic stimulus packages, to shore up the battered banking institutions, encouraging banks to lend to needy commercial firms.

Some banks, considered to be too big to fail, are bailed out by the US government for fear of causing more panic to the fragile financial system. The US government was given a downgrade in its foreign credit rating due to a high foreign debt/GDP ratio. The US dollar was devalued against other strong currencies, and this caused the price of crude oil to soar, and, hence, a ripple effect of rising cost of living in other countries. The crisis impacted the United States severely with 9 million job losses, representing 6 percent of US workforce.

A single dominant currency used in world trade could cause havoc to the stability of economic development of the world, and such currency has immense political influence on bilateral relationship between two countries in settling political conflicts. It is an opportune time for China's currency, RMB, to take a new position as an alternate foreign exchange currency in world trade.

The world cannot afford to continue to depend on one national currency to control international trade and international relations. It is like putting all the eggs of international faith in one basket.

The Subprime Mortgage Crisis's Effect on China's Export Markets

Concurrently, Eurozone is in deep economic crisis due to a combination of sovereign debt crisis, banking crisis caused by banks being under-capitalized, laden with worthless MBS, and lack of liquidity. Some European governments were given a downgrade in their credit rating. Government austerity measures exacerbated the high unemployment problem among the younger population. Economic recessions and heavy national debt burden in the United States and EU, the two largest trading partners of China, caused a cut back on imports from China, the factory of the world. This results in a chain reaction with downstream effects of reduction of China's imports of raw materials from other trading countries like Australia that exports less iron ore to China. China's GDP has been decreasing in the past few years due to lackadaisical global trading.

International trades and financial systems are much intertwined like a chain that if one major trading nation in the chain suffers a setback, other nations in the chain will be affected as well. The world has seen some nations using their devalued currency as a means to leverage their export trades to overcome an immediate social problem. The present global decline in the commodities sector and pricing has alarmed the treasuries of many affected countries due to reduced demand from China. When China announced devaluation of its currency by 2 percent, in August 2015, a shockwave reverberated throughout the world with a flurry of currency devaluation by many countries in response. In the period of June to August 2015, when the Shanghai Composite index shed 38 percent of its value, it caused a tsunami wave of stock sell off in other countries, signaling the importance of China in the world financial market and economic well-being.

There are a slew of economic measures by countries mired in economic malaise to avert an economic meltdown. To subsidize an export commodity to earn back production cost without a profit is one measure which is better than doing nothing and then suffering from uncontrollable unemployment with calamitous consequential social problems. A tourniquet measure is better than none.

The subprime mortgage crisis has affected the economic wellbeing of the Chinese migrant workers who are laid off because of declining export market.

Hence, the government has to rework its economic policy to seek new job opportunities for the tens of millions of unemployed migrant workers. The Eco-World project is one tonic that can create new hope and opportunity for China's economic advancement.

To maintain a healthy economic growth to feed the 1.36 billion people and to reduce the income gap between the rich and poor, especially the urban-rural disparity, the Chinese government continues to work relentlessly on sustainable and high income projects that can increase the purchasing power of the rural population of about six hundred million poverty stricken people. The most tangible and long-term economic growth project is the establishment of an Eco-World. The six hundred million poor rural residents will move up the value chain by upgrading their intellectual levels in the eco-cities with production of high value products and services. Their increase in income will stimulate economic growth of the domestic market and, thus, raising the GDP figure.

Economic Impact Due to the Eco-World Project

China to Invest in Eco-World Project to Expand Market Economy

The Eco-World project is a proactive investment of about US$1 trillion that not only can generate discernible and positive future earnings and wealth for the country, but also can avert a potential national disaster arising from domestic sociopolitical discontent. Eco-cities will be self-sufficient in foods, water, and energy, thereby annually saving hundreds of billions of dollars in foreign exchange, generating trillions of dollars of value-added industries, and eliminating problems of air and water pollutions that entail hundreds of billions of dollars of environmental damages for decades and human health degradation.

There is never a perfect time to implement the Eco-World project, especially when the economic recessions in the United States and Europe, who are the most important trading partners of China, would take many years to recover. The United States Federal government is mired in a $18 trillion national debt and a potential problem, as predicted by speculators, of currency devaluation due to persistently printing of money out of thin air.

Meanwhile, there are still many trillions of US dollars from the US Treasury's QE packages and private fund managers floating around looking for a safe home for investment. China's Eco-World project would be the home for such cheap investment money. China can afford to repay the loans easily and cheaply in digital numbers when its currency appreciates significantly against the US dollars in the future, with the GDP exceeding that of the United States, and when Chinese currency CNY becomes the preferred international trading currency instead of the US dollar.

Eco-World Banking Rules and Regulations

New Prudent Banking Rules and Regulations

The Chinese leaders have acquired the wisdom, through lessons learned, of how to avoid the pitfalls of having foreign hot money flooding the housing and stock markets by enacting stricter rules and regulations to control the operations of all the state banks, including the shadow banking systems that has been operating without strict control and regulations. Hot money could easily filter into the shadow banking system and hence, fuel excessive funding in the property market that could lead to housing bubble. No individual is permitted to borrow from a bank an amount exceeding 50 percent of his realizable assets to purchase a property during the period of rapid housing price increases.

The Internet provides easy fund transfers throughout the world to facilitate seamless and real-time trading operations on money matters and financial transactions; however, without prudent control and supervision, a click of the mouse could cause a bank to go bankrupt like Barings Bank, founded in 1762 and collapsed in 1995.

There will be, in the Eco-World of China, stringent and watertight rules and regulations and close monitoring to control and manage the financial markets just like the systems used in aviation and food manufacturing industries to ensure the safety of the public is not compromised or abused. In all the eco-cities, every bank must comply with ISO 9001 standard, and is to undertake and pass a Basel III stress test to obtain the ISO 9001 certificate. Illegal trading would attract criminal prosecution of the bank CEO. Deviation from the ISO 9001 procedures incurs heavy fine. The fiascos of financial meltdowns in the United States serve to remind the Chinese government to be on guard on fraudulent activities in loan applications and approval by all banks in housing transaction.

Stringent and Tight Rules to Guard against Dubious Financial Products

Every eco-city establishes a credit rating organization that analyses and do a due diligence on credit worthiness of each mortgage, derivative, loan, unit trust, bond, and any other financial product with tangible and proven collateral asset backing. Foreign financial products, with two other international reputable banks as underwriters, can apply to get a government approval before it is allowed to be sold in the Chinese market. External audits are done annually to ensure there is absolute compliance with rules and regulations.

Unrestrained and unethical banking operation will be severely dealt with under the new banking regulation in which the bank CEO has to face a court hearing for any financial product that is sold without proper scrutiny and evaluation and asset backing. The government has the power to withdraw the license at any time when an illegal operation is discovered.

The new reformed banking rules and regulations seek to prevent a bank like Lehman Brothers Investment Bank and Barings Bank from mismanagement leading to bankruptcy. Constant contact and dialogue between the bank and regulators ensure proper conduct in the banking business and protection of the interests of the bank's depositors and investors. Hot and speculative money will be closely monitored to prevent it from being used in the property market.

The banks would need to report regularly its financial positions and its credit rating. Any serious irregularities must be rectified promptly or else its license will be revoked. In addition, there is a cap on fees charged by the bank as a retailer of any foreign financial products to discourage a frenzied mood of greedy bankers who are too greedy to sell to novice investors to earn overtly high income for doing little work. There will be different independent external auditors to audit the bank's accounts annually to prevent cozy relationship between the bank and the auditing firm.

The Society for Worldwide Interbank Financial Telecommunication (SWIFT) is a cooperative society under Belgian law and owned by its financial institution members around the world. It deals with services in the financial marketplace involving securities, treasury, trade services, and cash payments and management. Every institution and bank has a SWIFT code for identification.

China is wary of using the SWIFT code as the secrecy of the SWIFT system is compromised by the US government's security agencies that have a "terrorist finance tracking program" to access the SWIFT transaction database after the September 11 attacks. In addition, the United States has control over the transaction between two foreign countries. The US National Security Agency also monitors SWIFT banking and credit card transactions. The SWIFT system is also being used by the United States to block financial transactions in trade sanction against another country. The Chinese government is wary that China will lay bare its trade and financial secrets to the United States when its SWIFT accounts are assessed by the US government. The use of a SWIFT code is discouraged in Chinese banking operations. Using SWIFT as a political tool is unacceptable to China.

Bank Notes

With advancements in IT, cash card, and cell phone technology, the use of bank notes and coins will be gradually phased out. New cell phones will incorporate microchips embedded in the phone, which will be used for all daily transactions using apps. The cost of business operations will be reduced without the need to deal with bank notes and coin deposits and withdrawals, and ATMs will become obsolete. The online shopping e-commerce that is prevalent in China allows money transactions using online digital payment.

Politics and Financial Liberalization

The Chinese government is well aware of the needs to reform and restructure its banking system and operation so as to integrate and synchronize with the international banking systems and operations as the globalization of the financial markets are intimately intertwined among all countries. Such needs entail relaxing the Chinese government's overly tight rein on currency control, leading toward globalization and free interchangeability of its CNY. It is to be noted that the Chinese banks have been operating in the past with prudence and conservatism that help stabilize the financial markets in the world.

With CNY being a global currency, Chinese political development will lean toward more democratic and less communistic ideology. It is a natural process. All the Chinese state banks have been issued IPOs and operate under the rules and regulations of the stock exchanges. Their annual financial reports are published for scrutiny by all investors. All these banks now have branches around the world.

When more countries begin to use CNY for international trade through Asia Infrastructure Investment Bank, Shanghai Cooperation Organization, Silk Road Economic Belt, and the Twenty-First Century Maritime Silk Road organizations, China helps the world become unshackled by the mighty US dollar that has been used as a political weapon on trade sanctions, casino chips for foreign exchange speculators, and as a means to control global monetary policy. There should be checks and balances in the financial market. The world should have a choice of currency for international trade, free from unsavory political pressure and interference.

Export-Import Bank

There is no one-size-fits-all bank that caters to the plethora of needs of the private individual, commerce, and industries. Banking rules and regulations need to be rigid and transparent to ensure there is a fair playing field, compliance with the banking laws, and to protect the banks and their customers. An export-import bank controlled by the government is needed to help industries and commercial firms in the export markets. There is a slew of problems in the export business that could confront both the exporters and the importers which the banks of the exporters could not handle.

Problems of untrustworthy private banks in the importing countries being delinquent in payments on due dates, currency fluctuations and control, political crises, and industrial actions could derail export business transactions. An export-import bank that deals with the importing country's national bank could be the answer to help the exporter in taking over the financial transaction risk. In addition, the export-import bank can offer attractive interest rate to the exporters.

Private Micro-Banking Institutions and Incubator

The SME (Small and Medium size Enterprise) private companies have had troubles getting loans from the state-owned banks that prefer to give loans only to big state-owned enterprises. In the new Eco-World, private investors are encouraged to set up micro-banking institutions to lend small amounts of money to SME companies that are shunned by large commercial banks. To help the novice businessman without adequate knowledge and resources in conducting a successful business operation, these micro-banking institutions will conduct training classes, especially on how to maintain a healthy cash flow on their balance sheets.

China adopts a similar US financial incubator system for any entrepreneur who has invented new products but lacks in financial and other resources to promote and market his products. The financial investors will perform a feasibility study of his products, market survey, barrier-to-entry, legal matters, intellectual property, business payback, and product lifecycle.

Asian Infrastructure Investment Bank (AIIB)

China will have come of age when the Asian Infrastructure Investment Bank (AIIB) is up and running in 2015. AIIB was initiated by China mainly as a result of its unhappiness with the way the World Bank and Asian Development Bank were being dominated by the United States and Japan and was lacking in funds for large-scale infrastructure projects in Asia. Many nations concur with China's assessment, and China is smart enough to seize the opportunity to set up AIIB, which has met with approval from like-minded nations. The United States expresses reservations over its transparency and has urged other nations not to join AIIB, whose founding membership application expired on March 31, 2015.

In defiance of US opposition, fifty-seven countries, including many US allies in Europe, decide to join as founding members of AIIB, which will have US$100 billion as seed capital. With AIIB as the driving force in the Asian economic development led by China, it signals the beginning of the end of United States' monetary monopoly and its waning supremacy in international politics. With China as the driving force of a loan provider, Chinese currency (CNY) will play a significant role in financing projects under the auspices of AIIB.

The Asian Development Bank estimates that US$8 trillion is needed to fund Asia's infrastructure requirements from now until 2020. AIIB will assume more significant role in Asian economic development projects in the future without political string attached. China might likewise establish a similar investment bank for Africa and South America to strengthen the position of the CNY in the world economy. It is to be noted that China was the largest economy in the world in the eighteenth century. Chinese banks need to establish more branches worldwide to support the Chinese CNY as an international reserve currency in international trade.

In the past decade China has been concentrating on building bridges of economic friendship with many foreign countries around the world while the United States has been busy fighting expensive proxy wars in distant lands and spending valuable energy and time getting involved in the internal affairs of other countries. It is a common knowledge that whoever has the money calls the shots, and the Chinese government is ultra-rich, with a foreign reserve of US$4 trillion that is growing annually. Meanwhile, China's foreign minister is happy that the United States continues in its role as the international police and keeps fighting proxy wars in various distant lands.

Chapter 21

E-Government

Present Social and Political Discontents

The thirty-year-old urbanization program has helped China's social and economic progress immensely but also generated many sociopolitical problems that could threaten the foundation of the government. Proliferating corruption, water and environmental pollution, unsafe factory foods, unemployment, soaring foods prices, housing and medical fees, and galloping inflation are pressing social problems that cannot be put on a back burner. They need to be tackled immediately before a perfect storm erupts. Six hundred million poverty-stricken rural residents remain a time bomb that cannot be ignored by the government for long. There are many matured politicians calling for immediate sociopolitical reform before the Communist Party meets the "dead end." Finally, the Communist Party leaders decide to abandon the present urbanization program, and adopt a new innovative program of creating a new Eco-World with an E-government in every one of the four hundred eco-cities.

Participation of Netizens on Social Media

Politics in China traditionally has been in the domain of the Communist Party hard core members who are the founding members of the party and their descendants. However, with the advent of Internet and social media proliferation, netizens of four hundred million strong begin to enter the political arena to voice their opinion on social and political issues affecting "the man on the street." They are not politicians wanting to take on an opposition role but as a concerned civil community. Their opinion can be vociferous and intolerant toward social injustice and corruptions. They can spot government officials who wear expensive watches that are beyond their normal purchasing power. Chinese political system has to change to keep abreast with time and the aspiration of the citizens in order to progress constantly. The world of today is not the same as that in Mao Zedong's era when there were no cell phones or multimedia Internet access.

The participation of the netizens can act as whistle-blowers that the government leaders can take heed of when there is a cover-up by pockets of party members usurping their power to oppress the local citizenry or engage in corrupt practices. Even some local political party secretaries can subjugate the judiciary to their own whims and fancies causing detrimental effect on the Communist Party reputation. China is too big to govern fairly even with a massive Communist Party security force and strict party rules.

It is imperative that the Communist Party must accept the netizens' feedback to curb the abuses of power by government officials and party members. The Communist Party needs to rework its membership criteria and renewal qualification, and to take positive measures to eliminate the antisocial and anti-Party behavior of party members. The Communist Party's manifesto must change to adapt to the prevailing social environment.

Economic Benefits from the Eco-World Project

The Eco-World will be acclaimed as the most ambitious socioeconomic political system transformation that ever happened in human history. Maintaining the status quo incurs the consequent costs of worsening climate change effect of greenhouse gases, air and water pollution, vast administrative expenses to manage the welfare of the six hundred million poor farmer families and civil services in the rural areas, increasing medical expenses and diseases, unrelenting corruption, and payments of hundreds of billions of dollars for oil and foodstuff imports. The annual costs of more than a trillion dollars to deal with all of these social issues have become annual expenses without realizable benefits to the nation and people now or in the future.

Annual Savings from the Eco-World Project

With the Eco-World project, the government secures great savings by not having to dole out annually billions of CNY to relieve the farmers who suffer perennially from natural disasters like drought and floods. Other sources of project funds come from the subsidies to farmers, closures of hundreds of thousands of rural county governments, and savings of foreign reserves of US$400–500 billion and US$100–200 billion each year by not importing oil and agricultural products respectively.

The government will save hundreds of billions on health care costs that will be drastically reduced due to the eradication of harmful effects of greenhouse gases and pollutants liberated by burning of coal and fossil fuel which will be banned in the Eco-World. The government derives significant economic benefits in the Eco-World from reduction of traffic accidents which accounts for nearly one million people being killed and permanently disabled annually. The direct and indirect costs of these accidents represent 1.5 percent of China's GDP.

With e-governments, the hundreds of billions of dollars that used to grease the corrupt officials will remain intact in the national treasury for the people. Hence, the Chinese national coffer will be enriched annually by the investment of US$1 trillion spent on the Eco-World project plus a windfall of beneficial knock-on effect. The vast economic and social benefits of Eco-World are incalculable, including value for money on public spending, significant synergistic effects on social advancements, enhanced national security, and clean and green environment sustainable to the next millennium.

Clean Environment

There will be no more greenhouse gases escaping the chimneys of coal-fired power stations or internal combustion engines using fossil fuel. Renewable energy power from the other sources of wind turbine, solar, hydro, biodiesel, and tidal waves will be the sources for energy production, replacing fossil fuel and coal. The residents will enjoy a green and pollution free environment. People's health will be significantly improved, and medical bill is correspondingly reduced.

Eco-City Infrastructures and Social Amenities

To live in the eco-city is to enjoy a feast of social harmony, stress- and crime-free environment, and mutual trust in the community. There is time for everyone to smell the flowers. In the many parks, located on various housing estates, residents are free to walk about and dance in the morning and evening hours that are the usual social interaction of the housewives and homemakers.

Safety is assured by robotic security guards keeping the nights free of loiterers and drunks off the streets. The roads are cleaned every day by an automatic water sprinkler system. Automatic firefighting systems are installed along the center road divider with two pylons supporting a movable and remotely controlled water jet that can spray water to extinguish fires on any building. The pylons also serve as street lamp posts and supports for solar panels. There is no shortage of water in the eco-cities.

Trees are planted along the sides of the streets, and flowerpots are dotted along various street junctions. Many canals meander through the city to provide waterway transports to commuters and freight cargo and add color to the city panorama. They also serve as a flood control conduit to divert excess water to outskirt reservoirs. Sculptures of historical figures and well-known personalities are placed at various parks and government buildings. Traffic noise pollution is nonexistent as train and bus traffic is underground and all private vehicles are driven electrically.

Every eco-city has an open-air theatre for concerts, plays, and art performances. Regular sporting activities for different seasons and games are held at a large stadium. The stadium is covered in winter to prevent inclement weather affecting the games and spectators. Various cultural clubs, like calligraphy, chess, painting, pottery, dance, martial arts, cooking, and yoga would hold regular meets for their members and the public. Schools and higher educational institutions also hold cultural and sporting activities for the students.

The traditions and cultures of the former farmers are encouraged to continue in the new eco-city. Music and arts are the foods for the soul. Sports are energizers for the physical body. Every festive season is celebrated fervently by all citizens. A special day is picked as the founding day of each eco-city, and to be remembered by special events, celebrations, remembrances, and mass participation. The government encourages young people to participate in sports rather than playing computer games in their spare time. With abundance of social and sporting activities, it is envisaged that the eco-city residents will be in the pink of health.

People are well educated and healthy. They understand the importance of keeping fit and healthy with sports, proper diet and healthy living style. Smoking marijuana or illicit drug use is nonexistent. Documentary films about the harmful effects of drugs are shown to school students. They learn Chinese traditional medicine at a young age in schools to understand the common diseases and their causes.

Fostering harmonious relationships between government officials and the citizens is a good recipe for continuing governance; this being the axiom expounded by Confucius (551 BC) more than two thousand years ago. There is a community hall in every housing estate where the residents intermingle and help one another in their daily lives, solving immediate problems in their own neighborhoods. They form a close-knit society. In schools, the children will be imbued with care and love for the family, the environment, and the country.

Work-life balance is a topic that receives attention in the eco-cities by young people who prefer a working life without burnout and contracting health-related diseases such as heart attack, stroke, depression, and sleep disorders. Overtime work is discouraged by companies, and the government lays down rules and regulation to stop workers from working more than a stipulated time per week, just like the conditions imposed on airline flight attendants and crews. Maintaining a balanced working life is essential for good health and harmonious family life.

In the eco-city, there is a strong social interaction between the people and government officials and grass-root leaders who hold monthly meet-the-people sessions to hear their daily life problems. Quality of life, mutual respect and love for the community and country are the ingredients for national cohesion and are taught in schools. The local community will have a website to connect with the people on social issues.

One important aspect of working life in the co-city is that there is no pressure of rushing to and from work. Dinner can be arranged within your estate with the community club whose members are your neighbors who are willing to prepare favorite dishes for a token fee. Residents can engage Michelin-grade freelance cooks to prepare special dinner for a group dining. Many working couples employ robots to do household chores. To save time and trouble, residents prefer to do online shopping with home delivery for foodstuffs and other daily essentials.

E-hospital and Health Care

Hospitals and health care services are revamped entirely with revolutionary systems and management. The new system and operation eliminate prevailing rampant corruption and can deliver affordable and quality medicare services to patients. Young children in schools will be taught how to stay healthy and avoid contracting ailments. Hospital operations and administration are fully computerized. Online booking for hospital admission is required, with the patient's medical history recorded prior to admission.

Robotic surgeries could be performed by surgeons from remote locations. Robots are deployed to provide nursing care duties in hospital and at home.

Post-surgery aftercare consultation is done online to track the patient's recovery at home. Robots are available for hire to help lonely patient at home and to provide health care services.

E- Education

The new e-education system is a game changer in opening up the potential of future young Chinese to be creative, entrepreneurial, and receptive to new ideas in the world through using state-of-the-art IT and Internet media. China wants to be the leader in innovation and production of high quality consumer products that can sustain longer product life cycle and market longevity. With e-education, the system aims to produce well-rounded students and develop their minds, seeking the truth of nature, finding new answers to old problems, and be broadminded to absorb new ideas and explore new frontiers of knowledge.

Commerce and Industries

To continuously raise the people's standard of living in China, manufacturing industries are encouraged, with financial assistance from the government and university support, to innovate, design and manufacture quality products that can command higher selling price and greater profit margin in the market place. The government provides incentives to industries to automate their production and to use IT for management and operations. The aim is to increase productivity per employee. Automation eliminates all the problems related government's financial provisions for pension and social security.

There are various commercial organizations that can offer assistance to anyone who intend to set up a business by attending a business course that covers the legal requirements of business operations, labor laws, and cash flows. The government encourages private investment companies to offer loans to small- and medium-size enterprises.

The e-government encourages entrepreneurs, investors, and innovators to specialize in being system integrators for product planning, design, and manufacturers like Apple and Boeing, whose products are the results of integrating various quality components from sources around the world. Their products command top dollars. Other innovations include material science and technology that could produce alternate manmade materials to replace materials from nature. Every large company is encouraged to spend 5–10 percent of its revenue on R&D with tax incentive. Every e-government is tasked to provide the right environment to support industries and commerce in order to help China continuously move up the value chain of quality living.

The e-government establishes R&D funds to help start-up companies venture into developing the latest IT apps and technological innovations and products, such as robots and automatic machines for industrial and medical applications. 3-D printing is a special project that the government emphasizes for greater development. The Eco-World will use many types of robots in the daily lives of many disabled persons, industries and farming. Robots will be the caretakers in the future for the increasing population of aged persons.

National Projects

The Chinese government has a blueprint for developing China's industries for the next millennium in the following arena:

1. Battery-driven cars—China shall manufacture battery-driven cars of various standards for the world market using 3-D printing techniques and software for mass production car models or custom-made model. Interior furnishings can be made in China or overseas countries to suit local conditions and demand.
2. Ships—China shall build ships of various tonnages and applications using 3-D printing technique in China and overseas countries. The ships will run on biodiesel fuel and incorporate anti-pirate security and latest navigational systems.
3. Apparel—In conjunction with dress designers in various countries, China shall manufacture dresses for various designers and sales/marketing companies using mannequins specially designed for making dresses of various types and sizes of dresses using new sewing techniques.
4. Robotic chefs and robotic restaurants—Outside dining is becoming common practice worldwide. China will design robotic chefs and restaurants operated by robots to cater to various cuisines from different countries. China's robotic restaurants will operate in various countries, overtaking McDonald's fast-food restaurants. The robotic restaurants will feature their menu on their website and the pricing of every dish. Take-out service is also available.
5. Robotic surgical instruments—designing robotic platform for single-entry or multi-entry site surgical operations using flexible endoscope, mini-cutting tools, and high-definition vision systems to perform a minimally invasive surgery at a hard-to-reach anatomical location.

6. Ceramic matrix composites—these manmade composites will be used exclusively in high temperature application such as rockets and commercial and military jet engines that are worth hundreds of billions.
7. Residential condominiums—Using 3-D printing technique, China will have a fully integrated housing design and fabrication company to build low-cost housing for the world market using experience from the Eco-World project. Raw materials for interior furnishings can be made available from local sources.

China will use its experience and technological advances to develop various fully integrated manufacturing industries to produce consumer products of the highest quality with affordable price. China will leverage its prowess in manufacturing and to have joint ventures in foreign counties to achieve global multinational companies across the globe.

Foreign talents will be employed to leapfrog the learning process to achieve early attainment of product quality on par with or surpassing the competitors. To attract foreign talents, China sets up numerous recruitment agencies around the world to interview interested candidates to migrate to China. Special recruitment agencies at various Japanese cities are engaged to recruit Japanese professionals who are experts in quality engineering and testing. This should help Chinese manufacturers upgrade their product quality and precision manufacturing skill.

Like the United States, which recruited many scientists, technologists and other professionals after WW2 from European countries to help US industries advance by leaps and bounds, China at this opportune time would do likewise especially when many European countries presently suffer from high unemployment.

China sets a long-term goal to take over the Japanese global markets of cameras, video equipment, cars, motor cycles, precision machineries, watches and other high quality industrial products. This should cripple Japanese industries. With fewer exports, decreasing income, growing aging population and inflation, and depleting tax revenues, Japan would not have the financial resources to build up offensive military hardware for aggression. China wants to extinguish eternally the flame of Japanese desire of aggression against its neighbor.

In due course, the United States and Japan's military alliance would dissolve as it becomes obsolete. The US's Seventh Fleet ships would leave the

East and South China seas due to increasing military defense cuts, increasing national debt burden, the diminishing of US leadership in international affairs, and lack of military sales opportunity in Asia. China would win the battle of wits with the United States without firing a bullet as time is on China's side with increasing wealth, power, and business relations with its neighbors. The United States is never China's neighbor, and China never wants to treat the United States as an enemy now or in the future. Peaceful coexistence, a Confucius teaching, is a virtue.

Recycling of Raw Materials

Recycling of waste materials is a statutory requirement for all households and commercial establishments in the eco-city. Biodegradable materials are collected for composting for use in the eco-farms. Other recycling materials include glass, paper, plastic and metal. Every block of apartment is provided with waste bins which are emptied at regular intervals. Special bulky items can be collected by special arrangement.

The recycling policy is to reuse raw materials to protect the environment by reducing the energy it takes to reprocess recycled materials into final products. Rather than processing the raw materials from their natural state, recycling conserves natural resources that are limited in supply and reduces pollution. More importantly, landfills will not be required, therefore keeping the environment free from contamination. Recycling paper will reduce the need to cut down trees, which are required to absorb CO_2 from the atmosphere.

Special Innovation Projects with Government Funding

The government has a program of innovation projects that offer special incentives for industries to take up. The following projects are some examples:

1. Intelligent Mannequin

One of the innovation projects is to develop a computerized intelligent inflatable mannequin that can take human body's physical measurements. A person wearing the master mannequin dress will have his or her physical dimensions measured and a code number assigned. The code number can be used to inflate another mannequin to the same dimensions. This process is useful for a dress maker to make a 100 percent fitting dress for a client. A retailer can find a ready-made dress that meets the buyer's body measurements using the mannequin's information.

The company that owns the inflatable mannequins establishes branches all over the world offering such mannequin measurement services gratis. Subscribers to the database of the company's mannequin measurements for a fee can make dresses to match various bodies' measurements. This innovation is useful to many people whose body has changed shape with ages, and these people find difficulty in buying ready-made dresses off the shelf for a perfect fit. In the future, people can order dresses online with design and material that suit individual requirements using their own mannequin measurements for perfect fitting. Online shopping for a perfect dress for any person is available anywhere in the world.

Computer-controlled dressmaking machines using special glue and the mannequin dimensions will be available in the future to make a dress within minutes without the conventional sawing and stitching machines. This new method of dressmaking offers quality and reasonable costs for making a dress even of intricate design. It also saves materials as the computer-operated cutter cuts the exact material for making a customized dress. There will be no more seamstresses employed in the apparel industry. Automatic dressmaking factories will be established worldwide.

2. Other Intelligent Models

Similar innovation can also be made for shoemakers to make a pair of shoes that best fit the left and right foot of an individual. Our pair of left and right feet do not necessary have the identical length or width. Different people have different toe shapes and heel curves. Intelligent inflatable shoes are now available to take measurements of the left and right feet of an individual. The measurements are coded and can be used by a 3-D printer to make a pair of shoe last for a customer. Together with 3D CAD/CAM technology, a pair of best fit shoes can be ordered and custom-made from the shoe last model. A shopper can order a pair of shoe online, quoting the personal feet measurement codes for the right size of shoes to be made. Similar innovations can be applied to custom-make brassiere and underwear tailored to an individual's requirements.

3. Automatic Robotic Chefs

In order to make available to the people of China and the world all kinds of Chinese cuisines and the special food dishes from every village, town, and city, the government has set up special culinary schools to develop robotic chefs that can take over the chores of a human chef. Every robotic chef specializes in only one type of dish. These culinary schools will transform the entire Chinese food industry. Every dish is given a specification with a proper name, recipe, cooking process, and nutritional values.

The robotic chef and the kitchen facility will be designed and approved by the Chinese Food and Beverage Association (FBA), which will issue the franchise license to any local or foreign restaurant owner who wants to lease the robotic chef and manage the restaurant facility. All the ingredients for making the dishes will have to follow the ISO 9001 process as stipulated by the FBA and will be monitored closely by professional food tasters to ensure food quality and hygiene standards are maintained per specifications. The Chinese government is aware that with declining population, there are less people willing to become a chef because of hard work and long working hours. Also, local special dishes will vanish in the future as not many young people willing to take over the small family business. Robotic chefs will fill in the vacancies.

Other Innovation Projects

Other projects that can receive government funding involving the following:

1. Perovskites—for use in making more efficient solar panels and semiconductor devices in electronics and medical fields
2. Graphene—stronger than steel, more conductive than copper, and as flexible as rubber for use in making faster computer chips, solar cells, flexible touch screens, and other commercial applications.
3. Carbon nanotubes—application of carbon nanotubes on new industrial products in the field of electronics, medical, sensors, and energy
4. 3-D printing—producing various products with quality, speed and low costs
5. Robots—to replace manual workers in industries that are shunned by many people and also in the health care services
6. Battery—invention of a lighter weight and durable car battery

Seal of Approval of Quality (SAQ)

Every company strives for an iconic image for its product lines. An iconic product is recognized as a quality product anywhere in the world irrespective where it is made. In every eco-city there is a nonprofit quality organization, represented by various professional bodies, to seal an approval on any company that achieves the highest five-star standard of quality in the country. A company that has acquired the Seal of Approval of Quality (SAQ) stands to gain recognition of professionalism and quality from the consumers. It is like the Royal Seal of "By Appointment to the Queen" in the UK, given to industries that meet the high quality standard of the royal family.

China wants to emulate the high-quality standard of engineering products made in the western countries. It wants to erase the memory of a country that used to make cheap consumer products. ISO 9001 will be the norm for all industries and a way of life in China. Like every violinist who would like to possess a 1716 Antonio Stradivari violin, China wants to be a torchbearer for quality living in the world with the highest happiness rating. Professionalism and ethics will rule Chinese industries. The culture of quality will be imbued to students in schools and higher institutions. China must move up the value chain when it becomes the richest country in the world.

Traffic Safety Measures

Private vehicular and pedestrian traffics are separated for different levels of the roads. To reach the city centers, all the buses and trains use the underground levels. Such a system design is to provide commuters protection against the elements and contact with private vehicles. The surface roads are designed to be through-flow such that there is no traffic junction to stop any traffic flow. Diversions signs and traffic information are available on internet and on electronic boards above the roads whenever there is traffic jam.

Every street corner is marked with an electronic coordinate for ease of location search by road users. Using this coordinate and the vehicle's sensors, it is easy to locate any vehicle on the road and its speed. Such a system is used to catch speed limit violators and tailgate drivers. Vehicle theft is nonexistent as the system can easily locate the stolen vehicle. Robots, controlled by vigilante corps at home, are deployed at night to do night patrol on the streets in the local estate in all seasons. Using a vigilante corps promotes better understanding of the security situation in the housing estate. It involves community living.

Food Safety Measures

Frequent food safety incidents reported in the mass media in the past decade have caused concerns in China and in other countries. There are several factors that are related to these incidents: lack of supervision of and enforcement by health inspectors, no standalone food safety policy, corrupt officials, and too many small food production units spread over a wide area in remote places. Food safety incidents involved gutter oil, milk powder contaminated with melamine, expired meat recertified for use, fake drugs, alcoholic drinks, and food products contaminated with insecticides.

The government takes the opportunity of Eco-World establishment to revamp the entire food and drug administration with advice from the US Food and Drug Administration (FDA). In addition, the government wants to follow the same principles adopted by the Federal Aviation Authority (FAA), which has cradle-to-grave records of every item used on an airplane. Approved records are requires to identity source of every food item, the processes involved in production of the final food product and chemical laboratory test results in accordance with approved specifications. Any deviation in food source, process, and production must be approved before being allowed for sale.

Every company that produces a food product for sale must comply with ISO 9001 and engage a government-licensed quality assurance inspector who reports directly to the local FDA. A self-monitoring system will be in place just like in the airline operations where the airline quality assurance inspector must inspect and approve all the tasks and processes performed by the maintenance staff. No deviation is allowed unless approved by FAA inspector. The food products produced in the eco-farms are safe from insecticides and other chemicals that are harmful to human. All food exports must be stamped with the Seal of Quality Approval.

E-Government Structures and Policy

In order that every eco-city can be sustained to the next millennium with prosperity and harmony, the central government decides every eco-city is to be governed by an e-government that is for the people and by the people, and it is to be compatible with the environment. The local people are the masters of their own destiny. The local government will hold a general election to select candidates for local government officials who have had certain number of years of grassroots experience and are known to the local citizens. The central government will have a legal representative in the provincial government to

1. approve the provincial government budget
2. control the police department and internal security operations
3. control the administration of anti-corruption operations

Such a political process, as adopted in the Hong Kong self-governing administration, ensures that the economic development of the province is progressive and healthy and subject to the scrutiny of the local citizens. There is no need for local officials to seek favors from the central government to get elected as has happened in the past.

E-government civil administration system will adopt a pro-citizen approach where the civil servants will not be talking down on citizens. To stay connected with the citizens, the e-government has a website listing the heads of department and their e-mail addresses. Grassroots leaders, either party or non-party affiliated, will assist the provincial government minister to solve personal and social problems. The size of the e-government is controlled by the central government, and mirrors the setup similar to that practiced by the Singapore government for efficiency and transparency.

Ironclad Anti-corruption Measures

With e-government, the problems of deep-rooted corrupt practices that prevail in the old world of China will be eradicated as all procedures and processes of getting approval from government departments will be processed online 24/7 for the public. The purpose of the e-government is to eliminate the need for citizens to physically contact any government employee to obtain approval, especially for doing business.

The cost of living and conducting business will be drastically reduced without corruption. Tax payment by small and medium size companies could be performed online without having to visit the tax department to pay cash. Payment for government services can be done online, via bank portals or kiosks that accept credit cards.

The Corruption Investigation Bureau, manned by a senior minister of the National People's Congress, reports directly to the State Council. It is open 24/7 online for feedback. To wipe out the age-old corruption practice from the nation with an ironclad policy, a punishment as powerful as a hyena's bite will be meted out to government officials who receive bribes. Any citizen offering a bribe to a government official receives a treble amount of punishment by law.

Members of the judiciary organization are reminded by the Supreme People's Court to treat every court case impartially and without prejudice. Any corrupt practice and improper conduct committed by any lawyer or judge receives double punishment and banned for life in any government and civil services, and his license to practice as a lawyer may be revoked. Every government department and civil service organization must follow their ISO 9001 standard. Any civil service official who attends functions or dinner engagement with businessman will need to fill up a form for approval. Any gift received from the public has to be surrendered to the government.

Salary paid to the senior public administrator and government officials is comparable to or even higher than the equivalent job in the private sector, under a similar pay scheme practiced in Singapore where the government officials receive the highest salary in the world in order to maintain a clean image and integrity of the government. All Chinese officials receive handsome retirement benefits without the need to look for extra income in retirement.

People-Centered E-Government

E-government uses its portals to interact with the population, to disseminate information, and to exchange information and idea on a real-time basis. The netizens using Weibo media (similar to Twitter) are alerted to the latest news in the country. Every minister has a Weibo account to interact with the population. The present judicial system needs to upgrade to enforce the court's independence to conduct its legal proceedings. Swift corrections to injustice cases by the government will be the testimony of upholding the integrity of the government. The bonanza for such quick remedial actions would earn the political party immeasurable goodwill, accolade and trust from the populace.

The conduct of the government officials will subject to the crosshairs of netizen's surveillance to prevent corruption. The government will compensate generously all the government officials for their arduous work in order to attract competent staff and to retain their service. It is not easy to balance between a good private family life and a demanding 24/7 public service.

Every eco-city will have a balanced or surplus annual budget as standard eco-city governance and operations. It will remember the fate that befell Detroit in the United States that has gone bankrupt. A referendum will be needed to pass a deficit annual budget. Like the central government, the eco-government will have its top officials replaced by new bloods after a term of not more than ten years. To prevent civil service getting bloated with staff, staff salary expenditure does not exceed the limit set by the central government. Annual auditing of each e-government and civil service is performed to check the financial accounts and compliance with standard procedure of operations in accordance with the ISO 9001 standard. Any notable discrepancies will be published and announced in the news media.

Self-renewal Process for Communist Party Members

Since the advent of market economy introduced by Deng Xiaoping, China had transformed slowly from pure Communism to a hybrid of Communism, Capitalism, and Socialism (COCASO) with varying degree of weightage for each system. With experience and confidence, the Communist Party begins to relax its control on civil services. It has to change with time. The central committee of the Communist party is aware that it is impossible for good governance sake to micromanage every aspect of local government and civil service operations.

Delegation of power does not mean erosion of control as long as there is a good and effective system in place just like running a huge multinational corporation, for example, Foxconn, a subsidiary of Taiwanese Hon Hai Precision Company in China employing one million people. It would be suicidal for the CEO in Taiwan to micromanage such a huge multinational corporation on a daily basis. He has to employ trusted and qualified people to effectively and profitably manage the company.

It is time to revolutionize the Communist Party machineries to catch up with the latest sociopolitical development internally and externally. The old practice of emphasizing on inducting increasing number of membership is changed to quality membership. Annual renewal of membership is introduced to get rid of members with dubious character and infringement of party constitution.

Selection of Suitable Candidates for Office Bearers

Talent scouting by an elite group of party officials searches for high-caliber members who can be groomed to take the fast track of promotion to the higher echelon of party organization. Just like in the ancient days of government examination conducted by the Imperial Court of the Emperor, the Communist Party also conducts similar examination to scout for candidates with impeccable character and integrity to assume high positions in e-governments. Potential candidates will attend an interview with the senior Communist Party members before being selected for general election. The successful candidates will go through rigorous training and scrutiny to serve the public and not be tainted with any iota of corrupt practices that are considered the Communist Party's Achilles' heel. Potential candidates have been working for some time at the grassroots levels to gain practical experience and have received favorable feedback from the masses.

Politics Evolves with Time

History has shown there is no perfect political system that is universal and suitable for all countries at all times. There is history, culture, and tradition, and the prevailing national social and economic condition to be considered when the people would decide what is best for them at the material time. China is a unique communist country that has gone through six decades of changes in its political and doctrinal changes. It has five thousand years of history with many dynasties, some of which led China to be the largest economy in the world. It experienced a short spell of democracy but failed to attract the support of the majority of poor farmers in the rural areas. They opted for regime change and selected the Communist leaders to rule the country, not because of political ideology but for the promise of a better life.

Today, fear of social uprising or people power by six hundred million poor farmers is the driving force that propels the Communist Party to adopt the Eco-World project to eliminate poverty forever from China. Communism with Chinese characters, as they call it in China, would prevail for a long time, just like the glorious days of China ruled by benevolent emperors who cared for the masses of farmers who were the backbone to pay taxes to the imperial court. When the farmers were happy, so were the emperors.

To the poor farmers, political doctrines remain as plain theories that have no relevance to their daily lives of basic survival—food, water, and shelter. Empty rhetoric by politicians pays no dividend in the Eco-World. The Eco-World of China is one for the common people with shared values and common destiny.

Free education, affordable medical services and housing are available to the population in the Eco-World. It has state-of-the-art communication, transportation, and high-tech public administration systems. The people will enjoy better health and higher education standard and a congenial environment. Petty crime is non-existent as everyone can get a job in the eco-city. It is a Utopian life.

Turning an annual expense of US$1 trillion into an investment that creates an Eco-World could generate an economic return of many trillions of dollars is a real winner especially it can also eliminate poverty, pollution, high inflation, social discontent, and fear of political uprising against the government and the Chinese Communist Party.

Chapter 22
Tourism

Present State of Tourism in China

China earns little from Tourism Compared to Others

Tourism is a lucrative industry for many countries. According to The World Bank, the United States receives US$214 billion in 2013 from seventy million inbound international tourists, representing US$670 per capita. China earns US$56 billion from fifty-six million inbound tourists or US$41 per capita. This is a paltry sum compared to tiny country Singapore's US$3,000 per capita. Hence, China has a long way to go to catch up with other countries to earn its fair share of international tourist receipts.

Investment in tourism can also produce handsome returns of tax receipts and infrastructural and financial developments. Chinese outbound tourists spend US$129 billion in 2013, which is more than double its inbound foreign tourist receipts. Many foreign countries ease their visa requirement to attract Chinese tourists who are big spenders on shopping.

Tourism Is a Lucrative Business

China is a vast country for sightseeing, hiking, and exploring. It is endowed with natural scenic attractions stretching from the cold regions of the far north, high mountains in the west, and the forests in the south. The cultural heritage in China is one of the oldest in the world, spanning more than five thousand years. There is a kaleidoscope of attractions for foreign tourists with varying interests. These include historic relics, sculptures, temples, pagodas, Chinese paintings, arts and crafts, and a spectrum of different costumes and dances of various ethnic minority groups, natural scenic sites, and varieties of foods and cuisines. China is indeed a country worth visiting as a tourist.

The famous Great Wall, built as early as the fifth century BC, Terracotta Warrior of the first Chinese emperor Qin Shi Huang (259 BC–210 BC), Imperial Palaces of the Ming Dynasty (1368–1644), Dazu Rock Carvings, a series of Chinese religious sculptures, and carvings in the seventh century AD are some of the popular tourist attractions. With such a rich endowment, there is no reason for China not to promote tourism as a worthwhile industry, which is evergreen. Tourism not only produces a good source of foreign exchange income, it is also an effective marketing tool to showcase to the world that China is a peaceful country with a rich culture, and its people are friendly.

Tourism as an Image Promotion Tool for China

China still remains a mysterious country to many people around the world. Some foreigners still have the notion that China is a backward country run by a tyrannical communist dictator. They picture China as in the timeframe of WW2. They do not know China has the second largest economy in the world, the world's longest high-speed railway network, and has sent astronauts into space. Soon China may overtake the United States as the strongest economy in the world. China's success in economic development in a short time is a miracle many people still do not believe.

Therefore, to help promote a better understanding of China by foreigners, the Chinese government decided to set up the Tourism Ministry to take charge of tourism to encourage foreigners to visit China. Tourism is a cash cow industry that should be treasured by the government and the Chinese people.

Tourism Is an Industry worth US$4 Trillion Annually

Foreign tourism is worth at least US$816 billion based on US$600 per capita initially and US$3,000 per capita in the next decade when all the tourism infrastructures are in place. By then, tourism could produce a staggering US$4 trillion of foreign receipts, equivalent to the current Germany's GDP. When eco-cities are established, many more foreigners will visit China to see China's new wonders of eco-farms, unlimited supply of freshwater and foods, and inexhaustible renewable energy production, eradication of water and air pollution, and a carbon-free environment. China will showcase to the world it can say good-bye forever to fossil fuels to save the world from being devastated by greenhouse gases. All private vehicles operating in the eco-cities are powered by batteries.

Present Hurdles in Tourism Promotion

There are presently many problems that impede the development of tourism in China. The industry is fragmented. There is no integrated effort to coordinate the various counties, cities and central government departments in the proper maintenance and promotion of the tourist sites. The infrastructures in many of the tourist sites are inadequate to cater to large crowds, and are lacking in facilities such as hotels, parking, toilets, rest areas, and restaurants. During peak seasons there are insufficient tour guides to manage all the tourists arriving in droves.

Many local government officials treat the tourist sites as a source of income and not a national treasure to be maintained for future generations. Even though tourist attractions are given accreditation on quality of facilities, security, management and services by China National Tourism Administration (CNTA), few places receive the highest rating of 5A.

During peak periods of national holidays like Chinese New Year and National Day, large numbers of tourist just overwhelm the tourist sites, generating complaints of long lines, overcrowding, and lack of space to move about. There is a cry of insufficient time to enjoy the sites or scenery. Tempers flare and scuffles among irate tourists often occur, resulting in a state of chaos and spoiling the fun of many tourists. Highway congestion, overcrowded transportation and accommodations at popular tourist resorts are perennial occurrences.

Many local counties and governments collect fees from the tourists but hardly invest money to maintain and develop the sites which fall into disrepair over time. Moreover, many local county governments do not have the resources to market the local tourism industry. Malpractices are prevalent concerning rampant collection of fees for viewing of natural sites like mountains and seaside beaches, forcing tourists to buy souvenirs at inflated prices, profiteering at temples selling expensive incense and unscrupulous seafood restaurant owners at Sanya in Hainan Province overcharging tourists to the hilt. Dirty public toilets and overflowing of rubbish bins are common complaints raised by tourists.

All in all, tourism in China is neglected, underdeveloped, and chaotic, and in dire need of overhauling. Many government agencies have overlapping responsibility of overseeing and control of the tourism industry. Tourism bugs do not seem to stop anywhere. Sustainable tourism has to come under a centralized government ministry to manage, develop and promote the tourist sites which are the country's treasures and cultures. The local county and regional governments cannot be a safe keeper of heritage of national importance without resources, knowledge and expertise. The CNTA does not seem to enforce the standards and quality of preservation and maintenance of the tourist sites.

Tourism Objectives

Tourism Is a Goodwill Industry and Employment Generator

Tourism is an important industry to China, as it not only could generate US$4 trillion tourist receipts annually but can offer employment to tens of millions of workers, and to the government hundreds of billions of dollars of tax revenue and development of infrastructures. The Chinese government understands that to promote tourism properly as an important sustainable industry, with a long-term investment in mind and as a marketing tool to spread the goodwill of the Chinese people to the outside world, the CNTA must be revamped to comply with ISO 9001 standard and national aspiration and objectives.

The rich culture, heritage and treasures shall be maintained and protected effectively for future generations. Too much is at stake without an effective organization and system. China welcomes tourists from every country and it wants to ensure that they return home with a good impression of China and a memorable and enjoyable experience of touring China. Returning foreign visitors will be a testimony of China's success in promoting a good image to the world.

China has many historic buildings and tourist sites that have been neglected and fallen into disrepair. Historic sculptures and rock paintings have been vandalized. Some scenic places are destroyed by pollution. Many parts of Great Wall are crumpling. The tourism department is tasked to set up restoration projects to repair damaged sites, historic treasures, and erect fences to protect scenic sites. The famous sixty-four hundred mile Silk Road will be restored to attract tourists who feel nostalgic to relive the bygone days of international businessmen who traded between China and countries in Europe and Middle

East dating back to the Han Dynasty (206 BC–220 AD). The Great Wall will be repaired and restored to the grandeur of the past.

Blueprint for National Tourism Promotion

The various subcommittees in the Tourism Ministry will establish a blueprint incorporating ISO 9001 industry standards for hotels, ground transportation, restaurants, public hygiene, safety, protection, and maintenance of tourist sites. To maintain quality standards, the government establishes guidelines, procedures, and training for the employees in the industry in order to meet the demands of foreign tourists with satisfaction. Members of the various committees will visit the tourist sites to collect relevant information and interview the tourists, tour guides and local officials. They also visit renowned tourist attractions in foreign countries around the world to study their formula of success in their tourism industries.

A subcommittee will monitor and audit the various government departments to ensure their compliance with the government's tourism regulations and rules, and publish recommendations for improvements. Universities and colleges will offer courses on tourism and graduates will find employment in the tourism industries which will be considered of national importance by the government.

China Tourism Ministry

Multidiscipline Tourism Setup with Focused Objectives

The tasks of building up a first-class tourism industry are arduous as the tourism industry involves the Ministries of Industry, Culture, Education, Environment, Finance, and Internal and Foreign Affairs. The first step toward building a cohesive tourism industry is to collect information from the relevant local governments that collect receipts from tourists, the high and low seasons, important problems facing the officials, tourists, and all the people and organizations that deal with the tourists. Feedback and suggestions from tour agents are also sought for possible solutions to existing problems. The perennial problems of overcrowding at popular tourist sites throughout China during the long national holiday periods will have to be resolved to ensure that both the domestic and international tourists will get their fair share of enjoyment without being crushed by huge crowds.

The Tourism Ministry establishes a blueprint for a ten-year tourism project capable of drawing in US$4 trillion receipts from foreign tourists. The project involves building hotels, all the necessary infrastructures at the tourist sites in towns and cities, amenities for tourists and workers, and parking bays for buses and private cars. High-speed rail stations will be built on all the tourist sites. The problems concerning different foreign languages and cultural and religious differences will be solved by dedicated tour guides with foreign language proficiency and working experience.

The department will establish an office in various countries to perform marketing efforts and answer inquiries. A comprehensive website with different languages will be set up to advice tourists of all the renowned attractions, descriptions of tour sites, historical background of heritage sites and accommodations. Every tour site has a wi-fi connection for the tourists to download information concerning the site.

Unique Solutions for Unique Problems

Tourist Sites Must be Regulated to avoid Overcrowding

Tourism in China is unique compared to other countries for one reason. It is that China's internal tourist population is too large to handle during the public holiday seasons when all the tourist sites are jammed with people. Unlike in other countries where holiday makers would stagger their vacations throughout the year, local tourists prefer to take vacation during the Spring Festival and National Day Week. Scuffles and fights often break out in the crowds. Such ugly occurrence does not augur well for a civilized country and definitely does not score well with foreign visitors.

The government decides to regulate the number of local visitors who can visit the popular tourist sites during peak seasons. Such measure should allow local visitors to enjoy the tourist sites with more space and time, and less pressure. At the same time, foreign visitors could have a chance to visit the popular tourist sites without facing the problem of overcrowding. Foreign visitors are encouraged to visit China during a lull, with discounts so as to avoid congestion during national holiday period.

The ministry appreciates such measures might not be welcome by many people. However, with increasing wealth and population, more local people will definitely find it harder to visit the tourist sites if there is no regulation and control to manage the huge volume of crowd. Moreover, the ministry has to endeavor to maintain a zero-accident safety standard for all tourists, which could number one billion annually. It is analogous to the problem of managing the maximum number of spectators that can be accommodated in a football stadium.

Global Marketing

In order for a good and friendly image to be propagated to the outside world as quickly as possible and from the views of the outsiders, the Chinese Tourism Ministry decides to engage an American advertising company that specializes in global advertising. The company will make documentary films about Chinese history, social and economic progress, scientific and technological developments, and arts and cultures. Adequate funds are available for engaging international multimedia and magazines to spread favorable news and articles about China. Good marketing of China to the outside world is necessary to promote better and positive image in the early stage of tourism development in China until the market reaches maturity. Annual review will be conducted to examine the areas of tourism that need improvement and update. Foreign tourism professionals are invited to provide input and critiques.

Internet-Based Tourism

In order to enhance satisfaction for tourists in the future, the ministry's website will store short feature films depicting the history of various historic and scenic sites, and the cultures of the ethnic people. For example, feature films are produced for the Great Wall, Terracotta army, Ming Tomb, Forbidden City, Three Gorges Dam, Potala Palace in Tibet, the giant panda at Sichuan, and many other famous mountainous resorts with narration of their back ground and history.

Films about various cultural festivals, such as Dragon Boat and Mid-Autumn are also stored on the website. Contemporary and traditional arts and dance festivals are also broadcast on the website. China's famous cuisine at various locales are also featured and stored in the website for free download. Exquisite and expensive Chinese antiques and paintings are also featured in the advertisement.

China Central Television has many good programs covering documentary, entertainment, and social topics that would appeal to foreigners. These programs are to be translated into several foreign languages to be broadcast to foreign countries.

Advanced Booking of Tour Sites

Advance online bookings to visit the various tourist sites are required to ensure there is sufficient space to accommodate the maximum numbers of tourists. Such measure is similar to the pre-booking of seats to attend a concert or football game. The official website can offer tourists tour packages to suit individual requirement. Inclusive of tour packages are tour guides who can speak the foreign language, accommodation, type of foods, transport, and wi-fi passwords for downloading of information and feature films about each of the tour sites. In China, all the tour sites provide free wi-fi connections. Feature films are in various foreign languages.

Preservation and Restorations of Important Tourist Sites

From the receipts income of tourists, the Tourism Ministry begins a long-term project to restore and preserve the grandeur of the thirteen thousand one hundred seventy mile Great Wall, where many sections have fallen into disrepair. With the completion of renovation, the Department builds a cable car system that takes tourists along the side of the Wall and stops by the watch towers to have spectacular panoramic sights around the Wall. With cable cars, many more tourists could climb the Wall to view the remarkable structures on the rugged mountains and surrounding sights.

The famous Silk Road will be restored to its past condition, as many adventurous tourists would like to ride the camels for a taste of living in the bygone days of the Han Dynasty (206 BC–220 AD). Many adventurous tourists would hire buses and cars to traverse the great length of the Silk Road between China and its neighboring countries in a desert setting. All the buses and cars are powered by battery, which can be replaced or charged along the Silk Road stations where electrical power is provided by solar and wind power. Battery shops will be open 24/7 to provide battery services. Emergency services are available for tourists in need of urgent help along the Silk Road.

Specialty Tour for Iconic Sites

Campsites are built along the Silk Road, with supplies of refrigerated foods and fresh water. Accommodations in motels managed by robots are also available for families with children. Restaurants managed by robots are open 24/7 to tourists to prepare various cuisines from different countries that were popular during the bygone days along the Silk Road. At every battery station and restaurant along the Silk Road, there is wi-fi connection for the tourists to download all the information about the history of the Silk Road.

The Silk Road tourists will have an opportunity to see the vast expanse of deserts being rejuvenated into arable lands, hundreds of thousands of trees being planted and numerous oases, lakes and wetlands created to restore the ecosystems for wildlife and vegetation. The visitors would be impressed by the river waters being recycled for rejuvenation of deserts and arid lands that have spread across the vast areas along the long Silk Road.

Development of More Tourist Attractions and Cruise Industries

To cater to increasing numbers of domestic and international tourists, and to lessen the stress on the existing tourist sites, many new tourist sites are developed in every province, especially in the southern provinces along the coasts with nice seaside beaches for swimming and water sports catering to the summer and winter vacationers from the northern parts of China and from foreign countries. There are many hidden scenic places with water falls and lakes and archaeological sites waiting for development as tourist attractions. When more new tourist sites are being developed together with new infrastructures and facilities, the pressure on the existing tourist sites will decline, and the quality of tourism would improve.

The CNTA will have a list of tour packages for foreign visitors to select. It has a unique tour program for foreign tourists wanting to see the uniqueness of eco-city's infrastructures and city design, eco-farms producing food crops, biodiesel plants, animal husbandry, and the massive fishing industries using state-of-the-art technologies. Visitors who are keen on social developments will have their eyes wide open when they visit the eco-city's new primary and secondary schools where all the students who are in small classes, interact with robotic teachers and using electronic textbooks for self-studies and homework.

The Ministry also introduces medical tourism to promote China as one of the top countries that can provide a high standard of medical care for patients who are in dire need of medical treatment. The eco-city health care services are considered to be best in the world. The medical tourism in eco-city attracts many foreigners seeking various medical treatments in the public hospitals that have undergone an unprecedented evolution in treatment and aftercare service, especially for geriatric patients who need twenty-four-hour-observation and physical assistance.

Many surgical operations are performed by off-site specialist surgeons appointed by the hospitals using remote surgery procedures. Some patients seek traditional Chinese medicine—for example, acupuncture for ailment that cannot be cured by Western methods of treatment. Local hospitals can tie up with foreign doctors and hospitals to provide treated foreign patients with aftercare services similar to those in China. Such aftercare services include robots specially designed for the foreign patient's special personal needs that are unavailable in the patient's home.

Cruise Ship Tours

China will introduce cruise liners to ply along the coasts of China and to other countries in the Pacific and Atlantic oceans and South China Sea. Currently, the cruise industry is in the infant stage. China wants to develop and promote the cruise industry to be at least on par with if not overtaking Royal Caribbean Cruise Line of Norway. The Chinese cruise line will introduce passengers to special packages which include traditional Chinese medicine treatment of illness using acupuncture and massages, honeymoon celebration with relatives and friends, special cuisines, virtually conducted tours on board scenic places, and tourist attractions in China and learning of Chinese martial arts. Long-term leasing of cabins is available to couples who are retired and would like to cruise around the world.

Tours-on-Wheels

China will introduce a tour-on-wheel package for domestic and foreign tourists. Tourists can hire a caravan which is furnished with a sleeping berth, shower, and toilet and cooking facilities. Such a caravan design is popular in Western countries where people take vacations with the whole family to a location not too far from home. Usually the location is deserted during quiet periods, and there are few hotel accommodations. China will build a caravan park at every popular tour site to accommodate tourists 24/7.

The caravan park will provide sleeping quarters, shower, toilet, and laundry facilities. The park has a large waste bin to collect all the wastes from the caravans. The toilet waste can be discharged from the caravan into a collector tank in the park. A convenience store open 24/7 is available for tourists to buy daily essentials. All purchase transactions are done on the internet. The purchaser can collect his orders from a special counter. All the sale items are recorded and the sale information is dispatched to the supplier for replenishment.

Power supply to the store and park comes from the solar panel and wind turbine. The facility is managed by robots which can make the bed, clean and mop the place. Robotic cooks are available to do cooking for the tourists.

Security and surveillance of the park is performed by robots that are controlled by a security firm. CCTVs are installed at strategic locations of the park. Many domestic and international tourists prefer to drive a caravan to tour the whole of China. Such tours-on-wheels is cheaper, more fun, and enjoyable for a family than a conducted tour. Moreover, self-driving provides an opportunity for tourists to see more of the countryside and scenic places at their own leisurely pace. Also, they can savor local cuisine in small towns and villages that is normally unavailable in big cities.

Every caravan is installed with GPS and a transponder for safety reason and for location detection of the caravan by the tour agency. Emergency stations are located at various towns and cities for tourists to request assistance.

Author's Note

China has been spending about US$1 trillion each year on oil and food grain imports, fighting industrial pollution, paying billions of dollars in aid to farmers when their crops are damaged by perennial droughts and floods, and increasing health care expenditures due to the effects of air and water pollutions. Six hundred million poverty-stricken rural residents are still living in primitive conditions. Official corruptions are rampant. Social discontents are widespread caused by escalating inflation, increasing costs of foods, housing, education and health care. The Chinese government solves all of the above problems in one fell swoop by investing US$1 trillion on the Eco-World project.

The Eco-World is game changer for the people of China. The Chinese people will have unlimited supplies of food, energy, and water for sustenance for centuries. The new eco-cities will have affordable state-of-the-art housing and public transport systems, efficient judicial and banking systems, and universal education and health care services. Recycling of waste, wider use of robots in daily life and industries, promotion of cultural and sporting activities, and tree planting across the nation would improve quality of life. Renewable energy will be used instead of fossil fuels, thereby eliminating greenhouse gases.

Social etiquette, community living spirit, and close social interaction amongst citizens are encouraged by the local government. All government departments will have a one-stop shop service to facilitate ease of communication with the people. Inflation and crime are curbed. Shorter working hours in the new Eco-World allow parents to have more free time with family and children.

Poverty is eradicated. The country is annually managed with a surplus budget and keeps inflation in check.

China will become the richest country in the world. The Eco-World, made in China, will serve as a model for other nations to emulate to achieve a similar sustainable economic and peaceful development compatible with the environment.

About The Author

The author was born in Malaysia and received Engineering Degrees from universities in Australia. He is a frequent traveler to China since 1978, He has two daughters, and lives with his wife in Singapore. He has published a book entitled "The Essentials of Airplane Maintenance".